MORE PRAISE FOR *AUTOMATING INEQUALITY*

"In this remarkable chronicle of 'how the other half lives' in the age of automation, Eubanks uncovers a new digital divide—a totalizing web of surveillance ensnaring our most marginalized communities. This powerful, sobering, and humane book exposes the dystopia of data-driven policy and urges us to create a more just society for all."

—**Alondra Nelson, author of** *The Social Life of DNA*

"In this illuminating book, Eubanks shows us that in spite of cosmetic reforms, our policies for the disadvantaged remain dominated by the ancient credo of the poor law, obsessed with the exclusion and punishment of the neediest in our communities."

—**Frances Fox Piven, author of** *Regulating the Poor*

"The single most important book about technology you will read this year. Today everyone is worrying about the Internet's impact on democracy, but Eubanks shows that the problems facing us run much deeper than 'fake news'—automated systems entrench social and economic inequality by design and undermine private and public welfare. Eubanks dives into history and reports from the trenches, helping us better understand the political and digital forces we are up against so we can effectively fight back."

—**Astra Taylor, author of** *The People's Platform: Taking Back Power and Culture in the Digital Age*

"*Automating Inequality* powerfully exposes how U.S. institutions, from law enforcement to health care to social services, increasingly punish people—especially people of color—for being poor. A must-read for everyone concerned about the modern tools of inequality in America."

—**Dorothy Roberts, author of** *Killing the Black Body* **and** *Shattered Bonds*

"This book is for all of us: community leaders, scholars, lawyers, recipients of government assistance, and anyone alive whose survival depends upon a better understanding of how nations made wealthy by digital industries are using technology to create and maintain a permanent underclass. It is a book for our times."
—Malkia A. Cyril, executive director and co-founder, Center for Media Justice—home of the Media Action Grassroots Network

"*Automating Inequality* is one of the most important recent books for understanding the social implications of information technology for marginalized populations in the US. As we begin discussing the potential for artificial intelligence to harm people, Eubanks' work should be required reading."
—Ethan Zuckerman, director, Center for Civic Media, MIT

"Startling and brilliant... As Eubanks makes crystal clear, automation coupled with the new technologies of ethical abandonment and instrumental efficiency threaten not only the lives of millions who are viewed as disposable but also democracy itself. If you want to understand how this digital nightmare is reaching deep into the institutions that attempt to regulate our lives, and how you can challenge it, this is a must read." —Henry Giroux, author of *The Public in Peril: Trump and the Menace of American Authoritarianism*

"*Automating Inequality* is a riveting, emotionally compelling story of vulnerable lives turned upside down by bad data, shoddy software, and bureaucrats too inept or corrupt to make things right. Everyone should read this book to learn how modern governance, all too often shrouded behind impenetrable legal and computer code, actually works."
—Frank Pasquale, author of *The Blackbox Society: The Secret Algorithms That Control Money and Information*

"Virginia Eubanks' new book shocks us with her gripping stories of the emerging surveillance state. The 'digital poorhouse' increasingly extends its web, not so much to aid as to manage, discipline and punish the poor. Read this book and join with Eubanks in pushing back against the injustice it sustains."
—Sanford Schram, author of *Words of Welfare* and *Disciplining the Poor*

AUTOMATING
INEQUALITY

Poorhouses were common enough that they often appeared in offensive, idealized, or ominous early-twentieth-century postcards.

AUTOMATING INEQUALITY

HOW HIGH-TECH TOOLS PROFILE, POLICE, AND PUNISH THE POOR

VIRGINIA EUBANKS

St. Martin's Press
New York

CONTENTS

For Sophie

AUTHOR'S NOTE

Fifty percent of the royalties from this book will be donated to the Juvenile Court Project of Pittsburgh, Indiana Legal Services of Indianapolis, and the Los Angeles Community Action Network (LA CAN).

AUTOMATING
INEQUALITY

Red Flags

In October 2015, a week after I started writing this book, my kind and brilliant partner of 13 years, Jason, got jumped by four guys while walking home from the corner store on our block in Troy, New York. He remembers someone asking him for a cigarette before he was hit the first time. He recalls just flashes after that: waking up on a folding chair in the bodega, the proprietor telling him to hold on, police officers asking questions, a jagged moment of light and sound during the ambulance ride.

It's probably good that he doesn't remember. His attackers broke his jaw in half a dozen places, both his eye sockets, and one of his cheekbones before making off with the $35 he had in his wallet. By the time he got out of the hospital, his head looked like a misshapen, rotten pumpkin. We had to wait two weeks for the swelling to go down enough for facial reconstruction surgery. On October 23, a plastic surgeon spent six hours repairing the damage, rebuilding Jason's skull with titanium plates and tiny bone screws, and wiring his jaw shut.

We marveled that Jason's eyesight and hearing hadn't been

damaged. He was in a lot of pain but relatively good spirits. He lost only one tooth. Our community rallied around us, delivering an almost constant stream of soup and smoothies to our door. Friends planned a fundraiser to help with insurance co-pays, lost wages, and the other unexpected expenses of trauma and healing. Despite the horror and fear of those first few weeks, we felt lucky.

Then, a few days after his surgery, I went to the drugstore to pick up his painkillers. The pharmacist informed me that the prescription had been canceled. Their system showed that we did not have health insurance.

In a panic, I called our insurance provider. After navigating through their voice-mail system and waiting on hold, I reached a customer service representative. I explained that our prescription coverage had been denied. Friendly and concerned, she said that the computer system didn't have a "start date" for our coverage. That's strange, I replied, because the claims for Jason's trip to the emergency room had been paid. We must have had a start date at that point. What had happened to our coverage since?

She assured me that it was just a mistake, a technical glitch. She did some back-end database magic and reinstated our prescription coverage. I picked up Jason's pain meds later that day. But the disappearance of our policy weighed heavily on my mind. We had received insurance cards in September. The insurance company paid the emergency room doctors and the radiologist for services rendered on October 8. How could we be missing a start date?

I looked up our claims history on the insurance company's website, stomach twisting. Our claims before October 16 had been paid. But all the charges for the surgery a week later—more than $62,000—had been denied. I called my insurance company again. I navigated the voice-mail system and waited on hold. This time I was not just panicked; I was angry. The customer service representative kept repeating that "the system said" our insurance had not yet started, so we were not covered. Any claims received while we lacked coverage would be denied.

I developed a sinking feeling as I thought it through. I had started a new job just days before the attack; we switched insurance providers. Jason and I aren't married; he is insured as my domestic partner. We had the new insurance for a week and then submitted tens of thousands of dollars worth of claims. It was possible that the missing start date was the result of an errant keystroke in a call center. But my instinct was that an algorithm had singled us out for a fraud investigation, and the insurance company had suspended our benefits until their inquiry was complete. My family had been red-flagged.

Since the dawn of the digital age, decision-making in finance, employment, politics, health, and human services has undergone revolutionary change. Forty years ago, nearly all of the major decisions that shape our lives—whether or not we are offered employment, a mortgage, insurance, credit, or a government service—were made by human beings. They often used actuarial processes that made them think more like computers than people, but human discretion still ruled the day. Today, we have ceded much of that decision-making power to sophisticated machines. Automated eligibility systems, ranking algorithms, and predictive risk models control which neighborhoods get policed, which families attain needed resources, who is short-listed for employment, and who is investigated for fraud.

Health-care fraud is a real problem. According to the FBI, it costs employers, policy holders, and taxpayers nearly $30 billion a year, though the great majority of it is committed by providers, not consumers. I don't fault insurance companies for using the tools at their disposal to identify fraudulent claims, or even for trying to predict them. But the human impacts of red-flagging, especially when it leads to the loss of crucial life-saving services, can be catastrophic. Being cut off from health insurance at a time when you feel most vulnerable, when someone you love is in debilitating pain, leaves you feeling cornered and desperate.

As I battled the insurance company, I also cared for Jason, whose eyes were swollen shut and whose reconstructed jaw and eye sockets burned with pain. I crushed his pills—painkiller, antibiotic, anti-anxiety medications—and mixed them into his smoothies. I helped him to the bathroom. I found the clothes he was wearing the night of the attack and steeled myself to go through his blood-caked pockets. I comforted him when he awoke with flashbacks. With equal measures of gratitude and exhaustion, I managed the outpouring of support from our friends and family.

I called the customer service number again and again. I asked to speak to supervisors, but call center workers told me that only my employer could speak to their bosses. When I finally reached out to the human resources staff at my job for help, they snapped into action. Within days, our insurance coverage had been "reinstated." It was an enormous relief, and we were able to keep follow-up medical appointments and schedule therapy without fear of bankruptcy. But the claims that had gone through during the month we mysteriously lacked coverage were still denied. I had to tackle correcting them, laboriously, one by one. Many of the bills went into collections. Each dreadful pink envelope we received meant I had to start the process all over again: call the doctor, the insurance company, the collections agency. Correcting the consequences of a single missing date took a year.

I'll never know if my family's battle with the insurance company was the unlucky result of human error. But there is good reason to believe that we were targeted for investigation by an algorithm that detects health-care fraud. We presented some of the most common indicators of medical malfeasance: our claims were incurred shortly after the inception of a new policy; many were filed for services rendered late at night; Jason's prescriptions included controlled substances, such as the oxycodone that helped him manage his pain; we were in an untraditional relationship that could call his status as my dependent into question.

The insurance company repeatedly told me that the problem was the result of a technical error, a few missing digits in a database. But that's the thing about being targeted by an algorithm: you get a sense of a pattern in the digital noise, an electronic eye turned toward *you*, but you can't put your finger on exactly what's amiss. There is no requirement that you be notified when you are red-flagged. There is no sunshine law that compels companies to release the inner details of their digital fraud detection systems. With the notable exception of credit reporting, we have remarkably limited access to the equations, algorithms, and models that shape our life chances.

Our world is crisscrossed with informational sentinels like the system that targeted my family for investigation. Digital security guards collect information about us, make inferences about our behavior, and control access to resources. Some are obvious and visible: closed-circuit cameras bristle on our street corners, our cell phones' global positioning devices record our movements, police drones fly over political protests. But many of the devices that collect our information and monitor our actions are inscrutable, invisible pieces of code. They are embedded in social media interactions, flow through applications for government services, envelop every product we try or buy. They are so deeply woven into the fabric of social life that, most of the time, we don't even notice we are being watched and analyzed.

We all inhabit this new regime of digital data, but we don't all experience it in the same way. What made my family's experience endurable was the access to information, discretionary time, and self-determination that professional middle-class people often take for granted. I knew enough about algorithmic decision-making to immediately suspect that we had been targeted for a fraud investigation. My flexible work schedule allowed me to spend hours on the phone dealing with our insurance troubles. My employer cared enough about my family's well-being to go to bat for me. We never stopped assuming we were eligible for medical insurance, so Jason got the care he needed.

We also had significant material resources. Our friends' fundraiser netted $15,000. We hired an aide to help Jason return to work and used the remaining funds to defray insurance co-pays, lost income, and increased expenses for things like food and therapy. When that windfall was exhausted, we spent our savings. Then we stopped paying our mortgage. Finally, we took out a new credit card and racked up an additional $5,000 in debt. It will take us some time to recover from the financial and emotional toll of the beating and the ensuing insurance investigation. But in the big picture, we were fortunate.

Not everyone fares so well when targeted by digital decision-making systems. Some families don't have the material resources and community support we enjoyed. Many don't know that they are being targeted, or don't have the energy or expertise to push back when they are. Perhaps most importantly, the kind of digital scrutiny Jason and I underwent is a daily occurrence for many people, not a one-time aberration.

In his famous novel *1984*, George Orwell got one thing wrong. Big Brother is not watching *you*, he's watching *us*. Most people are targeted for digital scrutiny as members of social groups, not as individuals. People of color, migrants, unpopular religious groups, sexual minorities, the poor, and other oppressed and exploited populations bear a much higher burden of monitoring and tracking than advantaged groups.

Marginalized groups face higher levels of data collection when they access public benefits, walk through highly policed neighborhoods, enter the health-care system, or cross national borders. That data acts to reinforce their marginality when it is used to target them for suspicion and extra scrutiny. Those groups seen as undeserving are singled out for punitive public policy and more intense surveillance, and the cycle begins again. It is a kind of collective red-flagging, a feedback loop of injustice.

For example, in 2014 Maine Republican governor Paul LePage attacked families in his state receiving meager cash benefits from Temporary Assistance to Needy Families (TANF). These benefits are loaded onto electronic benefits transfer (EBT) cards that leave a digital record of when and where cash is withdrawn. LePage's administration mined data collected by federal and state agencies to compile a list of 3,650 transactions in which TANF recipients withdrew cash from ATMs in smoke shops, liquor stores, and out-of-state locations. The data was then released to the public via Google Docs.

The transactions that LePage found suspicious represented only 0.03 percent of the 1.1 million cash withdrawals completed during the time period, and the data only showed where cash was withdrawn, not how it was spent. But the governor used the public data disclosure to suggest that TANF families were defrauding taxpayers by buying liquor, lottery tickets, and cigarettes with their benefits. Lawmakers and the professional middle-class public eagerly embraced the misleading tale he spun from a tenuous thread of data.

The Maine legislature introduced a bill that would require TANF families to retain all cash receipts for 12 months to facilitate state audits of their spending. Democratic legislators urged the state's attorney general to use LePage's list to investigate and prosecute fraud. The governor introduced a bill to ban TANF recipients from using out-of-state ATMs. The proposed laws were impossible to obey, patently unconstitutional, and unenforceable, but that's not the point. This is performative politics. The legislation was not intended to *work*; it was intended to heap stigma on social programs and reinforce the cultural narrative that those who access public assistance are criminal, lazy, spendthrift addicts.

LePage's use of EBT data to track and stigmatize poor and working-class people's decision-making didn't come as much of a surprise to me. By 2014, I had been thinking and writing about technology and poverty for 20 years. I taught in community technology centers, organized workshops on digital justice for grassroots organizers, led participatory design projects with women in low-income housing, and interviewed hundreds of welfare and child protective services clients and caseworkers about their experiences with government technology.

For the first ten years of this work, I was cautiously optimistic about the impact of new information technologies on economic justice and political vitality in the United States. In my research and organizing, I found that poor and working-class women in my hometown of Troy, New York, were not "technology poor," as other scholars and policy-makers assumed. Data-based systems were ubiquitous in their lives, especially in the low-wage workplace, the criminal justice system, and the public assistance system. I did find many trends that were troubling, even in the early 2000s: high-tech economic development was increasing economic inequality in my hometown, intensive electronic surveillance was being integrated into public housing and benefit programs, and policy-makers were actively ignoring the needs and insights of poor and working people. Nevertheless, my collaborators articulated hopeful visions that information technology could help them tell their stories, connect with others, and strengthen their embattled communities.

Since the Great Recession, my concern about the impacts of high-tech tools on poor and working-class communities has increased. The skyrocketing economic insecurity of the last decade has been accompanied by an equally rapid rise of sophisticated data-based technologies in public services: predictive algorithms, risk models, and automated eligibility systems. Massive investments in data-driven administration of public programs are rationalized by a call for efficiency, doing more with less, and getting help to those who really need it. But the uptake of these tools is occurring at a time when programs that serve the poor are as unpopular as they have ever been. This is not a coincidence. Technologies of poverty management are not neutral. They are shaped by our nation's fear of economic insecurity and hatred of the poor; they in turn shape the politics and experience of poverty.

The cheerleaders of the new data regime rarely acknowledge the impacts of digital decision-making on poor and working-class people. This myopia is not shared by those lower on the economic hierarchy, who often see themselves as targets rather than beneficiaries of these systems. For example, one day in early 2000, I sat talking to a young mother on welfare about her experiences with technology. When our conversation turned to EBT cards, Dorothy Allen said, "They're great. Except [Social Services] uses them as a tracking device." I must have looked shocked, because she explained that her caseworker routinely looked at her purchase records. Poor women are the test subjects for surveillance technology, Dorothy told me. Then she added, "You should pay attention to what happens to us. You're next."

Dorothy's insight was prescient. The kind of invasive electronic scrutiny she described has become commonplace across the class spectrum today. Digital tracking and decision-making systems have become routine in policing, political forecasting, marketing, credit reporting, criminal sentencing, business management, finance, and the administration of public programs. As these systems developed in sophistication and reach, I started to hear them described as forces for control, manipulation, and punishment. Stories of new technologies facilitating communication and opening opportunity became harder to find. Today, I mostly hear that the new regime of data constricts poor and working-class people's opportunities, demobilizes their political organizing, limits their movement, and undercuts their human rights. What has happened since 2007 to alter so many people's hopes and dreams? How has the digital revolution become a nightmare for so many?

To answer these questions, I set out in 2014 to systematically investigate the impacts of high-tech sorting and monitoring systems on poor and working-class people in America. I chose three stories to explore: an attempt to automate eligibility processes for the state of Indiana's welfare system; an electronic registry of the unhoused in Los Angeles; and a risk model that promises to predict which children will be future victims of abuse or neglect in Allegheny County, Pennsylvania.

The three stories capture different aspects of the human service system: public assistance programs such as TANF, the Supplemental Nutrition Assistance Program (SNAP), and Medicaid in Indiana; homeless services in Los Angeles; and child welfare in Allegheny County. They also provide geographical diversity: I started in rural Tipton County in America's heartland, spent a year exploring the Skid Row and South Central neighborhoods of Los Angeles, and ended by talking to families living in the impoverished suburbs that ring Pittsburgh.

I chose these particular stories because they illustrate how swiftly the ethical and technical complexity of automated decision-making has increased in the last decade. The 2006 Indiana eligibility modernization experiment was fairly straightforward: the system accepted online applications for services, checked and verified income and other personal information, and set benefit levels. The electronic registry of the unhoused I studied in Los

Angeles, called the coordinated entry system, was piloted seven years later. It deploys computerized algorithms to match unhoused people in its registry to the most appropriate available housing resources. The Allegheny Family Screening Tool, launched in August 2016, uses statistical modeling to provide hotline screeners with a predictive risk score that shapes the decision whether or not to open child abuse and neglect investigations.

I started my reporting in each location by reaching out to organizations working closely with the families most directly impacted by these systems. Over three years, I conducted 105 interviews, sat in on family court, observed a child abuse hotline call center, searched public records, submitted Freedom of Information Act requests, pored through court filings, and attended dozens of community meetings. Though I thought it was important to start from the point of view of poor families, I didn't stop there. I talked to caseworkers, activists, policy-makers, program administrators, journalists, scholars, and police officers, hoping to understand the new digital infrastructure of poverty relief from both sides of the desk.

What I found was stunning. Across the country, poor and working-class people are targeted by new tools of digital poverty management and face life-threatening consequences as a result. Automated eligibility systems discourage them from claiming public resources that they need to survive and thrive. Complex integrated databases collect their most personal information, with few safeguards for privacy or data security, while offering almost nothing in return. Predictive models and algorithms tag them as risky investments and problematic parents. Vast complexes of social service, law enforcement, and neighborhood surveillance make their every move visible and offer up their behavior for government, commercial, and public scrutiny.

These systems are being integrated into human and social services across the country at a breathtaking pace, with little or no political discussion about their impacts. Automated eligibility is now standard practice in almost every state's public assistance office. Coordinated entry is the preferred system for managing homeless services, championed by the United States Interagency Council on Homelessness and the U.S. Department of Housing and Urban Development. Even before the Allegheny Family Screening Tool was launched, its designers were in negotiations to create another child maltreatment predictive risk model in California.

Though these new systems have the most destructive and deadly effects in low-income communities of color, they impact poor and working-class people across the color line. While welfare recipients, the unhoused, and poor families face the heaviest burdens of high-tech scrutiny, they aren't the only ones affected by the growth of automated decision-making. The widespread use of these systems impacts the quality of democracy for us all.

Automated decision-making shatters the social safety net, criminalizes the poor, intensifies discrimination, and compromises our deepest national values. It reframes shared social decisions about who we are and who we want to be as systems engineering problems. And while the most sweeping digital decision-making tools are tested in what could be called "low rights environments" where there are few expectations of political accountability and transparency, systems first designed for the poor will eventually be used on everyone.

America's poor and working-class people have long been subject to invasive surveillance, midnight raids, and punitive public policy that increase the stigma and hardship of poverty. During the nineteenth century, they were quarantined in county poorhouses. During the twentieth century, they were investigated by caseworkers, treated like criminals on trial. Today, we have forged what I call a *digital poorhouse* from databases, algorithms, and risk models. It promises to eclipse the reach and repercussions of everything that came before.

Like earlier technological innovations in poverty management, digital tracking and automated decision-making hide poverty from the professional middle-class public and give the nation the ethical distance it needs to make inhuman choices: who gets food and who starves, who has housing and who remains homeless, and which families are broken up by the state. The digital poorhouse is part of a long American tradition. We manage the individual poor in order to escape our shared responsibility for eradicating poverty.

1

FROM POORHOUSE TO DATABASE

"You're going to send me to the poorhouse!"

Most of us reference the poorhouse only reflexively today. But the poorhouse was once a very real and much feared institution. At their height, poorhouses appeared on postcards and in popular songs. Local societies scheduled tours for charity-minded citizens and common gawkers. Cities and towns across the country still include streets named for the poorhouses once sited on them. There are Poor Farm Roads in Bristol, Maine, and Natchez, Mississippi; County Home Roads in Marysville, Ohio, and Greenville, North Carolina; Poorhouse Roads in Winchester, Virginia, and San Mateo, California. Some have been renamed to obscure their past: Poor House Road in Virginia Beach is now called Prosperity Road.

The poorhouse in my hometown of Troy, New York, was built in 1821. While most of its residents were too ill, too old, or too young for physical labor, able-bodied inmates worked on a 152-acre farm and in a nearby stone quarry, earning the institution its name: the Rensselaer County House of Industry. John Van Ness Yates, charged by the state of New York with conducting a year-long inquiry into the "Relief and Settlement of the Poor" in 1824, used Troy's example to argue that the state should build a poorhouse in every county. His plan succeeded: within a decade, 55 county poorhouses had been erected in New York.

Despite optimistic predictions that poorhouses would furnish relief "with economy and humanity," the poorhouse was an institution that rightly inspired terror among poor and working-class people. In 1857, a legislative investigation found that the House of Industry confined the mentally ill to 4½-by-7-feet cells for as long as six months at a time. Because they had only straw to sleep on and no sanitary facilities, a mixture of straw and urine froze onto their bodies in the winter "and was removed only by thawing it off," causing permanent disabilities.

"The general state of things described as existing at the Poor House, is bad, every way," wrote the *Troy Daily Whig* in February 1857. "The contract system, by which the maintenance of the paupers is let out to the lowest bidder, is in a very great measure responsible. . . . The system itself is rotten through and through." The county superintendent of the poor, Justin E. Gregory, won the contract for the House of Industry by promising to care for its paupers for $1 each per week. As part of the contract, he was granted unlimited use of their labor. The poorhouse farm produced $2,000 in revenue that year, selling vegetables grown by starving inmates.

In 1879, the *New York Times* reported on its front page that a "Poorhouse Ring" was selling the bodies of deceased residents of the House of Industry to county physicians for dissection. In 1885, an investigation into mismanagement uncovered the theft of $20,000 from the Rensselaer County poor department, forcing the resignation of Keeper of the Poorhouse Ira B. Ford. In 1896, his replacement, Calvin B. Dunham, committed suicide after his own financial improprieties were discovered.

In 1905, the New York State Board of Charities opened an investigation that uncovered rampant sexual abuse at the House of Industry. Nurse Ruth Schillinger testified that a male medical attendant, William Wilmot, regularly attempted to rape female patients. Inmates insisted that Mary Murphy, suffering from paralysis, had been assaulted by Wilmot. "They heard footsteps in the hall and they said it was Wilmot down there again," Schillinger testified, "and I found the woman the next morning with her legs spread apart and she couldn't move them herself because they were paralyzed."[1]

In his defense, John Kittell, the keeper of the House of Industry and Wilmot's boss, claimed that his management had saved the county "five to six thousand dollars per year" by reducing the cost of inmate care. Wilmot faced no charges; action to improve conditions was not taken until 1910. Troy's poorhouse remained open until 1954.

While poorhouses have been physically demolished, their legacy remains alive and well in the automated decision-making systems that encage and entrap today's poor. For all their high-tech polish, our modern systems of poverty management—automated decision-making, data mining, and predictive analytics—retain a remarkable kinship with the poorhouses of the past. Our new digital tools spring from punitive, moralistic views of poverty and create a system of high-tech containment and investigation. The digital poorhouse deters the poor from accessing public resources; polices their labor, spending, sexuality, and parenting; tries to predict their future behavior; and punishes and criminalizes those who do not comply with its dictates. In the process, it creates ever-finer moral distinctions between the "deserving" and "undeserving" poor, categorizations that rationalize our national failure to care for one another.

This chapter chronicles how we got here: how the brick-and-mortar poorhouse morphed into its data-based descendants. Our national journey from the county poorhouse of the nineteenth century to the digital poorhouse today reveals a remarkably durable debate between those who wish to eliminate and alleviate poverty and those who blame, imprison, and punish the poor.

America's first poorhouse was built in Boston in 1662, but it wasn't until the 1820s that imprisoning the indigent in public institutions became the nation's primary method of regulating poverty. The impetus was the catastrophic economic depression of 1819. After a period of extravagant financial speculation following the War of 1812, the Second Bank of the United States nearly collapsed. Businesses failed, agricultural prices dropped, wages fell as much as 80 percent, and property values plummeted. Half a million Americans were out of work—about a quarter of the free adult male population. But political commentators worried less about the suffering of the poor than they did about the rise of "pauperism," or dependence on public benefits. Of particular concern was outdoor relief: food, fuel, medical care, clothing, and other basic necessities given to the poor *outside* of the confines of public institutions.

A number of states commissioned reports about the "pauper problem." In Massachusetts, Josiah Quincy III, scion of a wealthy and influential Unitarian family, was appointed to the task. Quincy genuinely wanted to alleviate suffering, but he believed that poverty was a result of bad personal habits, not economic shocks. He resolved the contradiction by suggesting that there were two classes of paupers. The *impotent* poor, he wrote in 1821, were "wholly incapable of work, through old age, infancy, sickness or corporeal debility," while the *able* poor were just shirking.[2]

For Quincy, the pauper problem was caused by outdoor relief itself: aid was distributed without distinguishing between the impotent and the able. He suspected that indiscriminate giving destroyed the industry and thriftiness of the "labouring class of society" and created a permanently dependent class of paupers. His solution was to deny "all supply from public provision, except on condition of admission into the public institution [of the poorhouse]."[3]

It was an argument that proved alluring for elites. At least 77 poorhouses were built in Ohio, 79 in Texas, and 61 in Virginia. By 1860, Massachusetts had 219 poorhouses, one for every 5,600 residents, and Josiah Quincy was enjoying his retirement after a long and rewarding career in politics.

From the beginning, the poorhouse served irreconcilable purposes that led to terrible suffering and spiraling costs. On the one hand, the poorhouse was a semi-voluntary institution providing care for the elderly, the frail, the sick, the disabled, orphans, and the mentally ill. On the other, its harsh conditions were meant to discourage the working poor from seeking aid. The mandate to deter the poor drastically undercut the institution's ability to provide care.

Inmates were required to swear a pauper's oath stripping them of whatever basic civil rights they enjoyed (if they were white and male). Inmates could not vote, marry, or hold office. Families were separated because reformers of the time believed that poor children could be redeemed through contact with wealthy families. Children were taken from their parents and bound out as apprentices or domestics, or sent away on orphan trains as free labor for pioneer farms.

Poorhouses provided a multitude of opportunities for personal profit for those who ran them. Part of the keeper of the poorhouse's pay was provided by unlimited use of the grounds and the labor of inmates. Many of the institution's daily operations could thus be turned into side businesses: the keeper could force poorhouse residents to grow extra food for sale, take in extra laundry and mending for profit, or hire inmates out as domestics or farm-workers.

While some poorhouses were relatively benign, the majority were overcrowded, ill-ventilated, filthy, insufferably hot in the summer and deathly cold in the winter. Health care and sanitation were inadequate and inmates lacked basic provisions like water, bedding, and clothing.

Though administrators often cut corners to save money, poorhouses also proved costly. The efficiencies of scale promised by poorhouse proponents required an able-bodied workforce, but the mandate to deter the able poor virtually guaranteed that most inmates were unable to work. By 1856 about a quarter of poorhouse residents in New York were children. Another quarter were mentally ill, blind, deaf, or developmentally delayed. Most of the rest were elderly, ill, physically disabled, or poor mothers recovering from childbirth.

Despite their horrid conditions, poorhouses—largely through their failings—succeeded in offering internees a sense of community. Inmates worked together, endured neglect and abuse, nursed the sick, watched each other's children, ate together, and slept in crowded common rooms. Many used the poorhouse cyclically, relying on them between growing seasons or during labor market downturns.

Poorhouses were among the nation's first integrated public institutions. In his 1899 book, *The Philadelphia Negro*, W.E.B. Du Bois reported that African Americans were overrepresented in the city's poorhouses because they were refused outdoor relief by exclusively white overseers of the poor. Residents described as Black, Negro, colored, mulatto, Chinese, and Mexican are common in poorhouse logbooks from Connecticut to California. The racial and ethnic integration of the poorhouse was a sore spot for white, native-born elites. As historian Michael Katz reports, "In 1855, a New York critic complained that the 'poor of all classes and colors, all ages and habits, partake of a common fare, a common table, and a common dormitory.' "[4]

Poorhouses were neither debtors' prisons nor slavery. Those arrested for vagrancy, drunkenness, illicit sex, or begging could be forcibly confined in them. But for many, entry was technically voluntary. The poorhouse was a home of last resort for children whose families could not afford to keep them, travelers who fell on hard times, the aged and friendless, deserted and widowed, single mothers, the ill and the handicapped, freed slaves, immigrants, and others living on the margins of the economy. Though most poorhouse stays lasted less than a month, elderly and disabled inmates often stayed for decades. Death rates at some institutions neared 30 percent annually.[5]

Poorhouse proponents reasoned that the institution could provide care while instilling moral values of thrift and industry. The reality was that the poorhouse was an institution for producing fear, even for hastening death. As social work historian Walter Trattner has written, elite Americans of the time "believed that poverty could, and should, be obliterated—in part, by allowing the poor to perish." Nineteenth-century social philosopher Nathanial Ware wrote, for example, "Humanity aside, it would be to the best interest of society to kill all such drones."[6]

Despite their cruelty and high cost, county poorhouses were the nation's primary mode of poverty management until they were overwhelmed by the Panic of 1873. A postwar economic boom collapsed under the weight of Gilded Age corruption. Rampant speculation led to a run of bank failures, and financial panic resulted in another catastrophic depression. Rail construction fell by a third, nearly half of the industrial furnaces in the country closed, and hundreds of thousands of laborers were thrown out of work. Wages dropped, real estate markets tumbled, and foreclosures and evictions followed. Local governments and ordinary individuals responded by creating soup kitchens, establishing free lodging houses, and distributing cash, food, clothing, and coal.

The Great Railroad Strike of 1877 began when workers for the Baltimore & Ohio Railroad learned that their wages would be cut yet again—to half their 1873 levels—while the railroad's shareholders took home a 10 percent dividend. Railroad workers stepped off their trains, decoupled engines, and refused to let freight traffic through their yards. As historian Michael Bellesiles recounts in *1877: America's Year of Living Violently*, when police and militia were sent in with bayonets and Gatling guns to break the strikes, miners and canal workers rose up in support. Half a million workers—roustabouts and barge captains, miners and smelters, factory linemen and cannery workers—eventually walked off the job in the first national strike in US history.

Bellesiles reports that in Chicago the Czechs and the Irish, traditionally ethnic adversaries, cheered each other. In Martinsburg, West Virginia, white and Black railroad workers shut down the train yard together. The working families of Hornellsville, New York, soaped the rails of the Erie railroad track. As strike-breaking trains attempted to ascend a hill, they lost traction and slid back into town.

The depression also affected Germany, Austria-Hungary, and Britain. In response, European governments introduced the modern welfare state. But in America, middle-class commentators stoked fears of class warfare and a "great Communist wave."[7] As they had following the 1819 Panic, white economic elites responded to the growing militancy of poor and working-class people by attacking welfare. They asked: How can legitimate need be tested in a communal lodging house? How can one enforce work and provide free soup at the same time? In response, a new kind of social reform—the scientific charity movement—began an all-out attack on public poor relief.

Scientific charity argued for more rigorous, data-driven methods to separate the deserving poor from the undeserving. In-depth investigation was a mechanism of moral classification and social control. Each poor family became a "case" to be solved; in its early years, the Charity Organization Society even used city police officers to investigate applications for relief. Casework was born.

Caseworkers assumed that the poor were not reliable witnesses. They confirmed their stories with police, neighbors, local shopkeepers, clergy, schoolteachers, nurses, and other aid societies. As Mary Richmond wrote in *Social Diagnosis*, her 1917 textbook on casework procedures, "the *reliability* of the evidence on which [caseworkers] base their decisions should be no less rigidly scrutinized than is that of legal evidence by opposing counsel."[8] Scientific charity treated the poor as criminal defendants by default.

Scientific charity workers advised in-depth investigation of applications for relief because they believed that there was a hereditary division between deserving and undeserving poor whites. Providing aid to the unworthy poor would simply allow them to survive and reproduce their genetically inferior stock. For middle-class reformers of the period, like scientific social worker Frederic Almy, social diagnosis was necessary because "weeds should not have the same culture as flowers."[9]

The movement's focus on heredity was influenced by the incredibly popular eugenics movement. The British strain of eugenics, originated by Sir Francis Galton, encouraged planned breeding of elites for their "noble qualities." But in America, eugenics practitioners quickly turned their attention to eliminating what they saw as negative characteristics of the poor: low intelligence, criminality, and unrestricted sexuality.

Eugenics created the first database of the poor. From a Carnegie Institution–funded laboratory in Cold Spring Harbor, New York, and state eugenics records offices stretching from Vermont to California, social scientists fanned out across the United States to gather information about poor people's sex lives, intelligence, habits, and behavior. They filled out lengthy questionnaires, took photographs, inked fingerprints, measured heads, counted children, plotted family trees, and filled logbooks with descriptions like "imbecile," "feeble-minded," "harlot," and "dependent."

Eugenics was an important component of the wave of white supremacy that swept the nation in the 1880s. Jim Crow rules were institutionalized and restrictive immigration laws were passed to protect the white race from "outside threats." Eugenics was intended to cleanse the race from within by shining a clinical spotlight on what Dr. Albert Priddy called the "shiftless, ignorant, and worthless class of anti-social whites of the South." Both eugenics and scientific charity amassed hundreds of thousands of family case studies in what George Buzelle, general secretary of the Brooklyn Bureau of Charities, characterized as an effort to "arrange all the human family according to intellect, development, merit, and demerit, each with a label ready for indexing and filing away."[10]

The movement blended elite anxieties about white poverty with fears of increased immigration and racist beliefs that African Americans were innately inferior. Popular manifestations of eugenics theory reproduced and fed these distinctions: African Americans were utterly cast out, northern European–descended wealthy whites occupied the pinnacle of the eugenic hierarchy, and everyone in-between was suspect. Fitter family contests at state fair eugenics exhibits always had alabaster-skinned winners. The economically struggling hordes represented as drains on the public treasury were often racialized: "degenerate" genetic lines always had darker skin, lower brows, and broader features.

Widespread reproductive restrictions were perhaps the inevitable destination for scientific charity and eugenics. In the *Buck v. Bell* case that legalized involuntary sterilization, Supreme Court Justice Oliver Wendell Holmes famously wrote, "It is better for all the world if, instead of waiting to execute degenerate offspring for crime or to let them starve for their imbecility, society can prevent those who are manifestly unfit from continuing their kind. The principle that sustains compulsory vaccination is broad enough to cover cutting the Fallopian tubes."[11] Though the practice fell out of favor in light of Nazi atrocities during World War II, eugenics resulted in more than 60,000 compulsory sterilizations of poor and working-class people in the United States.

Unlike the intermittently integrated poorhouses, scientific charity considered African American poverty a separate issue from white poverty, and, according to social historian Mark Peel, "more or less deliberately ignored what late nineteenth-century Americans called the 'Negro Problem.' "[12] Thus, the movement offered paltry resources to a small number of "deserving" white poor. They used investigative techniques and cutting-edge technology to discourage everyone else from seeking aid. If all else failed, scientific charity turned to institutionalization: those who weren't morally pure enough for their charity or strong enough to support themselves were sent to the poorhouse.

The scientific charity movement relied on a slew of new inventions: the caseworker, the relief investigation, the eugenics record, the data clearinghouse. It drew on what lawyers, academics, and doctors believed to be the most empirically sophisticated science of its time. Scientific charity staked a claim to evidence-based practice in order to distinguish itself from what its proponents saw as the soft-headed emotional, or corruption-laden political, approaches to poor relief of the past. But the movement's high-tech tools and scientific rationales were actually systems for disempowering poor and working-class people, denying their human rights, and violating their autonomy. If the poorhouse was a machine that diverted the poor and working class from public resources, scientific charity was a technique of producing plausible deniability in elites.

Like the poorhouse before it, scientific charity ruled poor relief for two generations. But even this powerful movement could not survive the Great Depression. At its peak, an estimated 13–15 million American workers lost their jobs, with unemployment nearing 25 percent nationwide and topping 60 percent in some cities. Families who had been solidly middle class before the crash sought public relief for the first time. The always-fuzzy line between the deserving and the undeserving poor was swept away in the face of the nationwide crisis.

As the Great Depression gained steam in 1930 and 1931, scientific charity was stretched beyond its limits. Bread lines burgeoned, evicted families crowded into shared apartments and municipal lodging houses, and local emergency relief programs broke down in the face of overwhelming need. Poor and working people protested deteriorating conditions and rallied together to help one another.

Thousands of unemployed workers organized to loot food stores; miners carried off and distributed bootlegged coal. There were bread lines, soup lines, cabbage lines. As Frances Fox Piven and Richard Cloward report in *Regulating the Poor*, local aid agencies were harassed by protestors who picketed, shouted, and refused to leave until relief agencies released money and goods to waiting crowds. Rent strikers resisted foreclosures and evictions and reversed gas and electric shutoffs. In 1932, 43,000 "Bonus Army" marchers camped near the US Capitol in vacant lots and on the banks of the Potomac River.

Franklin D. Roosevelt rode to the presidency on this wave of citizen unrest. He launched a massive return to outdoor relief: the Federal Emergency Relief Administration (FERA), a program that distributed commodities and cash to families in need. His administration also created new federal employment programs, such as the Civilian Conservation Corps (CCC) and the Civil Works Administration (CWA), which put unemployed people to work in infrastructure improvement projects, construction of public facilities, government administration, health care, education, and the arts.

The New Deal reversed the trend toward private charity, and by early 1934 federal programs such as FERA, CCC, and CWA were assisting 28 million people with work or home relief. The programs were able to do so much for so many so quickly because of sufficient public funding—FERA alone eventually expended four billion dollars—and because they abandoned the in-depth investigations pioneered by scientific charity caseworkers.

As during the depressions of 1819 and 1873, critics blamed relief programs for creating dependence on public assistance. Roosevelt himself had serious misgivings about putting the federal government in the business of providing direct relief. He quickly capitulated to middle-class backlash, shuttering FERA, the program that provided cash and commodities, and replacing it with the Works Progress Administration (WPA). Against the protests of some in the Roosevelt camp who called for the creation of a federal department of welfare, the administration shifted its focus from distributing resources to encouraging work.

New Deal legislation undoubtedly saved thousands of lives and prevented destitution for millions. New labor laws led to a flourishing of unions and built a strong white middle class. The Social Security Act of 1935 established the principle of cash payments in cases of unemployment, old age, or loss of a family breadwinner, and it did so as a matter of right, not on the basis of individual moral character. But the New Deal also created racial, gender, and class divisions that continue to produce inequities in our society today.

Roosevelt's administration capitulated to white supremacy in ways that still bear bitter fruit. The Civilian Conservation Corps capped Black participation in federally supported work relief at 10 percent of available jobs, though African Americans experienced 80 percent unemployment in northern cities. The National Housing Act of 1934 redoubled the burden on Black neighborhoods by promoting residential segregation and encouraging mortgage redlining. The Wagner Act granted workers the right to organize, but allowed segregated trade unions. Most importantly, in response to threats that southern states would not support the Social Security Act, both agricultural and domestic workers were explicitly excluded from its employment protections. The "southern compromise" left the great majority of African American workers—and a not-insignificant number of poor white tenant farmers, sharecroppers, and domestics—with no minimum wage, unemployment protection, old-age insurance, or right to collective bargaining.

New Deal programs also enshrined the male breadwinner as the primary vehicle for economic support of women and families. Federal protections were tied to wages, union membership, unemployment insurance, and pensions. But by incentivizing long-term wage-earning and full-time, year-round work, the protections privileged men's employment patterns over women's. Another signature program of the New Deal, Aid to Dependent Children (ADC, called Aid to Families with Dependent Children, or AFDC, after 1962), was structured to support a tiny number of widows with children after the death of a male wage earner. Women's economic security was thus tied securely to their roles as wives, mothers, or widows, guaranteeing their continued economic dependence.

The design of New Deal relief policies reestablished the divide between the able and the impotent poor. But it flipped Josiah Quincy's script. The able poor were still white male wage workers thrown into temporary unemployment. But, reversing the preceding hundred years of poverty policy, they were suddenly considered the *deserving* poor and offered federal aid to reenter the workforce. The impotent poor were still those who faced long-term challenges to steady employment: racial discrimination, single parenthood, disability, or chronic illness. But they were suddenly characterized as *undeserving*, and only reluctantly offered stingy, punitive, temporary relief.

Excluded workers, single mothers, the elderly poor, the ill, and the disabled were forced to rely on what welfare historian Premilla Nadasen calls "mop-up" public assistance programs.[13] The distinctions between the unemployed and the poor, men's poverty and women's poverty, northern white male industrial laborers and everyone else created a two-tiered welfare state: social insurance versus public assistance.

Public assistance programs were less generous because benefit levels were set by states and municipalities, not the federal government. They were more punitive because local and state welfare authorities wrote eligibility rules and had financial incentive to keep enrollments low. They were more intrusive because income limits and means-testing rationalized all manner of surveillance and policing of applicants and beneficiaries.

In distinguishing between social insurance and public assistance, New Deal Democrats planted the seeds of today's economic inequality, capitulated to white supremacy, sowed conflict between the poor and the working class, and devalued women's work. By abandoning the idea of a universal benefits program, Roosevelt resurrected scientific charity's investigation, policing, and diversion. But rather than being directed at a broad spectrum of the poor and working class, these techniques were selectively applied to a new target group that was just emerging. They would come to be known as "welfare mothers."

Though all of the programs created by the Social Security Act are properly considered public assistance, the most controversial of the mop-up programs, ADC, has become synonymous with "welfare." If not for its eventual role as the focal point for a massively successful political movement of poor women, ADC/AFDC would be a historical footnote. For its first 35 years, the program was aimed narrowly at middle-class white widows. Very few families applied, and about half of those who did were turned away.

State and county rules excluded huge numbers of eligible recipients, especially women of color. "Employable mother" rules excluded domestics and farmworkers, whose wage labor was considered by legislators more important than caring for their children. "Suitable home" rules excluded never-married mothers, the divorced and abandoned, lesbians, and other women considered sexually immoral by welfare departments. "Substitute father" rules made any man in a relationship with a woman on public assistance financially responsible for her children. Residence restrictions denied benefits to anyone who moved across state lines. Welfare required that poor people trade their rights—to bodily integrity, safe work environments, mobility, political participation, privacy, and self-determination—for meager aid for their families.

Discriminatory eligibility rules gave caseworkers broad latitude to investigate clients' relationships, dig into all aspects of their lives, and even raid their homes. In 1958 police and welfare workers in Sweet Home, a small white working-class community in Oregon, planned a series of collaborative raids, all taking place between midnight and 4:30 a.m. In 1963, caseworkers in Alameda County, California, invaded the homes of 700 welfare recipients on one cold January night, rousting mothers and children from their beds in an attempt to uncover unreported paramours. Victims complained that raiders failed to identify themselves, used unnecessarily abusive language, and "even broke down doors when denied admittance," reported Howard Kennedy in the *Los Angeles Times*. The NAACP charged that the Alameda raids were "conducted mainly against Negro and Mexican-American ANC [Aid to Needy Children] recipients and that discrimination may be involved."[14]

The return to scientific charity–type investigation of ADC/AFDC recipients was a reaction to changing migration patterns and civil rights activism, which were shifting the racial composition of the program. Fleeing white supremacist terrorism and sharecropper evictions in the south, more than three million African Americans moved to northern cities between 1940 and 1960. Many found safer housing, better jobs, and more dignity and freedom. But discrimination in employment, housing, and education resulted in much higher unemployment rates for non-whites, and migrants reached out to public assistance to help support their families.

At the same time, the civil rights movement articulated a moral right to equal public accommodation and political participation for African Americans. The argument that supported the integration of public schools and the expansion of the vote was easily extended to the integration of public assistance. Mothers for Adequate Welfare, an early welfare rights group, was formed after several of its members attended the 1963 March on Washington for Jobs and Freedom. According to historian Premilla Nadasen, they were inspired by the march to fight back against the daily indignities and discrimination they suffered as Black welfare mothers and returned home to Boston eager to start a food distribution program.[15] Across the country, local organizations joined to form a national movement that challenged the unjust status quo: at least half the people eligible for AFDC were not receiving it.

The welfare rights movement shared information about eligibility, helped fill out applications, sat-in in welfare offices to challenge discriminatory practices, lobbied legislatures, crafted policies, and challenged all the assumptions that New Deal programs had left unquestioned. Most importantly, members of the movement insisted that motherwork *is work*. Though they supported any woman's right to paid employment if she desired, welfare rights organizations actively resisted all programs requiring that single mothers of young children work outside the home.

The successes of the welfare rights movement were extraordinary. It birthed the 30,000-member National Welfare Rights Organization (NWRO). It won increased access to special grants to obtain furniture, school clothing, and other household items. It spearheaded a fight for a guaranteed minimum income available to all poor families regardless of marital status, race, or employment. Recognizing that the exclusion of Black women and single mothers from public assistance was unconstitutional, the movement also mounted legal challenges to reverse discriminatory eligibility rules.

A victory in *King v. Smith* (1968) overturned the "substitute father" rule and guaranteed basic rights of personal and sexual privacy. In *Shapiro v. Thompson* (1969), the Supreme Court agreed that residency rules were unconstitutional restrictions of a person's right to mobility. *Goldberg v. Kelly* (1970) enshrined the principle that public assistance recipients have a right to due process, and that benefits cannot be terminated without a fair hearing. These legal victories established a truly revolutionary precedent: the poor should enjoy the same rights as the middle class.

AFDC became so embattled that President Richard Nixon proposed a guaranteed annual income program, the Family Assistance Program (FAP), to replace it in 1969. The program would guarantee a minimum income of $1,600 a year for a family of four. It would provide benefits to two-parent families earning low wages, who were excluded from AFDC. It would do away with the 100 percent penalty on earned income, allowing welfare beneficiaries to retain the first $720 of their yearly earnings without reducing benefits.

But the minimum income Nixon proposed would have still kept a family of four well below the poverty line. The NWRO proposed a competing Adequate Income Act that set the base income for a family of four at $5,500. Nixon's program also included built-in work requirements; this was a sticking point for single mothers with small children. Unpopular with both conservatives and progressives, the FAP failed, and pressure on AFDC continued to mount.

Emboldened by social movements, more families applied for public assistance; protected by legal victories, fewer were turned away. As eligibility limitations were struck down, AFDC expanded. The raw numbers are startling: there were 3.2 million recipients of AFDC in 1961 but almost 10 million in 1971. Federal spending on the program increased from $1 billion (in 1971 dollars) to $3.3 billion over the same decade. Most of the movement's gains went to poor children. Only a quarter of poor children received support from AFDC in 1966; by 1973, the program reached more than four-fifths of them.

The members of the NWRO were mostly poor African American women, but the welfare rights movement had middle-class allies and saw interracial organizing as crucial to achieving its long-term goals. Reflecting their disproportional vulnerability to poverty, African Americans accounted for roughly 50 percent of the AFDC rolls by 1967. But Johnnie Tillmon, first chairwoman of the NWRO, recognized that white welfare recipients were fellow sufferers and potential allies. As she explained in a 1971 interview, "We can't afford racial separateness. I'm told by the poor white girls on welfare how they feel when they're hungry, and I feel the same way when I'm hungry."[16]

But if welfare rights activists envisioned integration and solidarity, opposition to the expansion of AFDC drummed up white middle-class animosity to turn back the movement's successes. As backlash against welfare rights grew, news coverage of poverty became increasingly critical. "As news stories about the poor became less sympathetic," writes political scientist Martin Gilens, "the images of poor blacks in the news swelled."[17] Stories about welfare fraud and abuse were most likely to contain images of Black faces. African American poverty decreased dramatically during the 1960s and the African American share of AFDC caseloads declined. But the percentage of African Americans represented in news magazine stories about poverty jumped from 27 to 72 percent between 1964 and 1967.

Hysteria about welfare costs, fraud, and inefficiency increased as the 1973 recession took hold. Driven by Ronald Reagan and other conservative politicians, a taxpayer revolt against AFDC challenged the notion that the poor should have the full complement of rights promised by the Constitution. But the welfare rights movement's successes were enshrined into law, so exclusion from public assistance could no longer be accomplished through discriminatory eligibility rules.

Elected officials and state bureaucrats, caught between increasingly stringent legal protections and demands to contain public assistance spending, performed a political sleight of hand. They commissioned expansive new technologies that promised to save money by distributing aid more efficiently. In fact, these technological systems acted like walls, standing between poor people and their legal rights. In this moment, the digital poorhouse was born.

Computers gained ground in the early 1970s as neutral tools for shrinking public spending by increasing scrutiny and surveillance of welfare recipients. In 1943, Louisiana had been the first state to establish an "employable mother" rule that blocked most African American women from receiving ADC. Thirty-one years later, Louisiana became the first state to launch a computerized wage matching system. The program checked the self-reported income of welfare applicants against electronic files of employment agencies and unemployment compensation benefit data.

By the 1980s, computers collected, analyzed, stored, and shared an extraordinary amount of data on families receiving public assistance. The federal Department of Health, Education, and Welfare (HEW) shared welfare recipients' names, social security numbers, birthdays, and other information with the Department of Defense, state governments, federal employers, civil and criminal courts, local welfare agencies, and the Department of Justice. New programs searched burgeoning case files for inconsistencies. Fraud detection programs were carefully programmed and launched. Databases were linked together to track recipient behavior and spending across different social programs. The conflict between the expanding legal rights of welfare recipients and weakened support for public assistance was resolved by a wave of high-tech tools.

Because public assistance programs are federally funded and locally controlled, the uptake of welfare administration technology varied from state to state. But the route followed by New York provides an illuminating example. New York had the largest, most vocal welfare rights movement and the fastest expanding AFDC rolls in the country. By the late 1960s, one out of ten of the nation's welfare recipients lived in New York City, and they had organized into somewhere between 60 and 80 local welfare rights groups.

The movement began a campaign of daily demonstrations throughout the city in spring 1968, including a three-day sit-in at welfare department headquarters that was ended only by mounted police. Influenced by such visible activism, caseworkers began to see their role as advocating for applicants rather than diverting them from aid. According to a 1973 RAND Institute report titled *Protest by the Poor*, Bronx and Brooklyn caseworkers threatened to strike unless the city's Department of Social Services "cut red tape in order to process the flood of client demands."[18]

In 1969, the state of New York petitioned to participate in the Nationwide Demonstration Project, a HEW effort to develop a "computer-based management information system for the administration of public welfare." At the time, Republican governor Nelson Rockefeller was convinced that Nixon's FAP would pass, and that the state's welfare problems would be solved by a federal takeover of state and local welfare costs.

After the FAP failed to pass Congress in 1970, Rockefeller announced that New York had "no alternative but to continue to do its best to provide for the needs of its poor," while calling the state's current welfare system "outmoded" and a "tremendous burden." A few months later, in a statement to the legislature, he laid out his growing concern that if welfare was not radically changed, it "will ultimately overload and break down our society" because "rather than encouraging human dignity, independence and individual responsibility, the system, as it is functioning, encourages permanent dependence on government."[19]

Rockefeller announced a statewide welfare reform package that established one-year residency requirements and proposed a "voluntary resettlement plan" offering current welfare recipients transportation and a cash bonus if they agreed to move out of state. His proposed reforms required welfare recipients to take any available job or lose benefits, and removed caseworker discretion for deciding which recipients were "employable" and for determining the size of welfare grants. Rockefeller repealed minimum salary requirements for caseworkers, lowered educational qualifications for the job, and strengthened penalties against caseworkers "who improperly assist welfare recipients in obtaining eligibility or additional benefits."

Rockefeller also established a new office, the Inspector General of Welfare Administration, and appointed his campaign fundraiser George F. Berlinger to lead it. In the office's first annual report in February 1972, Berlinger charged that administrative mismanagement had allowed a "disease" of "cheats, frauds and abusers" to infect the city's welfare rolls. "Major surgery is in order," he wrote.

Berlinger proposed a central computerized registry for every welfare, Medicaid, and food stamp recipient in the state. Planners folded Rockefeller's fixation with ending the welfare "gravy train" into the system's design. The state hired Ross Perot's Electronic Data Systems to create a digital tool to "reduce well documented ineligibility, mismanagement and fraud in welfare administration," automate grant calculations and eligibility determinations, and "improve state supervision" of local decision-making.[20] Design, development, and implementation of the resulting Welfare Management System (WMS) eventually cost $84.5 million.

The rapid increase in the welfare rolls in New York plateaued in the mid-1970s, as the WMS was brought on line. Then, the proportion of poor individuals receiving AFDC began to plummet. The pattern was repeated in state after state. A combination of restrictive new rules and high-tech tools reversed the gains of the welfare rights movement. In 1973, nearly half of the people living under the poverty line in the United States received AFDC. A decade later, after the new technologies of welfare administration were introduced, the proportion had dropped to 30 percent. Today, it is less than 10 percent.

The Personal Responsibility and Work Opportunity Reconciliation Act (PRWORA) of 1996 is often held responsible for the demise of welfare. The PRWORA replaced AFDC with Temporary Assistance to Needy Families (TANF) and enforced work outside the home at any cost. TANF limited lifetime eligibility for public assistance to 60 months with few exceptions, introduced strict work requirements, ended support for four-year college education, and put into effect a wide array of sanctions to penalize noncompliance.

Sanctions are imposed, for example, for being late to an appointment, missing a volunteer work assignment, not attending job training, not completing drug testing, not attending mental health counseling, or ignoring any other therapeutic or job-training activity prescribed by a caseworker. Each sanction can result in a time-limited or permanent loss of benefits.

It is true that the PRWORA achieved striking contractions in public assistance. Almost 8.5 million people were removed from the welfare rolls between 1996 and 2006. In 2014, fewer adults were being served by cash assistance than in 1962. In 1973, four of five poor children were receiving benefits from AFDC. Today, TANF serves fewer than one in five of them.

But the process of winnowing the rolls began long before Bill Clinton promised to "end welfare as we know it." More aggressive investigation and increasingly precise tracking technologies provided raw material for apocryphal stories about widespread corruption and fraud. These stories birthed more punitive rules and draconian penalties, which in turn required an explosion of data-based technologies to monitor compliance. The 1996 federal reforms simply finished a process that began 20 years earlier, when the revolt against welfare rights birthed the digital poorhouse.

The advocates of automated and algorithmic approaches to public services often describe the new generation of digital tools as "disruptive." They tell us that big data shakes up hidebound bureaucracies, stimulates innovative solutions, and increases transparency. But when we focus on programs specifically targeted at poor and working-class people, the new regime of data analytics is more evolution than revolution. It is simply an expansion and continuation of moralistic and punitive poverty management strategies that have been with us since the 1820s.

The story of the poorhouse and scientific charity demonstrates that poverty relief becomes more punitive and stigmatized during times of economic crisis. Poor and working-class people resist restrictions of their rights, dismantle discriminatory institutions, and join together for survival and mutual aid. But time and again they face middle-class backlash. Social assistance is recast as charity, mutual aid is reconstructed as dependency, and new techniques to turn back the progress of the poor proliferate.

A well-funded, widely supported, and wildly successful countermovement to deny basic human rights to poor and working-class people has grown steadily since the 1970s. The movement manufactures and circulates misleading stories about the poor: that they are an undeserving, fraudulent, dependent, and immoral minority. Conservative critics of the welfare state continue to run a very effective propaganda campaign to convince Americans that the working class and the poor must battle each other in a zero-sum game over limited resources. More quietly, program administrators and data scientists push high-tech tools that promise to help more people, more humanely, while promoting efficiency, identifying fraud, and containing costs. The digital poorhouse is framed as a way to rationalize and streamline benefits, but the real goal is what it has always been: to profile, police, and punish the poor.

2

AUTOMATING ELIGIBILITY IN THE HEARTLAND

A little white donkey is chewing on a fencepost where we turn toward the Stipes house on a narrow utility road paralleling the train tracks in Tipton, Indiana. Michael "Dan" Skinner, 65-year-old ex-newspaper man and my guide to central Indiana, heaves his mom's 19-year-old sedan across the tracks and into the Stipes family's driveway a mile or so later. Their big white house is marooned in a sea of cornfields, but on this sunny day in March 2015, the stalks are cut back low and softened by snow melting to mud. Kim and Kevin Stipes joke that they've had to grow tall children: come July, the smaller ones disappear into the corn. I'm here to talk to Kim and Kevin about their daughter Sophie, who lost her Medicaid benefits during Indiana's experiment with welfare eligibility automation.

In 2012, I delivered a lecture at Indiana University Bloomington about how new data-based technologies were impacting public services. When I was finished, a well-dressed man raised his hand and asked the question that would launch this book. "You know," he asked, "what's going on here in Indiana, right?" I looked at him blankly and shook my head. He gave me a quick synopsis: a $1.3 billion contract to privatize and automate the state's welfare eligibility processes, thousands losing benefits, a high-profile breach-of-contract case for the Indiana Supreme Court. He handed me his card. In gold letters it identified him as Matt Pierce, Democratic member of the Indiana House of Representatives.

Two and a half years later, the welfare automation story brought me to the home of Sophie Stipes, a lively, sunny, stubborn girl with dark brown hair, wide chocolate eyes, and the deep brow characteristic of people with cerebral palsy. Shortly after she was born in 2002, she was diagnosed with failure to thrive, global developmental delays, and periventricular leukomalacia, a white-matter brain injury that affects newborns and fetuses. She was also diagnosed with 1p36 deletion syndrome, which is believed to affect between 1 in 5,000 and 1 in 10,000 newborns. She has significant hearing loss in both ears. Kim and Kevin were told that she might never sit up, walk, or speak. For her first two years, all she did was lie on her back. She barely moved.

Her parents contacted representatives of First Steps, a program of the Indiana Division of Disability and Rehabilitative Services that helps young children with developmental delays. Through the program, Sophie received therapy and nutrition services, and her family received counseling and support. Most important: she had a gastronomy tube implanted to deliver nutrition directly to her stomach; for the first two years of her life, she had not been eating very much at all. Shortly after they started feeding her directly through the G-tube, Sophie began to sit up.

At the time of my 2015 visit, Sophie is 13. She gets around on her own and goes to school. She knows all the letters of the alphabet. Though doctors originally told Kim that it wouldn't do any good to sign to her, Sophie understands 300 or 400 words in the family's pidgin sign language and communicates with her parents and friends. Sophie has been at school all day, so she is relaxing in her room watching *Elmo's World*, wearing orange-and-pink-striped pajamas. Kim Stipes introduces us, and we wave hello at each other.

I ask Kim to tell Sophie that I like her pink TV, and she laughs, signing the message. "Kudos to Sophie," says her mom, a blond with faded blue eyes, a gold thumb ring, and the slide-on Crocs worn by folks who spend a lot of time on their feet. "If other kids worked half as hard, they'd all be geniuses making millions. That's how hard Sophie has worked."

The Stipeses aren't strangers to hard work. In a greenhouse made of metal tubes and plastic sheeting, Kevin cultivates heirloom tomatoes, broccoli, lettuce, peppers, green beans, squash, and even peaches. They can and freeze produce to use throughout the winter. But 2008 was a rough year. Kevin lost his job, and with it, the family's health insurance. He and Kim were trying to support seven kids on what they could make selling auto parts on the internet. Their son Max had recently been diagnosed with type I diabetes. And Sophie had been very sick, throwing up all the time.

Without Medicaid Sophie's care would have been financially overwhelming. Her formula was incredibly expensive. She needed specialized diapers for older children with developmental delays. It cost $1,700 every time Sophie had a G-tube implanted. The cost of her care exceeded $6,000 a month.

Trouble really started in late 2007, when Kim applied for the Healthy Indiana Plan, which provides catastrophic health insurance for low-income adults. Though five of their children were covered by Medicaid, she and Kevin had no health insurance. Immediately after Kim started the application process, four members of the household became ill. Kim knew that she would not be able to fill out all the required paperwork while caring for them.

So she went to her local Family and Social Services Administration (FSSA) office in Tipton, spoke to a caseworker, and asked to have the application put on hold. The Tipton caseworker told her that, because of recent changes at FSSA, application decisions were no longer made at the local level. She would have to speak with a call center operator in Marion, 40 miles away. Kim called the Marion office and was told that her application "would be taken care of." Neither the Tipton caseworker nor the Marion call center operator told Kim that she had to sign paperwork declaring that she was stopping the application process. Nor did they tell her that her failed attempt to get health insurance for herself and her husband might impact her children's coverage.

Then, the family received a letter from the FSSA. It was addressed to six-year-old Sophie, and it informed her that she would be kicked off Medicaid in less than a month because she had "failed to cooperate" in establishing her eligibility for the program. The notice somehow managed to be both terrifyingly brief and densely bureaucratic. It read:

```
Mailing Date: 3/26/08
Dear SOPHIE STIPES,
MA D 01 (MI)
Your MEDICAID benefits will be discontinued
effective APRIL 30, 2008 due to the following
reason(s):
-FAILURE TO COOPERATE IN ESTABLISHING ELIGI-
BILITY
-FAILURE TO COOPERATE IN VERIFYING INCOME
SUPPORTING LAW(S) OR REGULATION(S) :
470IAC2.1-1-2
Important : If you believe you may be eligi-
ble for Medicaid benefits under another cat-
egory and have more information about your
```

> case, please contact us at the number listed
> at the top of this notice within ten days (13
> days if this notice is received by mail) of
> the date of this notice.

The notice arrived on April 5, 2008. It had been ten days since it was mailed. The family had three days left to contact FSSA and correct the mistake.

Kim sprang into action, composing a lengthy letter that explained her situation and faxing it to the Marion office on Sunday, April 6. In it, she stressed that Medicaid kept Sophie alive, that she had no other insurance, and that her medical supplies alone cost thousands of dollars a month. Sophie's medicines were due to run out in five days. Kim phoned the call center in Marion and was told that Sophie was being cut off because Kim had failed to sign the paperwork declaring that she was stopping her earlier applications for the Healthy Indiana Plan. Kim protested that no one had ever told her about the paperwork.

But it was too late.

According to the state of Indiana, the Stipes family had failed to cooperate with the eligibility determination process and, under state law, the punishment was total denial of medical benefits. The sanction would impact both Kim and Kevin, who were trying to get health insurance for themselves, and Sophie would be denied the Medicaid she was already receiving. When Kim asked why their other children were *not* being cut off, she was informed that they were. She should expect four more letters.

The Stipes family contacted Dan Skinner, who was spending his retirement as a volunteer with United Senior Action, working on behalf of elderly Hoosiers. In early 2007, United Senior Action started getting calls from individuals and organizations all over central Indiana: the shelves at food pantries were empty and the United Way was overrun by requests for emergency medical help. Skinner began an independent investigation in Howard County, visiting the mayor's office, the area agency on aging, Catholic social services, the senior center, and Mental Health America. He found that people were losing their benefits for "failure to cooperate" in alarming numbers.

Sophie's case stood out to him as particularly appalling. "She was six years old, and she was recovering. She learned how to sign. She was starting to walk!" Skinner said. "She was starting to be able to eat a little bit, and they said when she could take 3,000 calories, they would take the feeding tube out. She was right at that stage, and her Medicaid was cut off for failure to cooperate." By the time the Stipes family reached him, Skinner remembered, they were in a desperate situation and needed immediate action.

Dan called John Cardwell, founder and director of The Generations Project, an organization dedicated to addressing long-term health-care issues in the state of Indiana. The two gathered their colleagues from the AARP and the Alliance for Retired Americans, lobbied their contacts, worked the media, and called an emergency press conference. Dan took Sophie and her parents to the Indianapolis State House in a van. "She had a little dress on," Kim Stipes remembers. "She was not a happy camper then. Her little life was rough." They walked into the governor's office with Sophie in her wheelchair and "TV cameras in tow," said Skinner. "They didn't expect that."

At one point, Governor Mitch Daniels walked right by the group. "He did have an opportunity, quite frankly, to walk right over to us," Skinner recalled. "He just walked by. Mitch Roob [Secretary of the FSSA] was with him. They just stared at us and kept on going." Kevin Stipes yelled across the room to Daniels, inviting him to come talk with his family. But the governor and FSSA secretary failed to acknowledge them. "They get to that position they don't want to deal with that stuff. They want layers," Kevin theorized later, "They want people in between." The group asked for Lawren Mills, Governor Daniels' policy director for human services, who agreed to meet with them. The next day at four o'clock in the afternoon, Sophie had her Medicaid back.

Sophie's family was not alone. In 2006, Republican governor Mitch Daniels instituted a welfare reform program that relied on multinational corporations to streamline benefits applications, privatize casework, and identify fraud. Daniels had long been a foe of public assistance. In 1987, while serving as President Ronald Reagan's assistant for Political and Intergovernmental Affairs, he had been a high-profile supporter of a failed attempt to eliminate AFDC. Nearly 20 years later, he tried to eliminate TANF in Indiana. But this time he did it through high-tech tools, not policy-making.

Governor Daniels famously applied a Yellow Pages test to government services. If a product or service is listed in the Yellow Pages, he insisted, the government shouldn't provide it. So it was not surprising when, shortly after his election in 2004, Daniels began an aggressive campaign to privatize many of the state's public services, including the Indiana Toll Road, the Bureau of Motor Vehicles, and the state's public assistance programs.

Daniels appointed Mitch Roob as FSSA secretary. In *The Indianapolis Star,* Daniels praised Roob, then a vice president at Affiliated Computer Services (ACS), as being "deeply committed to the interests of the least fortunate among us and equally committed to getting the most service from every tax dollar." As their first order of business, Roob and his boss commissioned an audit of what Daniels called in a 2007 *South Bend Tribune* editorial "the monstrous bureaucracy known as the Family and Social

Service Administration." As the agency's audit report was released in June 2005, two FSSA employees were arrested and charged with theft, welfare fraud, and a panoply of other offenses. One of the employees was accused of collaborating with church leaders of the Greater Faith Missionary Baptist Church in Indianapolis to collect $62,497 in food stamps and other welfare benefits by creating dummy accounts for herself and fellow church parishioners. Between them, the two caseworkers had 45 years of experience at the FSSA.

Daniels seized the political moment. In public speeches, press releases, and reports, the governor repeatedly characterized Indiana's welfare system as "irretrievably broken," wasteful, fraudulent, and "America's worst welfare system." Citing the system's high error rate and poor customer service, Mitch Roob crisscrossed the state arguing that the system was broken beyond the ability of state employees to fix. In early 2006, the Daniels administration released a request for proposal (RFP) to outsource and automate eligibility processes for TANF, food stamps, and Medicaid. In the request, the state set very clear goals: reduce fraud, curtail spending, and move clients off the welfare rolls.

"The State is aware that poor policy and operations have contributed to a culture of welfare dependency among some of its clients," the RFP read. "Respondent will help address this issue by agreeing to use welfare eligibility and other programs to help clients reduce dependency on welfare assistance and transition into a paid work setting." While the state provided no incentives or support for matching applicants to available jobs, the RFP suggested that the FSSA would be willing to provide extra financial incentives for finding and denying ineligible cases. The state offered to "pay the Respondent for superior performance," for example, if the company can "reduce ineligible cases" by identifying "client misrepresentations."

At the time, the Indiana FSSA was helping about a million people access health care, social services, mental health counseling, and other forms of support. The 2006 agency was sizable: it had a budget of $6.55 billion and a staff of approximately 6,500. But it was much smaller than it had been 15 years earlier. In 1991, the Indiana General Assembly consolidated the departments of Mental Health, Public Welfare, and Human Services, and outsourced many of its functions. By the time of the automation, the FSSA had halved its public workforce and was spending 92 percent of its budget buying services from outside vendors.

Everyone—advocates, applicants, administrators, and legislators alike—agreed that the existing system faced serious challenges. FSSA offices were using an extremely out-of-date system called the Indiana Client Eligibility System (ICES) for daily administrative functions such as calculating eligibility and verifying income. Customer service was uneven at best. A 2005 survey found that applicants faced a slow intake process, a telephone system that rarely worked, and caseworkers who were difficult to reach. A U.S. Department of Agriculture (USDA) study found that food stamp applicants made up to four visits to county offices before receiving program benefits. Overstretched staff couldn't handle demand or keep up with towering piles of paper case files.[1]

The Daniels administration insisted that moving away from face-to-face casework and toward electronic communication would make offices more organized and more efficient. Even better, they argued, moving paper shuffling and data collection to a private contractor would free remaining state caseworkers to work more closely with clients. Daniels and Roob built a compelling case. And people listened.

However, many of Daniels's other assertions about the failures of FSSA have been contested. His claim that Indiana's welfare system was the worst in the country, for example, was based only on the state's record for moving Hoosiers *off* welfare. It is true that Indiana reduced the number of people on public assistance more slowly than other states in the decade after the 1996 welfare reforms. But Indiana had seen a significant drop in the welfare rolls years earlier. In the three years between the installation of ICES and the implementation of federal welfare reform, Indiana's caseload fell 23 percent. As Daniels began his term, only a tiny proportion of poor Hoosiers—38 percent—were receiving benefits from TANF, and only 74 percent of qualified individuals were receiving food stamps. Despite the administration's insistence that eligibility errors were spiraling out of control, the FSSA reported food stamp error rates consistent with national averages. The positive error rate—which measures those who receive benefits for which they are not actually eligible—was 4.4 percent. The negative error rate—which describes those who apply for benefits and are incorrectly denied them—was 1.5 percent.

Only two bids were submitted for the contract, one from Accenture LLC and the other from a coalition of companies called the Hoosier Coalition for Self-Sufficiency. The coalition was led by IBM and ACS, Roob's former employer. Accenture dropped out of the bidding process. On December 27, 2006, after holding a single public hearing on the topic, the governor signed a ten-year, $1.16 billion contract with the IBM/ACS coalition.

In a press release celebrating the plan, Daniels announced, "Today, we act to clean up welfare waste, and to provide Indiana's neediest people a better chance to escape welfare for the world of work and dignity. We will make America's worst welfare system better for the people it serves, a much fairer deal for taxpayers, and for its own employees."[2] According to the Daniels administration, the modernization project would improve access to services for needy, elderly, and disabled people while saving taxpayers' money. It would do this by automating welfare eligibility processes: substituting online applications for face-to-face inter-actions, building centralized call centers throughout the state, and "transitioning" 1,500 state employees to private telephone call centers run by ACS.

Daniels lauded his privatization plan and the automated system in the 2007 *South Bend Tribune* editorial. "Today's wel-fare system . . . is totally indefensible," he wrote. "For Hoosier taxpayers, reform means enormous savings: a half billion dollars over the next 10 years, and that's only on the administrative side. When today's high rates of errors and fraud are brought down, savings will probably exceed $1 billion."[3] By March, 70 percent of the FSSA workforce had moved to positions with private con-tractors. In October the Indiana automation project rolled out to 12 pilot counties in north central Indiana.

In the first nine weeks of the pilot, 143,899 people called the toll-free number and 2,858 applied online. System failures were immediate. "The telephone appointment system was a disaster," remembered Jamie Andree of Indiana Legal Services, an organ-ization providing legal assistance to low-income Hoosiers. "An interview would be scheduled from 10 to 12 in the morning. People would have to find a phone, sit by it, and wait to be called. Then the call wouldn't come, or they'd call at 11:45 saying [the interview] is being rescheduled for tomorrow."

Applicants who had taken time off work were often unable to wait by the phone the next day for a new appointment. Others received notices that required them to participate in phone inter-views scheduled for dates that had already passed. According to a 2010 USDA report, a food stamp (called the Supplemental Nutri-tion Assistance Program, or SNAP, after 2008) recipient added the call center number to her cell phone plan's "friends and family" list because she spent so much time on the phone with them. Applicants who failed to successfully complete their phone interview were terminated for failing to cooperate in eligibility determination. Says Andree, "It was a terrible, terrible, terrible system."

Private call center workers were not adequately trained to deal with the severity of challenges faced by callers, nor were they provided with sufficient information about applicable regulations. Advocates report call center operators bursting into tears on the phone. "The first person I called under modernization, I remember it vividly," reported Terry West, a patient advocate with 15 years' experience in central Indiana. "She was young, and . . . did not have any experience whatsoever. . . . There was a problem, a denial of a case. I talked to this young lady for about an hour. I kept citing [the appropriate regulations]. After about a half an hour, she just started crying. She said, 'I don't know what I'm doing.' That's exactly what she told me. I said, 'Look, it's okay. I was a caseworker. I'm reading right out of your policy manual what has to be done.' She just cried."

Millions of copies of drivers' licenses, social security cards, and other supporting documents were faxed to a centralized document processing center in Grant County; so many of them disappeared that advocates started calling it "the black hole in Marion." Each month the number of verification documents that vanished—were not attached properly to digital case files in a process called "indexing"—rose exponentially. According to court documents, in December 2007 just over 11,000 documents were unindexed. By February 2009, nearly 283,000 documents had disappeared, an increase of *2,473 percent*. The rise in technical errors far outpaced increased system use. The consequences are staggering if you consider that any single missing document could cause an applicant to be denied benefits.

Performance metrics designed to speed eligibility determinations created perverse incentives for call center workers to close cases prematurely. Timeliness could be improved by denying applications and then advising applicants to reapply, which required that they wait an additional 30 or 60 days for a new determination. Some administrative snafus were simple mistakes, integration problems, and technical glitches. But many errors were the result of inflexible rules that interpreted any deviation from the newly rigid application process, no matter how inconsequential or inadvertent, as an active refusal to cooperate.

The automation's impacts were devastating for poor and working-class Hoosiers. Between 2006 and 2008, the state of Indiana denied more than a million applications for food stamps, Medicaid, and cash benefits, a 54 percent increase compared to the three years prior to automation.

Michelle "Shelli" Birden, a soft-spoken and serious young woman from Kokomo, lost her benefits during the automation experiment. Shelli was diagnosed with epilepsy at six months of age; by the time she reached adulthood, she was suffering as many as five grand mal seizures a day. Despite having surgery to implant a vagus nerve stimulator—something like a pacemaker for the brain—she was still, in her own words, "violently ill" when the modernization hit. In late April 2008 she received a recertification notice from the FSSA. She faxed her response, a pile of forms, and other documentation eight days later. On June 25, Shelli received a letter dated June 12 informing her that her Medicaid benefits would be discontinued in five days for "failure to cooperate in establishing eligibility."

The failure to cooperate notice had originally been sent to an outdated address, which delayed its delivery. Now Shelli, in a panic, phoned the call center. An ACS worker told her to try to correct her application online. When that failed, she and her boyfriend Jeff Stewart phoned the call center several more times, trying to identify the problem. "I started reading her letters to

figure out what to do, and where to go, and who to call," Jeff remembered, "but you couldn't get anywhere on the phone. It was
like you were talking to a computer instead of a person."

On July 11, call center operators connected Shelli with one
of the few remaining state caseworkers in Marion, who told her
that she had neglected to sign a required form but did not tell
her which one. By this point, she was starting to run out of
her anticonvulsant medications. She would have to find a free
source for her drugs, which cost close to $800 a month, or risk
violent seizures, panic attacks, dizziness, insomnia, blurred vision, and an increased risk of death from going off them cold
turkey.

Shelli contacted the United Way, which provided her with a
few days of emergency medication. The staff also advised her to
immediately file an appeal of the "failure to cooperate" determination. She reached out to the Marion office again, on July 14,
and asked to lodge an appeal. But she was informed that the 30-
day deadline to contest the June 12 decision had passed. It was
too late to appeal the FSSA's decision. She'd have to reapply.

A new determination would take 45 days. She had three days
of medication left.

The governor and the FSSA promised that an automated eligibility system would offer increased client control, a fairer application process, and more timely decisions. The problem with the
existing caseworker-centered system, as they saw it, was twofold.
First, caseworkers spent more time manually processing papers
and collecting data than "using their social work expertise to help
clients." Second, the outdated data system allowed caseworkers to
collude with outside co-conspirators to illegally obtain benefits
and defraud taxpayers. The old system involved caseworkers developing one-on-one relationships with individuals and families
and following cases through to completion. The new system was

"self-serve," technology-focused, and presented call center workers with a list of tasks to complete rather than a docket of families to serve. No one worker had oversight of a case from beginning to end; when clients called the 1-800 number, they always spoke to a new worker. Because the Daniels administration saw relationships between caseworkers and clients as invitations to fraud, the system was designed to sever those links.

The FSSA packed up all its existing records and moved them to a central storage facility in Indianapolis. These paper records were set aside in case the state needed them for appeal hearings, but were not scanned into the modernized system. All current recipients of TANF, food stamps/SNAP, and Medicaid were required to turn in all their supporting documentation *again*, no matter how long they had been receiving benefits. "All of the documents that identified the members of the household—birth certificates and that sort of thing—were in the local office until the modernization. And then they were gone," remembered Jamie Andree. "It was as if they had never existed. So one of the things that happened with modernization is that people [were] asked to turn in [obscure] stuff, like the title to a vehicle that they hadn't owned since 1988. They were being asked to turn in things that the agency already had."

When clients did manage to find decades-old documents, delays between the document center receiving paperwork and the contractors processing it were consistently interpreted as the fault of the applicant. Chris Holly, a Medicaid attorney in Bloomington, estimated that 95 percent of the Medicaid applications he handled during the automation resulted in eligibility determination errors. According to Holly, all the errors were generated by the state and its contractors, not his clients. "We knew we had submitted everything by the deadline," he said in December of 2014, "and we were still getting denials for failure to cooperate." It would take three or four days for documentation to get processed, but "they never waited. They would deny it on the [deadline], or even before. And if people get denied, they assume the system knows what it's doing. They'll accept that they're just ineligible and give up."

Still, many applicants fought to retain their health insurance or food assistance against these formidable odds. Like Shelli, they became tenacious detectives, trying to ferret out a single error in complex applications running dozens of pages. Failure to cooperate notices offered little guidance. They simply stated that *something* was not right with an application, not *what specifically was wrong*. Was a document missing, lost, unsigned, or illegible? Was it the fault of the client, the FSSA, or the contractor? "Failure to cooperate was the operative phrase," noted Glenn Cardwell, a retired caseworker and administrator now living in Vigo County, "because then it was the client's problem and not the city, not the contractor."

Under the previous system, mistakes or omissions in an application were troublesome and time-consuming, requiring caseworkers and clients to collaborate to secure documents like birth certificates, medical reports, proof of income, social security cards, and rental receipts. "Before modernization, they had someone to call up and say, 'Listen, I received this notice. What do I need to do?'" recalled ACLU attorney Gavin Rose. "And the answer was 'Run it down to me, fax it over right now. I'll make sure it gets in your file and we'll take care of this.'" Before the automation, "failure to cooperate" had been a last-ditch punishment caseworkers used against a few clients who actively *refused* to participate in the eligibility process. After the automation, the phrase became a chain saw that clearcut the welfare rolls, no matter the collateral damage.

Shelli Birden was wary of talking about what she remembers as one of the most confusing and terrifying times of her life. Ultimately she discovered the lone signature she had missed. "I had to go back through my papers," she said. "I always copied my papers. I missed one question, and boom, they shut me off." When we spoke in 2015, she remembered feeling completely alone in a life-threatening situation. "They didn't give us enough information," she said. "They didn't send us in with our social workers anymore. They made us do it on our own."

But Shelli, as smart and tenacious as she is, didn't do it entirely on her own. She received help from advocate Dan Skinner, whose contacts with FSSA staff fast-tracked solutions. Her boyfriend took on navigating the debacle like it was a second job. She received help from the United Way, which provided advice and support. Birden was reinstated to Medicaid on July 17. She received her medication in time to save her life. Seven years later, with her health stabilized, Shelli was holding a job at Wal-Mart. "I'm doing really good," she said. "I'm actually able to get back to work, and I feel like my life matters."

But many others were not so lucky. "As attorneys, we had access to people that could fix things," noted Chris Holly. "But average well-meaning people that needed help? They were the ones that suffered the most." Jane Porter Gresham, a retired caseworker with nearly 30 years' experience at FSSA, agreed. "The most vulnerable of our population—the parents of children who didn't have food to eat, who needed medical treatment, and the disabled who were not able to speak for themselves—were the ones who took it on the chin, took it in the gut, and in the heart."

Lindsay Kidwell of Windfall also lost public benefits during the modernization experiment. Six months after giving birth to her first child, Maddox, in December 2008, Lindsay was informed that she was due to recertify for food stamps/SNAP and Hoosier Healthwise, Indiana's Medicaid program for low-income parents, pregnant women, and children. She participated in a phone interview on December 10 with a call center worker in Marion, who told her what documentation she needed to provide. Among the documents requested were pay stubs for her partner, Jack Williams, who made about $400 a week before taxes at the Buckhorn Restaurant and Lounge. Lindsay faxed everything except the pay stubs to the document center on December 19, because Jack got paid by bank check and didn't have any stubs. His boss at the Buckhorn called the document center to find out how to supply proof of his wages. Following their directions, she wrote out a list of paychecks and amounts and faxed them to the document center on December 23.

On January 2, Lindsay received a medical bill informing her that her Medicaid had been denied, and that she would be responsible for paying $246 out of pocket for her recent postnatal check-up. When she went out to do some grocery shopping on January 4, her EBT card—the debit-like card holding her food stamp/SNAP benefits—was denied. On January 15, she received a letter from FSSA.

```
Mailing Date: 1/13/09
Dear LINDSAY K KIDWELL,
FS01 (XD)
Your application for FOOD STAMPS dated DECEM-
BER 10, 2008 has been denied.
You are not eligible because:
—FAILURE TO COOPERATE IN VERIFYING INCOME
SUPPORTING LAW(S) OR REGULATION(S) :
7CFR273.2(d)
   .  .  .
MA C 01 (MI)
Your HOOSIER HEALTHWISE benefits will be
```

```
discontinued effective JANUARY 31, 2009 due to
the following reason(s):
—FAILURE TO COOPERATE IN VERIFYING INCOME
SUPPORTING LAW(S) OR REGULATION(S) : 470IAC2.
1-1-2
```

A week later, well within the 13-day window to submit the "missing" documents, Lindsay went to her local Tipton County FSSA office, submitting a more complete listing of wages and photocopies of Jack's last three paychecks.

Lindsay had the wage report and canceled paychecks stamped "Received" and asked for a copy. She watched the employee scan her paperwork into the system and took a copy of the "Scan Successful" notice confirming it was received by the document center. She also filed an appeal of the earlier "failure to cooperate" determinations. If she began a fair hearing process, her food stamps/SNAP and Medicaid would be reinstated until an administrative law judge ruled whether or not the decision to terminate her benefits was correct.

The Tipton County worker told Lindsay that she should file a new application for benefits rather than an appeal. It would be faster and easier, she insisted. Lindsay refused. She didn't want to reapply; she wanted to appeal what she saw as an incorrect FSSA decision.

Three weeks later she received a phone call from a young man who informed her that she would receive a notice in the mail soon—a hearing on her Medicaid case had been scheduled. Then he advised her to drop her appeal. He was looking in the computer, he said, and because Lindsay had never submitted payroll information for Jack, she would lose her case. But Lindsay had copies of his payroll information stamped "Received." She had the canceled checks and the scan confirmation. It must be some kind of mistake, she insisted. It didn't matter. Lindsay recalls that the man on the phone simply said, "I found no documentation of recent payroll information in the computer. The judge will simply look in the computer, see this, and deny you."

One of the great victories of the welfare rights movement of the 1960s and '70s was the redefinition of welfare benefits as the personal property of the recipient, rather than as charity that can be bestowed or denied on a whim. Activists successfully challenged inequitable access to public assistance by appealing decisions and demanding access to administrative law procedures known as fair hearings.

In 1968, eight individuals denied due process in New York launched a class action lawsuit that led to a Supreme Court decision in *Goldberg v. Kelly*. This landmark case found that all welfare recipients have a right to an evidentiary hearing—a process that includes timely and adequate notice, disclosure of opposing evidence, an impartial decision-maker, cross-examination of witnesses, and the right to retain legal representation—*before their benefits can be terminated*.

By successfully reframing public benefits as property rather than charity, the welfare rights movement established that public assistance recipients must be provided due process under the Fourteenth Amendment of the Constitution. The case hinged on the understanding, expressed by Justice William Brennan, that abrupt termination of aid deprives poor people of both their means of survival and their ability to mount an adequate challenge to government decisions. "From its founding, the Nation's basic commitment has been to foster the dignity and well-being of all persons within its borders," Brennan wrote. "Public assistance, then, is not mere charity, but a means to 'promote the general Welfare, and secure the Blessings of Liberty to ourselves and our Posterity.'"[4]

The far-reaching and fundamental changes introduced by Indiana's automated system put it on an inevitable collision course with the poor's right to due process guaranteed by *Goldberg*. A class action lawsuit, *Perdue v. Murphy*, was filed by Gavin Rose and Jacquelyn Bowie Suess, staff attorneys from the ACLU of Indiana, on behalf of more than a dozen individuals in north central Indiana who had lost their Medicaid, food stamps/SNAP, or TANF assistance for failure to cooperate. The case explicitly challenged the loss of due process under the automated system.

The ACLU alleged that notices were incomplete, "failure to cooperate" was being used too broadly, and the new caseworkerless system denied the disabled equal access to public programs. They also claimed that the last resort of wrongly denied applicants—a fair hearing—was made increasingly difficult to access. Call center workers defaulted to the decisions of the automated system over the administrative law process, discouraging appeals in favor of reapplication, and failed to notify applicants of their rights. Applicants felt that they had nowhere to turn for redress.

After successes for the ACLU in lower courts, *Perdue v. Murphy* eventually went to the Indiana Supreme Court, which found that the state's "failure to cooperate" notices were unconstitutional and did not provide adequate due process protections. But, reversing a lower court's decision, Indiana's highest court held that the state *does* have a right to deny applicants for "failure to cooperate" because at some point "failing" and "refusing" to cooperate converge. The case forced the FSSA to create more complete and specific notices, but did little to return the individualized attention of caseworkers to the Indiana eligibility process, or to stop the use of "failure to cooperate" to clearcut the rolls.

"The judge will simply look in the computer . . . and deny you," the call center operator said to Lindsay Kidwell in February 2009.

The words were a nightmare. Despite the fact that she had stamped proof that she submitted all the appropriate payroll information, Lindsay wavered. Should she cancel her appeal? If she lost, she'd be responsible for repaying all the benefits she received while waiting for a decision—months of medical and food bills.

Even though Lindsay knew she was in the right, there was no guarantee she would win the case. A loss would mean more debt for her young family. She asked the man on the phone if she could talk to an advisor before deciding whether or not to continue her appeal. He said, "No. I need an answer now. Are you going or not?" Gathering her courage, she re-affirmed that she wanted a fair hearing.

He hung up on her.

Lindsay remembered that the appeal hearing was pretty straightforward. "I went to my appeal," she said in 2017. "They said basically that they messed up. I didn't owe them money." Her family met all of the eligibility requirements of the program; their Hoosier Healthwise and food stamp benefits were officially reinstated.

But her experience with the FSSA still haunts her today. Her family was self-supporting for nearly a decade after the eligibility automation. Then she went through a divorce. When I spoke with her in 2017, she knew she was probably eligible for help from FSSA. "I'm going through a tough time," she said. "I'm a single mom. I work full time, but it doesn't always cut it." Her experience during the automation makes Lindsay hesitant to apply for benefits again. "They make it so difficult. If I applied now I could probably get it, but that experience with being denied . . . I mean, I cried. I did everything that they asked me to do. I don't even know if it's worth the stress."

Applicants for TANF, food stamps/SNAP, and Medicaid were not the only Hoosiers impacted by the shift to automated decision-making. That's why I traveled to Fort Wayne in March 2015 to talk to caseworkers about their experience with the Indiana experiment.

Fort Wayne, the second-largest city in Indiana, is in the northeast, 18 miles west of Ohio and 50 miles south of Michigan. General Electric and International Harvester had factories there that closed or scaled their workforces back significantly during the 1970s and 1980s. Driving to my first appointment of the afternoon, I pass the local headquarters of the National Association of Letter Carriers; George's International Market with its incredible selection of house-made salsas and bottled hot sauces; and Uncle Lou's Steel Mill Tavern, which sports a sign in the window that reads "Honk if you like beer." I cross the railroad tracks and the St. Marys River, swollen from recent flooding, into a neighborhood of modest two-story houses.

Jane Porter Gresham welcomes me into her tidy white home, where we sit on a blue velveteen couch in her front parlor. Gresham's wooden cross contrasts sharply with her matching blue t-shirt and cardigan set. Gresham worked for the FSSA for 26 years, from 1985 to 2011, when she retired in the wake of the automation. Even four years later, rage and frustration flicker across her round face as we speak. "People who are [at FSSA] for the first time, you can see it in their eyes—fear. Fear of what I'm going to do. People say to me, 'I never thought I'd have to be here.' They're not trying to cheat the system; they don't know where else to turn. Our responsibility as public employees is to make certain that people who are eligible get the benefits they're entitled to."

With decades of experience and seniority, Gresham managed to hold on to her state job when the automation rolled out to Allen County. But under the new system, she no longer carried a caseload. Rather, she responded to tasks that were assigned by the new Workflow Management System (WFMS). Tasks bounced between 1,500 new ACS employees and 682 remaining state employees, now known as "state eligibility consultants."

The governor promised that no state workers would lose their jobs due to the automation and that salaries would stay the same or rise. But the reality of the new ACS positions created a wave of retirements and resignations. After reapplying for jobs they already held, sometimes for decades, and submitting to criminal background checks and drug tests, workers found their positions moved from their home county office to a regional call center. They were offered moving bonuses if their new job was more than 50 miles from their current work site, but many declined to uproot their lives for the insecure new positions.

Under the eligibility automation, no single employee "owned" or oversaw a case; staff were responsible for responding to tasks that dropped into their queue in the WFMS. Cases were not handled in the county where applicants lived. Now, any employee could take any call from any county using the new system, even if they knew nothing about the caller's local context. "We got calls from all over the state," says Gresham. "I had never heard of Floyds Knobs [in southeastern Indiana] until we started that process! I had no idea of services that were available in that area."

Reducing casework to a task-based system is dehumanizing, she suggests, for both worker and client. "If I wanted to work in a factory, I would have worked in a factory. . . . You were expected to *produce*, and you couldn't do that if you listened to the client's story." The majority of clients Gresham saw during her long career were traumatized—by flood or fire, illness or accident, domestic violence or extended unemployment. "People who have gone through a trauma want some hope that it's going to get better. That somebody's paying attention, that they're not in this alone," she says. "That's what I think we did [before the automation]. We listened to what they had to say and acted on it so that things could get better."

"We became slaves to the task system," said Fred Gilbert, a 30-year FSSA employee specializing in refugee assistance. "Like any other private call center, it's 'just the facts.' But the welfare system is very complicated. That's the job of caseworkers, to help people wade through the mess."

The governor and the IBM/ACS coalition promised more timely decisions, more efficient use of resources, and better customer service. But caseworkers experienced cascading technical failures, an explosion of errors that slowed or terminated applications, and poorly trained private workers who passed the problems they created on to the remaining public employees. Mistakes made by ACS workers were referred to state workers for correction, piling an outsized workload on the handful of long-term employees that remained.

By summer 2009, there was a backlog of nearly 32,000 cases and 6,500 people were waiting for appeal hearings. According to their monthly management reports, the FSSA was reporting incredibly high food stamp eligibility error rates to the USDA. Between 2006 and 2008, the combined error rate more than tripled, from 5.9 percent to 19.4 percent. Most of that growth was in the negative error rate: 12.2 percent of those applying for food stamps were being incorrectly denied. The state's long wait times for food stamps decisions attracted notice and threats of financial penalties from the USDA.

The pressure to keep timeliness numbers high to fulfill the basic requirements of the contract, combined with an ever-growing backlog of cases, led to mass application denials and the now-habitual advice from call center workers to "just reapply." Fred Gilbert reflected, "The rules became brittle. If [applicants] didn't send something in, one of thirty documents, you simply closed the case for failure to comply. . . . You couldn't go out of your way to help somebody."

Back in her living room, Jane Porter Gresham turns reflective.

"It didn't take long for word to get out on the street: If you want your benefits on time, go to the office [in person] because they have to give you a face-to-face appointment," she says. "We were inundated with people who knew that. It was bogging everybody down.... We didn't save space and rent. We didn't save workers.... We were inundated at the end."

Gresham saw great workers burn out, and her own health began to deteriorate. "Morale was at an all-time low. There couldn't be reassurance, there couldn't be any camaraderie. It was just you out there," she says wistfully. "Towards the end, I realized this was affecting my health, my relationships. I was one of the last holdouts."

When failed by FSSA, Indiana's poor and working-class families relied on local governments, volunteers, and each other. Faced with lines of desperate people waiting for help, recalcitrant state agencies, and dismissive private call center workers, Hoosiers fought back. One of the centers of their resistance was Muncie, Indiana, the largest city in the automation experiment's first pilot area.

Following State Route 32 through "Middletown, USA" provides a drive-by tour of the city's recent industrial past. The abandoned million-square-foot BorgWarner plant haunts the town as you arrive from the west. In the 1950s, it employed 5,000 people assembling transmissions for Ford trucks, but it closed in 2009. Two miles later on your right, you roll by an enormous asphalt field, site of the old General Motors plant. Workers made the famous Muncie M-22 "Rock Crusher" four-speed transmission for the muscle cars of the 1960s there, but the plant closed in 2006. When I visited Muncie in 2015, the job board in the Center Township of Delaware County Trustee's office offered only a handful of employment opportunities: gardener, custodian, food service, Pepsi delivery.

The state of Indiana is broken up into 1,008 six-square-mile townships, each with a local government office funded by property taxes and run by a township board and an elected trustee. Though each township office works a little differently, one of their primary responsibilities is to manage local poverty relief. Almost immediately after its rollout in October 2007, the failures of the automated system overwhelmed the Delaware County Trustee's office. "People were devastated," Lead Case Coordinator Kim Murphy said. "I mean they were just lost. Lost, lost, lost." Already suffering through the rash of plant closures, Muncie families were now getting kicked off food stamps, cash assistance, and Medicaid. "They were confused, and they didn't know where to turn," said Marilyn "Kay" Walker, Center Township trustee. "There was no case management, no personal connection, no communication among agencies. It was just the biggest mess."

According to the *Muncie Star Press,* by February 2008, the number of households receiving food stamps in Delaware County dropped 7.47 percent, though the number of households receiving food assistance had climbed 4 percent in Indiana overall. Calls to the LifeStream 211 telephone hotline requesting information about food pantries doubled. The Second Harvest Food Bank of East Central Indiana faced severe shortages. The municipal graveyard complained it had not been paid for thousands of dollars worth of funerals for poor and indigent people.

The public was encouraged to apply for services through the new online system; but low-income families in Muncie, as elsewhere, did not have regular access to the internet. The majority of applicants had to rely on a community partner such as a local library, food pantry, or health clinic to access the online application. The FSSA aggressively recruited community organizations to support the new system by becoming part of a Voluntary Community Assistance Network (V-CAN).

Asked to use her office's existing computers and staff to help

Muncie citizens submit applications for public assistance, Walker resisted. "When it came out that this is what they were going to do, I was like, 'Excuse me, but, hell! You are not!' They were trying to get all these other organizations involved to *do their work*," she remembered. "We're already overloaded." Walker made her office available to people who needed to fax documents and participate in phone appointments, and her staff went out of their way to help applicants, but she drew the line at becoming a V-CAN partner. "I didn't think it was our responsibility to start doing FSSA's work."

Public libraries were particularly hard-hit by the automation project. "We had lines of desperate people waiting for help," said Muncie Public Library director Ginny Nilles, now retired. V-CAN partners received little to no compensation, training, or oversight to do what amounted to volunteer casework. Librarians trained community volunteers to help patrons submit welfare applications, but the library was quickly overwhelmed. The situation worsened when budget cuts required reducing hours and laying off staff.

Library staff and volunteers did a great job, said Nilles, but there were serious issues. "Confidentiality is very important to librarians. The forms ask very personal questions. If they couldn't use the computer, it was incumbent on us to read the questions out loud and get the answers: social security numbers, mental and physical health. Volunteers are great, but if you pay someone to do a job, it's their responsibility. It's about accountability."

"Local agencies were victimized," said John Cardwell from the Generations Project, who worked closely with local non-profits throughout the automation. "They were being dumped on, serving thousands of people they shouldn't have been serving, scrambling to help people get their benefits restored. They knew these people. They weren't going to leave them without medical care or food."

Faced with system failures, increasing need, and little help from the state, public assistance recipients, community organizations, and trustee's offices began to organize. A group called Concerned Hoosiers set up a website where FSSA and ACS workers could share their experiences with the modernized system. The Indiana Home Care Task Force held press conferences on the automation experiment's impacts and drafted model legislation to reverse damage. A subcommittee of service providers, advocates, and welfare recipients calling themselves the Committee on Welfare Privatization Issues provided emergency interventions for recipients facing benefits termination, organized press tours highlighting impacts on Hoosier families, and launched campaigns to increase pressure on policy-makers to stop the automation rollout and terminate the IBM/ACS contract. With typical Hoosier humor, their acronym, COWPI, made it clear what they thought about the new system.

Town Hall meetings on the welfare modernization spread across the state. Anderson was first in April 2008, then Muncie, Bloomington, Terre Haute, Kokomo. One of the most successful was the Muncie People's Town Hall meeting, held on May 13, 2008. Walker and Murphy proved to be shrewd organizers. They printed flyers for the meeting and delivered them to social service agencies, convenience stores, and libraries. They convinced the Dollar Tree to put a flyer in every customer's bag. They scheduled the meeting to coincide with a free food distribution by the Second Harvest Food Bank. They invited local lawmakers, including State Senator Sue Errington, State Senator Tim Lanane, and State Representative Dennis Tyler, who listened to hours of testimony from impacted constituents. They invited Mitch Roob, who at first demurred. As the town hall date approached, he changed his mind and asked Walker to make space for a small army of caseworkers, eight computers, and a photocopier, to help attendees solve their eligibility problems on-site.

More than 500 people attended. A room-spanning line of public assistance recipients testified about unanswered phones, lost documents, and benefits denied capriciously. Melinda Jones of Muncie, the mother of a ten-month-old with cancer, was fighting to keep her Medicaid and food stamps. "I have to beg and borrow from my family to give my daughter her food," she said, "and I think it's utterly ridiculous that we do our children like this."

Christina King, a diabetic and working mother of three, lost her Medicaid during the modernization. She was unable to afford insulin for seven months and her blood sugar was out of control, putting her at risk of stroke or coma. "What good does it do when my seven-year-old walks in and I physically cannot get out of bed?" she asked. "I spent two days in the ICU because I have no medicine. My kidneys are now at risk. My eyes are at risk. But I get up every day and I go to work, because I think it's important for me to show my kids, 'Don't be dependent on the system.' I need a hand up, not a handout. I'm raising three kids by myself. I am trying to show my kids, 'Don't be like me—do better.'"

Deaf, blind, disabled, and mentally ill clients were particularly hard-hit. "I'm deaf. How can I do a telephone interview?" asked Dionna McGairk through a sign-language interpreter. "I tell [call-center operators] to use my relay service. They don't understand what relay service is." When operators told her she needed to get help to apply for public services, she responded: "*No*—I can answer my questions myself. You are discriminating against the deaf."

The day after the Muncie Town Hall meeting, State Representative Dennis Tyler sent a letter to his colleagues in the Indiana House of Representatives requesting a summer General Assembly meeting to address ongoing problems with the automated system. "The state of Indiana isn't doing its job," he said to Joe Cermak of *NewsLink Indiana*. "You don't want to think this system is put in place to fail these people, but what can you think when it's failing this bad?" A few days later, on May 19, the IBM/ACS coalition, receiving a "go ahead" order from the FSSA, rolled out the automated system to 20 more counties in northeastern and southwestern Indiana.

The modernized system had now reached 59 of 92 Indiana counties, and was serving 430,000 social services clients, a bit less than half of the state's caseload. On May 30, a severe weather system—including tornadoes, torrential rain, and high winds—battered the state, causing widespread flooding. The IBM/ACS coalition pulled employees away from regular operations to pitch in for the flood effort, easing the way to emergency benefits for thousands but worsening the already significant backlog for regular public assistance applicants.

At a Bloomington Town Hall meeting a few weeks later, State Senator Vi Simpson and State Representatives Peggy Welch and Matt Pierce listened to client testimony and grilled Zach Main, director of the Division of Family Resources at FSSA and Mitch Roob's right-hand man. Participants in the forum raised similar concerns to those in Muncie: telephone lines were always busy, Help Center offices had multi-day waits, failure to cooperate notices were arbitrary and unclear, V-CAN partners were not trained or supported. Main, visibly frustrated, responded to criticism of the new system. "I'm not here today to argue, to defend," he said. "I'm certainly not here to tell you that everything is perfect with the system. What I will tell you is that we're working very hard. . . . When Governor Daniels came into office, Indiana was first in the nation in child deaths and last in the nation in welfare-to-work. We had a system that was undeniably broken, and the results speak for themselves on that."

He faced a skeptical, even incredulous, room. If the results spoke for themselves, what were they saying, exactly? Simpson and Welch, who had been responding to constituent complaints for three months, weren't buying it. They pressed him with questions about the ambiguity of failure to cooperate notices, inadequate caseworker support, lack of FSSA accountability to its own processes, and failure to levy penalties against IBM and ACS for poor performance.

Peggy Welch shot back, "I'm sorry Zach, but what we've heard over and over again is about this telephone interview time, that they tell you, 'We're going to call between 2 and 4 and you better be there,' and the call doesn't come through. They call at 8 o'clock the next morning and then say 'failure to cooperate.' That's a real problem." Simpson added, "People don't know what it means when they get 'failure to cooperate' on a denial notice. In the old days, they used to be able to *call their caseworker* and find out what piece of paper they were missing, or what signature line they forgot to sign, or whatever the problem was. Now they don't have anyone to call."

The press was printing poignant human interest stories emerging from the modernization: a nun denied Medicaid, desperately ill patients spending their final months fighting to get their health care back, food banks picked clean. Ollice Holden, regional administrator of the Food and Nutrition Service, which administers food stamps for the USDA, wrote a letter to Secretary Roob requesting that the FSSA delay further implementation. The federal government was concerned over long determination wait times.

The governor faced increasingly vocal challenges from state legislators. "I asked for a point of personal privilege on the House floor," said Matt Pierce, a Democrat. "I said, 'This is a train wreck and everybody ought to know. This thing is hurting people. We've really got to fix it.'" The governor attacked complaints as partisan sniping. "Let me tell you what," Daniels fired back in an interview with the *Evansville Courier & Press*, "[Legislators] are hearing complaints from people who made money off the past system. That's where the complaints are principally coming from."[5]

But Daniels' contention that the only people harmed by the automation experiment were welfare chiselers proved unsustainable when members of his own party began to attack the project. In October 2008, State Representative Suzanne Crouch and State Senator Vaneta Becker, both Republicans, drafted legislation that would halt the expansion of the new eligibility system until the Select Joint Commission on Medicaid Oversight could perform a thorough review. At the close of the year, Daniels announced that he was moving his friend and colleague, Mitch Roob, out of the FSSA and making him the state's secretary of commerce and CEO of the Indiana Economic Development Corporation. He appointed Anne Waltermann Murphy, Roob's chief of staff, to lead the troubled agency.

Within three months of taking control, Murphy demanded that IBM submit a corrective action plan to improve 36 different service deficiencies, including excessive wait times, lost documents, inaccurate data, interview scheduling problems, slow application processing, and incorrect instructions to clients.

IBM argued that nothing in their contract required that they respond to a corrective action plan, but agreed to evaluate existing operations and suggest areas for system improvement. According to Ken Kusmer of the *News and Tribune*, IBM released a 362-page plan to fix problems, including "inaccurate and incomplete data gathering" and "incorrect communications to clients" in late July.[6] Secretary Murphy encouraged two longtime welfare officials, Richard Adams and Roger Zimmerman, to come up with a "Plan B" in case IBM was unable or unwilling to make these changes. According to Adams' testimony in *Perdue v. Murphy*, the two sketched out a "hybrid system" that would bring back some aspects of the pre-automated FSSA process on a napkin over lunch.

Daniels continued to defend the automation experiment, insisting that Indiana would not back down from high-tech welfare reform and that "over time this issue will resolve itself." But the political winds had changed. Daniels was now the subject of speculation about a presidential run, and the failed automation was embarrassing to the state and to his administration. In October 2009, with his eye on a national audience, the governor did something unexpected. He admitted that the experiment had failed and canceled the contract with IBM, calling the project a "flawed concept that simply did not work out in practice."

In May 2010, Indiana sued IBM for $437 million, claiming breach of contract. The state claimed that the automation experiment led to faulty benefit denials that harmed needy Hoosiers, and demanded that the company pay back the nearly half-billion dollars they had received for running the modernization plus damages for lawsuits, federal penalties, and state employee overtime. IBM countersued for about $100 million for the server, hardware, automated processes, and software that the state was still using to determine benefit eligibility. IBM won the suit, and was awarded more than $52 million.

"Neither party deserves to win this case," wrote Marion Superior Court Judge David Dreyer in his judgment in favor of IBM. "This story represents a 'perfect storm' of misguided government policy and overzealous corporate ambition. Overall, both parties are to blame and Indiana's taxpayers are left as apparent losers. . . . There is nothing in this case, or the Court's power, . . . [to] remedy the lost taxpayer money or personal suffering of needy Hoosiers."

In its suit against IBM, the state charged that the company had misrepresented its ability to modernize complicated social service programs and failed to meet the performance standards contained in the contract. Automated counties lagged behind "as-is" counties in almost every area of performance: timeliness, backlogs, data integrity, determination errors, and number of appeals requested.

The state even accused IBM of jury-rigging its processes to make its performance look better. "A major cause of the dramatic rise in appeals in the Modernized counties," the private attorneys hired to represent the state argued, "was that the IBM Coalition workers were so far behind in processing applications that they would often recommend denial of an application to make their timeliness numbers look better, but then would tell the applicant to appeal the decision. While the appeal was pending, the Coalition workers would actually process the application and benefits would be granted before the hearing date." According to the suit, "for the three-year period, IBM was achieving higher-than-projected profit margins at the same time that its modernized system was floundering."

IBM argued on the contrary: the state had consistently praised their efforts. In May 2008, Secretary Roob reported to the General Assembly that, "We are serving more people statewide and in a timelier manner than we ever have before."[7] In December 2008 Governor Daniels stated that the new system "was far better than what preceded it." IBM admitted that there were problems with managing overload in the new system. But the company claimed the problems that arose were due to factors beyond its control. The Great Recession, the new Healthy Indiana Program, and the 2008 floods had pushed application levels beyond what either party had imagined.

Judge Dreyer saw incompetence and negligence on *both* sides. He noted that the state invited IBM to keep working on the project even as they rolled out the hybrid system, which was based on IBM's tools, software, and skills. But since the Senate had stripped the FSSA budget "bare" in early 2009, there was no money to pay for change orders or modifications to the contract. Secretary Murphy wrote in an email to her colleagues that IBM would "not commit to moving forward at no cost.... [T]hey want more money! We don't have money now and we won't have money for the remainder of [State Fiscal Year] '10. What a mess."[8] When IBM refused to do more work without more pay, the state simply cut out the middle man, terminating their contract while keeping their equipment, processes, and subcontractors in place.

The state and IBM both blamed forces out of their control for the plan's collapse. But in reality the coalition delivered exactly what Indiana officials had asked for: smaller welfare rolls, whatever the cost.

In the lawsuit, both the state and IBM avoided talking much about the impact of the failed automation experiment on the people of Indiana. The state knew from the beginning that what it was doing posed enormous risks for public assistance recipients and their families. The state identified "several areas of potentially significant risk" with the automated system, but "concluded that 'the status quo is not acceptable'" and moved forward with the plan anyway.[9]

The goals of the project were consistent throughout the automation experiment: maximize efficiency and eliminate fraud by shifting to a task-based system and severing caseworker-to-client bonds. They were clearly reflected in contract metrics: response time in the call centers was a key performance indicator; determination accuracy was not. Efficiency and savings were built into the contract; transparency and due process were not.

Judge Dreyer found that the problem with the automation experiment was not contractor negligence. There was no material breach of the Indiana/IBM contract. "The heart of the contract remained intact throughout the project," he concluded in his findings, "although sometimes beating irregularly." The state achieved its goal of containing the cost of social service programs. The contractor, accountable only to its employer and its shareholders, had no obligation to measure the automation experiment's impact on poor and working-class Hoosiers. The problem with the automation experiment was not that the IBM/ACS coalition failed to deliver, it was that the state and its private partners refused to anticipate or address the system's human costs.

After an expensive series of appeals of Judge Dreyer's decision, in March 2016 the Indiana Supreme Court ruled that IBM did in fact materially breach its contract with the state. But the legal case only seeks to apportion blame and levy penalties. *Indiana v. IBM*, as Judge Dreyer pointed out, was about material breach of contract, not the public trust or public injury. The real cost of the privatization experiment—the loss of life-saving benefits for struggling families, the cost of the contract and legal disputes to taxpayers, and the weakening of the public service system and democratic process—has yet to be calculated. It is perhaps incalculable.

"There's a cost to *people*," said Jamie Andree of Indiana Legal Services. "The cost of just waiting around without Medicaid benefits is enormous; it's really hard to make somebody whole. Most people will stop getting medical care while eligibility is being determined. There's no way to compensate them for that."

The state now uses the hybrid eligibility system, which combines face-to-face interactions with public employees with the electronic data processing and privatized administration of the automated system. Its design allows applicants to contact a team of regional caseworkers assigned to their case by phone, by internet, by mail, or in person, providing increased contact with state workers. But the hybrid system still relies on privatized, automated processes for many core functions and retains the task-based case management that caused so many problems during the modernization. In the hybrid system, re-staffed local offices function as problem resolution centers, while regional and statewide "change centers"—run by Xerox, which bought ACS in 2009 for $6.4 billion—review applications, collect and digitize documents, schedule appointments, screen applications for fraud, process fair hearing requests, provide a first point of contact for clients, and perform most updates to cases.

The move to the hybrid system in 2009 certainly quieted the automated system's most vocal detractors. But it is unclear if it works better to secure benefits for those who deserve them. "They got marginally better when they ditched IBM and did the hybrid thing," said Chris Holly in December 2014. "They got better for people like me. People who *help* poor people have access to the local office directly to solve problems. So they took care of us. I don't think they took care of the normal person. I won't say they bought us off, but they responded to us. We were the ones that were complaining the loudest."

Representative Gail Riecken of Evansville agreed with Holly in an op-ed she wrote in the *Fort Wayne Journal Gazette* in May 2010. "[FSSA Secretary Anne] Murphy reported that fewer people are filing appeals for mistakes and wrong decisions [under the hybrid system]. But it is not clear why the appeals have decreased. Is it because the system is better, or have people simply given up fighting the system?"[10]

For some caseworkers, the hybrid system is just the automated system with a different name. "I don't see any change," said Jane Porter Gresham. "We're still working mandatory overtime. We still have the same number of people clamoring to be heard in face-to-face interviews. The workload has not diminished. . . .

The people that were the most vocal had their needs met." When I asked her why we weren't hearing more about the problems of the hybrid system, she replied, "Experienced workers who knew how it was supposed to be aren't there any more." Glenn Cardwell, retired FSSA worker and advocate, agreed. "Yeah," he said, "We're not satisfied [with the hybrid system], but that's partly a matter of energy. We won a big battle, but we weren't ever sure we won the war."

"They set that system up to just slide stuff under the rug and hide it," argued Kevin Stipes, Sophie's dad. "People [on public assistance] don't have a voice. That's one of the reasons we went down [to the state house]." Kim chimed in, "To put a face on it!" Kevin nodded at his wife. "We didn't mind standing up," he said. But there were a lot of people who didn't know what to do, or felt too vulnerable to rally to their own defense. "My wife is persistent, intelligent—I mean, it should have been a breeze for her to get the paperwork turned in correctly. I just can't imagine people with lesser skills . . . I know they couldn't, they *didn't* do it."

"The system doesn't seem to be set up to help people. It seems to be set up to play gotcha," said Chris Holly. "In our legal system it is better that ten guilty men go free than one innocent man go to jail. The modernization flipped that on its head." Automated eligibility was based on the assumption that it is better for ten eligible applicants to be denied public benefits than for one ineligible person to receive them. "They had an opportunity to make a system that was responsive and effective, and ensure people who qualified for benefits received those benefits," Holly said. "My gut feeling is that they did not respect the people who needed their help."

In the fall of 2008, Omega Young of Evansville missed an appointment to recertify for Medicaid because she was in the hospital suffering from terminal cancer. The cancer that began in her

ovaries had spread to her kidneys, breast, and liver. Her chemo-
therapy left her weak and emaciated. Young, a round-faced,
umber-skinned mother of two grown sons, struggled to meet the
new system's requirements. She called the Vanderburgh County
Help Center to let them know that she was hospitalized. Her
medical benefits and food stamps were still cut off for failure to
cooperate.

"The 50-year-old Young, who lived alone in a tiny apartment,
was frantic," reported Will Higgins in the *Indianapolis Star*.[11] She
called Cecilia Brennan, a staffer with Evansville-based Southwestern Indiana Regional Council on Aging who had been helping with her case, crying, asking, " 'What am I going to do?' " Her
sister, Christal Bell, refrained from telling the press that the
Medicaid denial hastened Young's death, but she did blame the
automated system for making her last days full of extra worry and
trouble. Her brother-in-law, Tom Willis, told Higgins that he
routinely hid Young's medical bills from her so she would not ob-
sess about the $10,000 she owed.

Because she lost her benefits, Young was unable to afford her
medications. She lost her food stamps. She struggled to pay her rent.
She lost access to free transportation to medical appointments.
Omega Young died March 1, 2009. The next day, on March 2, she
won her FSSA appeal for wrongful termination and her benefits
were restored.

The public welfare system has never been simple, particularly
for Black women. The most restrictive eligibility rules were historically aimed at them. "Suitable home" and "employable mother"
rules were selectively interpreted to block African American
women from claiming their benefits until the rise of the welfare
rights movement in the 1970s. "Man in house" and "substitute
father" rules legitimized intrusion into their privacy, judgment of
their sexuality, and invasions of their homes. Ronald Reagan's
1976 stump speech about the lavish lifestyle of "welfare queen"

Linda Taylor was intended to make the face of welfare both Black and female. "There's a woman in Chicago," he said during the New Hampshire Republican presidential primary contest. "She has 80 names, 30 addresses, 12 Social Security cards and is collecting veterans' benefits on four non-existing deceased husbands. She's got Medicaid, getting food stamps and she is collecting welfare under each of her names. Her tax-free cash income alone is over $150,000."[12] Ms. Taylor was eventually charged with using 4 aliases, not 80, and collecting $8,000, not $150,000, but Reagan's overblown claims found fertile ground, and the image of the welfare queen has remained central to our country's understanding of public assistance.

Even today, audit studies find that nonwhite applicants in welfare offices face more unprofessional behavior from caseworkers than whites: withholding crucial information, refusing to provide applications, and other forms of outright rudeness.[13] States with higher African American populations have tougher rules, more stringent work requirements, and higher sanction rates.[14] Casework is a complex, human endeavor that relies on relationships, requires a difficult mix of canniness and compassion, and is vulnerable to all the biases about race, class, and gender that are woven through our society. Concerns about discretionary excesses are valid. Caseworkers do turn down individuals based on bigotry or unconscious bias.

The majority of public assistance recipients in Indiana are white, but race still played a major role in the automation experiment. Governor Mitch Daniels played on rural-urban tensions and white racial anxiety when he persistently framed problems in terms of dependency, cheating, criminality, and collusion despite evidence that only a small proportion of those eligible for public assistance benefits actually claimed them and that fraud was not a particularly severe problem at FSSA. The fraud case he held up as indicative of the worst problems in the system—the Greater Faith

Missionary Baptist scam—involved Black defendants. It's hard not to suspect that Daniels, like his anti-AFDC mentor Ronald Reagan, cagily stoked Hoosiers' stereotypes about race, class, and public assistance to drum up support for the move to an automated, privatized welfare system.

The Indiana counties with the smallest African American populations were transitioned to the automated system first, and the experiment was halted before it reached Indianapolis and Gary, the two cities a large share of Black Hoosiers call home. But despite being tested primarily on poor whites, the automation experiment had profound impacts on African Americans. According to census data, in 2000, African Americans made up 46.5 percent of the state's TANF rolls, and whites held a very slim majority in the program, at 47.2 percent. At the end of the automation experiment in 2010, the gap between white and African American TANF and food stamp/SNAP recipients had widened precipitously. Despite the fact that the African American population of Indiana had grown over the decade, the TANF rolls were now 54.2 percent white and only 32.1 percent African American. Though eligibility modernization was tested on primarily white communities, Black families still felt its worst effects.

Removing human discretion from public assistance eligibility may seem like a compelling solution to the continuing discrimination African Americans face in the welfare system. After all, a computer applies the rules to each case consistently and without prejudice. But historically, the removal of human discretion and the creation of inflexible rules in public services only compound racially disparate harms.

For example, in the 1980s and 1990s Congress and many state legislatures enacted a series of "Tough on Crime" laws that established mandatory minimum sentences for many categories of crime and removed a great deal of discretion from judges. Ironically, the changes were a result of organizing both by conservative law-and-order types *and* by some progressive civil rights activists who saw the bias in judicial discretion as creating racially disparate outcomes in sentencing.

The evidence of the past 30 years is clear: racial disparity in the criminal justice system is a great deal worse. As the Leadership Conference on Civil and Human Rights wrote in a 2000 report called "Justice on Trial," "Minorities fare much worse under mandatory sentencing laws and guidelines than they did under a system favoring judicial discretion. By depriving judges of the ultimate authority to impose just sentences, mandatory sentencing laws and guidelines put sentencing on auto-pilot."[15]

Automated decision-making can change government for the better, and tracking program data may, in fact, help identify patterns of biased decision-making. But justice sometimes requires an ability to bend the rules. By removing human discretion from frontline social servants and moving it instead to engineers and private contractors, the Indiana experiment supercharged discrimination.

The "social specs" for the automation were based on timeworn, race- and class-motivated assumptions about welfare recipients that were encoded into performance metrics and programmed into business processes: they are lazy and must be "prodded" into contributing to their own support, they are sneaky and prone to fraudulent claims, and their burdensome use of public resources must be repeatedly discouraged. Each of these assumptions relies on, and is bolstered by, race- and class-based stereotypes. Poor Black women like Omega Young paid the price.

New high-tech tools allow for more precise measuring and tracking, better sharing of information, and increased visibility of targeted populations. In a system dedicated to supporting poor and working-class people's self-determination, such diligence would guarantee that they attain all the benefits they are entitled to by law. In that context, integrated data and modernized administration would not necessarily result in bad outcomes for poor communities. But automated decision-making in our current welfare system acts a lot like older, atavistic forms of punishment and containment. It filters and diverts. It is a gatekeeper, not a facilitator.

The Indiana automated eligibility system enhanced the state's already well-developed diversion apparatus, turbo-charging what must be seen as a remarkably efficient machine for denying applications. By narrowing the gate for public benefits and raising the penalties for noncompliance, it achieved stunning welfare roll reductions. Even under the hybrid system and during the greatest economic downturn since the Great Depression, drops in the state's TANF caseload continued to outpace national averages. As poverty in Indiana increased, caseloads dropped. When the governor signed the contract with IBM in 2006, 38 percent of poor families with children were receiving cash benefits from TANF. By 2014, the number had dropped to 8 percent.

Struggling people like Omega Young, Lindsay Kidwell, and Shelli Birden were the first victims of the automation, and they bore the system's most terrifying impacts. Though the Stipes family managed against incredible odds to reestablish their daughter's Medicaid, the experience took a dreadful toll. "During that time, my mind was muddled because it was so stressful," said Kim Stipes. "All my focus was getting Sophie back on that Medicaid. Then crying afterwards because everybody was calling us white trash, moochers. It was like being sucked into this vacuum of nothingness."

In the seven years between the Stipes' battle with the automation experiment and my visit, Sophie's life improved: She gained weight, learned sign language, went to school and made friends. But eight days after I interviewed the family in their Tipton home, Dan Skinner sent me an email. "Sad news," it read. "Kim Stipes called and told me that little Sophie died. She had been sick and throwing up on Friday and when they found her dead on Saturday she was curled up in a fetal position looking peaceful. The doctor said her heart simply stopped."

In the end, the Indiana automation experiment was a form of digital diversion for poor and working Americans. It denied them benefits, due process, dignity, and life itself. "We were not investing in our fellow human beings the way we should be," said John Cardwell of The Generations Project. "We were basically saying to a large percentage of people in Indiana, 'You're not worth a shit.' What a horrible waste of humanity."

3

HIGH-TECH HOMELESSNESS IN THE CITY OF ANGELS

America's last Skid Row is a half square mile of open-air tent encampments on the edge of the Los Angeles downtown entertainment district. In 1947, Hal Boyle of the *Evening Independent* called the neighborhood "the poor man's underworld, a cross-section of American futility, the place where men who have lost hope go after they have jettisoned their dreams."[1] Fifty-eight years later, Steve Lopez at the *Los Angeles Times* described the neighborhood as "a rock-bottom depository and national embarrassment. A place [of] disease, abuse, crime and hard-luck misery . . . where business thrives in Porta-Potties . . . and urine still runs in the gutters."[2]

I arrived in Los Angeles in December 2015 to explore its coordinated entry system, which is intended to match the county's most vulnerable unhoused people with appropriate available resources. Touted as the Match.com of homeless services, the coordinated entry approach has become wildly popular across the country in the last half decade. Its supporters include the US Department of Housing and Urban Development (HUD), the National Alliance to End Homelessness, a myriad of local homeless service providers, and powerful funders, including the Conrad N. Hilton and Bill & Melinda Gates Foundations.

The proponents of coordinated entry argue that the system creates a "no wrong door" approach to the often dizzying array of services available to the unhoused and provides a standardized intake process to reduce waste, redundancy, and double-dipping across agencies. The system also collects, stores, and shares some astonishingly intimate information about unhoused people. It catalogs, classifies, and ranks their traumas, coping mechanisms, feelings, and fears.

For many, Skid Row personifies timeless corruption and hopelessness. But, like any too-simple story, this narrative hides more than it reveals. In the 1870s the neighborhood was mostly orange groves. By 1921 Skid Row offered all the necessaries for family living: a public school, an emergency hospital, streetcar transportation, churches, factories, workshops, warehouses, and retail. As the population of migrant workers swelled in the 1930s, it became known as the poor man's district. The neighborhood was filled with inexpensive housing and economic struggle, but also thriving community and vigorous politics. The Communist Party, for example, organized dozens of neighborhood Unemployed Councils under the motto "Don't Starve—Fight!," led protests of stingy soup kitchens, and resisted evictions during the Great Depression.

Despite the stereotype of Skid Row as home to older white men, the neighborhood has always been diverse. In a 1939 issue of the *Los Angeles Times Sunday Magazine*, Huston Irvine wrote, "The population is probably more motley than that in a similar district of any other American city,"[3] describing the Jews, Greeks, Italians, Germans, French, Egyptians, Chinese, Japanese, Native Americans, Mexicans, and African Americans who worked, lived, and played in the neighborhood. This population swelled during World War II, as new workers arrived looking for steady employment in the defense industries.

But the passage of the American Housing Act of 1949 spelled calamity. The legislation offered federal money to demolish blighted buildings, paired with support for developing 810,000 units of public starter housing geared to working-class families. Bunker Hill, a neighborhood of Victorian homes, boarding-houses, and low-cost hotels immediately northwest of Skid Row, was razed to the ground. The demolition removed 7,310 units of housing.

City building superintendent Gilbert E. Morris issued more than 65,000 building code violations in Skid Row alone. The violations required that building owners either rehabilitate and seis-mically retrofit their buildings, at their own expense, or demolish them. Many opted for demolition. The 1950s "rehabilitation" re-moved 4,165 hotel rooms and 1,379 other dwellings from Skid Row; nearly a thousand buildings were knocked down. A 1959 pamphlet written by Magner White for the *Los Angeles Examiner* bragged that Los Angeles was "Show[ing the] World How to End Slums."

The changes in the neighborhood between 1921 and 1957 were stark. Gone were the small businesses: the drugstores, book-binders, coffee roasters, and the Hippodrome Theater. Whole blocks of wood frame dwellings disappeared, their lots now used for automobile parking or sitting empty. Buildings that once boasted union halls now hosted missions of the "three hots and a cot" variety.

But when federally funded low-income housing was proposed to replace what had been demolished, white middle-class Angelenos vigorously resisted. Calling a plan to construct 10,000 affordable public units a "Red Plot to Control L.A. Housing," opponents blocked the creation of Elysian Park Heights, a racially integrated public housing complex, and organized to have the City Housing Authority investigated by the House Un-American Activities Committee on charges of Communism.

The battle against public accommodations had far-reaching impacts for Los Angeles, constricting available housing and deepening racial segregation. Demolition occurred primarily in neighborhoods that were home to large populations of people of color and poor whites: Bunker Hill had a sizable Native American population and the Chavez Ravine, the proposed home for Elysian Park Heights, was majority Chicano. After these neighborhoods were demolished, the white middle class thwarted plans to expand low-income housing through special referenda, hostility, and outright violence. Thus, Los Angeles built only a fraction of the number of public housing units of other cities its size, and most of it was built in communities of color. Half of the units built under the 1949 Housing Act were located in Watts, for example, one of the few neighborhoods where racially restrictive covenants had allowed African American residents to live.

In the 1960s available housing on Skid Row was halved again. The "Centropolis" master plan knocked down more buildings, constructed a band of light industry around the neighborhood, and focused redevelopment dollars on the nearby business district. Available housing stock shrank from roughly 15,000 units to about 7,500. Then, in the 1970s, planners prepared a proposal, popularly known as the Silver Book, which would clear the area of poor residents for good.

Named for its futuristic metallic cover, the Silver Book plan was a joint effort of a committee of downtown businessmen and the Los Angeles city government. It suggested that what was left of Skid Row, like Bunker Hill before it, be razed to the ground. Extensions of the University of Southern California and the University of California, Los Angeles, were to be built after the existing housing was demolished and neighborhood residents were sent to a massive detoxification and rehabilitation center.

But community activists and residents, led by the Catholic Workers, the Legal Aid Foundation, and the Los Angeles Community Design Center, produced a competing plan. Their Blue Book proposal protected the remaining single room occupancy (SRO) hotels on Skid Row and encouraged city government and local nonprofits to commit resources to improving housing and social services in the area. According to Forrest Stuart, author of *Down, Out, and Under Arrest: Policing and Everyday Life in Skid Row,* the Blue Book plan prevailed, at least in part, because organizers and community leaders adopted an unorthodox strategy of embracing the perception of Skid Row as lawless and frightening.

Activists threatened that a wave of homeless and indigent people would be unleashed on the suburban neighborhoods of Los Angeles if Skid Row was demolished. For some, the Blue Book plan was a *de facto* agreement to designate Skid Row as a sacrificial zone to contain the homeless. For others, it was a surprisingly successful battle to protect land and housing for Skid Row's poor and working-class inhabitants.

Until recently, the Blue Book's pioneering strategy to defend Skid Row worked. The neighborhood continued to be a "set-aside community" for the poor, working class, and unhoused. For four decades, its residents have worked hard to create community in the face of the city's strategy of malign neglect. But in the past decade, the neighborhood has undergone rapid transformation. Young professionals rejecting the suburbs and Los Angeles traffic sought out raw urban apartments and the services that cater to the wealthy followed: artisanal food shops, bespoke juiceries, craft coffee bars. Nightclubs capitalized on the neighborhood's colorful past but roped off their entrances and upscaled their drink prices.

The resident population of downtown LA grew by more than 23,500 between 2006 and 2013. A building boom in luxury rentals over the last half-decade has driven the vacancy rate in downtown Los Angeles to 12 percent—its highest level since 2000—but the median price of a one-bedroom is $2,500, and affordable housing is hard to find. The boundary between downtown and Skid Row slipped east from Main Street to Los Angeles Street, and then another block to Maple, as loft-style housing for the creative class expanded. The spread of the Little Tokyo neighborhood put similar pressure on Skid Row's northern border, which moved from 3rd Street to below 4th. Skid Row lost about 16 square blocks—a third of its size—in ten years.

Skid Row today is an area of highly visible, stark contrasts. On block after block, the neighborhood's professional middle-class residents inhabit live-work lofts with high ceilings and stainless appliances while its poor live in makeshift tents. On weekends, pedestrians nudge BabyBjörn jogging strollers past their neighbors' shopping carts of recyclables. On my first visit, I was stunned to see a man asleep on the sidewalk in front of the Pussy & Pooch pet boutique, which bills itself as "a design-forward, social experience for pets and people." A lanky young African American, he was stretched out with his head at the curb and his black t-shirt pulled over his face to block the hot midday sun. A svelte and leggy dog and its equally willowy owner stepped past him to enter the store, perhaps to eat raw meat at the "paw bar." The dog was wearing shoes; the man was not.

While many downtown residents—newcomers and old-timers alike—praise the area's ability to contain such contradictions, there are signs that the social fabric is fraying. As Hillel Aron reported in *LA Weekly*, when a mental health center housed in the Little Tokyo Lofts planned to expand to fill the available first-floor commercial space, neighbors resisted, successfully petitioning to block any expansion of social services. A proposal to turn the long-neglected Cecil Hotel into a permanent supportive housing complex for 384 chronically homeless people was killed by county supervisors in 2014.

Every night, approximately 2,000 Skid Row residents sleep in mission and emergency shelter beds. Another 6,500 are housed in SRO or supportive housing that includes social services for those struggling with mental illness, poor health, or addiction. Somewhere between 3,000 and 5,000 people sleep outside in encampments erected on the sidewalks of the neighborhood. Since 1950, more than 13,000 units of low-income housing have been removed from Skid Row, enough for them all.

The flophouses and tenements of the past have been replaced by rows of tents covered in blue and black tarps. Cardboard boxes, carefully cut down, provide floors and walls. Plastic storage bins protect clothing, food, dishes, and reading material from weather, dirt, and rats. Five-gallon buckets serve as storage, seats, and makeshift latrines. Shopping carts carry possessions from one area to another when police crackdowns or street cleaning crews arrive, moving the unhoused from block to block like human chess pieces.

On my walks around the neighborhood, I have been touched by the kindness and courage I've witnessed: a Bible laid on a neatly made-up sleeping bag inside a red tent, the affirmation "Let gratitude be your attitude" written in black magic marker inside a makeshift shelter on Gladys Avenue. I've had fascinating conversations on its street corners and been kindly chaperoned to the bus stop after dark by generous souls who then returned to sleep on the sidewalk. I've also been threatened by hustlers and knuckleheads, fondled, harassed, and followed by men muttering offers of drugs or "Dick . . . dick, dick, dick."

Residents face real challenges on Skid Row but also find

value and community here. As T.C. Alexander, a gravel-voiced 60-year-old community organizer living near the corner of Gladys and 6th, explained to me on my first tour of the area in January 2015, "It's so real down here. I find more love here than I have anywhere in the city. As down and out as people are, they'll stop and talk to you, shake your hand." My tour guide, Skid Row human rights defender General Dogon, finished T.C.'s thought, "On the other side of Main Street, they'll pass you like you a telephone pole."

The coordinated entry system was created in order to address the disastrous mismatch between housing supply and demand in Los Angeles County. Before coordinated entry, unhoused people navigated a complex system of waitlists and social service programs requiring a great deal of patience, fortitude, and luck. A rumor of an opening at one of the downtown single room occupancy hotels would create a rush of unhoused people who would wait outside in line for days for a chance at a room they could call their own.

Under the previous system, homeless service providers competed, both for limited funding and for rare available rooms for their clients. "Waiting lists before [coordinated entry] were often based on favors with property managers or the rental office," Patricia McHugh, a coordinated entry matcher with Lamp Community, a Skid Row social service agency that works to house adults with mental illness and other disabilities, said. "People have really bad stories about how things were before, how corrupt." At its worst, it was a system that rewarded the most functional people with housing that was not always an appropriate fit for their needs.

Coordinated entry is based on two philosophies that represent a paradigm shift in the provision of homeless services: prioritization and housing first. *Prioritization* builds on research by

Dennis Culhane from the University of Pennsylvania, which differentiates between two different kinds of homelessness: crisis and chronic. Those facing crisis homelessness tend to be experiencing "short-term emergencies [such as] eviction, domestic violence, sudden illness, or job loss, or reentering communities after incarceration."[4] The crisis homeless, Culhane argues, often self-correct: after a short stay in a shelter, they identify family members they can stay with, access new resources, or move away. A small, time-limited investment can offer them "a hand up to avoid the downward spiral" into chronic homelessness.

Those experiencing chronic homelessness, on the other hand, tend to be homeless frequently and for longer stretches. Chronically homeless adults, according to Culhane's research, "have higher rates of behavioral health problems and disabilities, and more complex social support needs."[5] For them, permanent supportive housing is an appropriate and effective solution. The shift to prioritization in Los Angeles acknowledged that the status quo was not serving the chronic homeless. There was a mismatch between needs and resources: the crisis homeless got resources most appropriate for the chronically homeless; the chronically homeless got nothing at all.

The other conceptual shift in coordinated entry is its *housing first* philosophy. Until very recently, most homeless services operated on a "housing readiness" model that moved individuals through different program steps before they could be housed. Someone who had been sleeping on the street or in their car might first enter an emergency shelter, then shift to a transitional housing program, and finally attain independent housing. At each stage, a set of behavioral requirements—sobriety, treatment compliance, employment—were gateways that controlled access to the next step. The housing first approach emerges instead from the understanding that it is difficult to attend to other challenges if you are not stably housed. Housing first puts individuals and families into their own apartments as quickly as possible, and then offers voluntary supportive and treatment services where appropriate.

Home for Good, a collaboration between the United Way of Greater Los Angeles and the Los Angeles Area Chamber of Commerce, combined prioritization, housing first, and technology-forward approaches to launch a coordinated entry program in 2013. They pledged to house 100 of the most vulnerable homeless people on Skid Row in 100 days. To achieve this ambitious goal, they needed to create a complete list of Skid Row's unhoused, ranked in order of need. They chose an assessment tool that collects vast amounts of information and sifts it for risky behaviors, built a digital registry to store the data, and designed two algorithms to rank the unhoused in order of vulnerability and to match them to housing opportunities.

The coordinated entry process begins when a social service worker or volunteer engages an unhoused person through an in-house service program, during a shelter admission, or as part of street outreach using the VI-SPDAT (Vulnerability Index—Service Prioritization Decision Assistance Tool). The survey includes incredibly intimate questions, including:

- "In the past six months, how many times have you received health care at an emergency department/room? Used a crisis service, including sexual assault crisis, mental health crisis, family/intimate violence, distress centers and suicide prevention hotlines?"
- "Do you ever do things that may be considered to be risky like exchange sex for money, run drugs for someone, have unprotected sex with someone you don't know, share a needle, or anything like that?"
- "Have you threatened to or tried to harm yourself or anyone else in the last year?"[6]

The survey also collects protected personal information: social security number, full name, birth date, demographic information, veteran status, immigration and residency status, and where the respondent can be found at different times of day. It collects domestic violence history. It collects a self-reported medical history that includes mental health and substance abuse issues. The surveyor will ask if it is OK to take a photograph.

The consent form that the unhoused are asked to sign before taking the VI-SPDAT informs them that their information will be shared with "organizations [that] may include homeless service providers, other social service organizations, housing groups, and health care providers," and refers them to a fuller privacy notice that can be provided on request. If survey-takers request the more complete privacy notice, they learn that their information will be shared with 168 different organizations, including city governments, rescue missions, nonprofit housing developers, health-care providers, hospitals, religious organizations, addiction recovery centers, the University of California, Los Angeles, and the Los Angeles Police Department (LAPD) "when required by law or for law enforcement purposes . . . to prevent a serious threat to health or safety." The consent is valid for seven years.

After assessment, their data is entered into a federally approved Homeless Management Information System (HMIS) for the Los Angeles area. The HMIS is not in itself a database: it is a set of universal data elements the federal government requires all organizations receiving homeless assistance funds to collect. There is no centralized federal registry of the homeless. But the information in HMIS, shorn of unique identifiers, is sent to the Department of Housing and Urban Development, aggregated, and used to produce an unduplicated count of the country's homeless, to facilitate trend analysis for the agency's reports to Congress, and to evaluate homeless service organizations.

Once the data from the VI-SPDAT is entered into the Los

Angeles HMIS, a ranking algorithm tallies up a score from 1 to 17. A "1" means the person surveyed is low risk and has a relatively small chance of dying or ending up in an emergency room or mental hospital. A "17" means the person surveyed is among the most vulnerable. Those scoring between 0 and 3 are judged to need no housing intervention. Those scoring between 4 and 7 qualify to be assessed for limited-term rental subsidies and some case management services—an intervention strategy called rapid re-housing. Those scoring 8 and above qualify to be assessed for permanent supportive housing.

Simultaneously, housing providers fill out vacancy forms to populate a list of available units. A second algorithm, the matching algorithm, is run to identify a person "who is in greatest need of that particular housing type (by virtue of their VI-SPDAT score)" and who "meets its specific eligibility criteria."

If a successful match is made, the unhoused person is assigned a housing navigator, a special caseworker who helps gather all necessary eligibility documentation. A birth certificate, photo ID, social security card, income verification, and other documents must be collected in about three weeks. Once documents are in hand, the unhoused person fills out an application with the Housing Authority of the City of Los Angeles (HACLA). HACLA then interviews the potential tenant, verifies their information and documentation, and approves or denies the application. If the application is approved, the unhoused person receives housing or related resources. If not, the match disappears and the algorithm is run again to produce a new applicant for the opportunity.

According to the system's designers and funders, coordinated entry upends the status quo in homeless services that privileged stronger clients. It builds new, deeper bonds between service providers throughout Los Angeles, leading to increased communication and resource sharing. It provides sophisticated, timely data about the nature of the housing crisis that can be used to shape more responsive policy-making. But most crucially, by matching homeless people to appropriate housing, it has the potential to save the lives of thousands of people. One of those people is Monique Talley.

I met Monique, a round-faced, freckled African American woman, at the Downtown Women's Center (DWC), a nearly 40-year-old organization dedicated to addressing the needs of poor and unhoused women. The DWC opened a facility on South San Pedro Street in 2010 with 71 permanent supportive housing units, a store that sells crafts produced by women from the center, a health clinic, and a variety of other services for women in the Skid Row community. The DWC goes to great lengths to make the building feel like home—there are cabinets that hold pottery, vases, and teapots, and blond wood benches where 75 or so women sat drinking coffee and talking on the day of my visit. There are showers and an open cafeteria-style kitchen. There is a box of neatly folded toilet paper for visitors to take before they go back to the tent encampments.

Monique had a history of unstable housing before ending up in a shelter. She bounced from place to place, helping a niece run a small daycare center and caring for an elderly family member before she found Pathways, a 430-bed shelter in a light-industry district of South Los Angeles. When Pathways turned her out of the shelter early every morning, Monique took the bus to the DWC for support, company, and sanctuary.

Monique faced enormous challenges: maintaining sobriety, being separated from her children, and dealing with mental and physical health issues that grew more severe the longer she lacked housing. But she was fortunate to have a strong support system. Her boyfriend and his mother welcomed her into their home most weekends, and she was able to wash her clothes, take her time in the bath, eat a family meal, watch some TV. "Just do what normal people do," she remembers, "have some normalcy in my life."

A DWC caseworker approached Monique one day to ask if she wanted to take the VI-SPDAT survey and be entered into the coordinated entry system. The survey was a challenge, Monique remembers, "Because it was like I was talking to my therapist." But Tracy Malbrough, a trusted ally and case manager at DWC, advised her to "just answer with all the honesty and pureness that your heart can offer," Monique remembers. "So I was honest."

"I would prefer to do [the VI-SPDAT] with somebody that I trust," she says, laughing and sorting through her monkey-shaped backpack. "But I would have done it with a stranger if I had to do that to get housed. . . . If it was to get me a roof over my head, I will talk to *you,* and tell you the truth, and tell you what you want to hear."

Malbrough called Monique one brisk day in December and asked her to come to the corner of South San Pedro Street and 5th. There, Monique got keys to an apartment in the Gateways Apartments, a $28 million permanent supportive housing complex built by SRO Housing Corporation. The nonprofit low-income housing developer had turned to the coordinated entry program to streamline the waitlist of more than 500 individuals competing for 107 units, and coordinated entry prioritized Monique. "It was December 17, 2013," she says, "It was the best Christmas gift I ever got; I got a home."

Her new apartment was a 350-square-foot studio with a closet, a kitchen, and her own bathroom. "I opened the door, I stood in the middle of the floor, and I cried," she says. "I thank God first because he made it all possible. I thank the Downtown Women's Center because they assisted God to get me off the streets."

Monique is still not sure why coordinated entry prioritized her for housing. No one ever shared her VI-SPDAT score with her.

"They never did explain to me how it worked," she says, thoughtfully touching a twisted brass hoop earring. After I tell her that the VI-SPDAT prioritizes the most vulnerable homeless people using a 1 to 17 scale, she guesses that she might have scored a 10. Her mental and physical health were fairly stable until just a few months before she got into the Gateways, though she had gone off some of her meds. "I managed," she says, "not to do anything stupid."

As grateful as she is, it bothers Monique a little that she got housed while so many others at the DWC, who seemed to be in a similar situation, did not. "I know a lot of women who did the CES," she reflects, "and almost three years later, they haven't been housed. I thought it was kind of odd. . . . They went through the same shit that I did, and three years later they're not housed. In the back of my mind it's like . . . something's wrong with that picture."

In the end, she attributes her housing success to her faith in God, her honesty and openness, and to luck. She is profoundly grateful and is working hard to be a stable presence in her children's lives. "I think things work out where they're supposed to be," she says. "I'm glad they worked out in my favor because if they didn't, I'd probably still be in a shelter or in the psycho ward. . . . You get tired of being mentally, physically, and emotionally beat the hell down. . . . There's three ways to go if you don't get housed: jail, institutions, or death. I would not want to send my momma through that pain."

"Uncle" Gary Boatwright has had less luck with coordinated entry. At 64, he's been on and off the street for ten years. On a blindingly bright day in May 2016, he is living in a gray and green tent on East 6th Street on the edge of Skid Row. There is a blue tarp over the top as extra rain protection and two shopping carts rolled up to protect the entrance. As I approach, calling out his name in lieu of a door to knock on, he is sweeping out the tent in preparation for my visit. He props the entrance open with a broom handle and offers me a folding chair (which I take) and a bottle of water (which I don't, because bottled water is a prime commodity on Skid Row).

His tent is immaculate. There are crates with OxyClean, laundry detergent, and a bottle of bleach. Science fiction novels, a copy of *It Can't Happen Here* by Sinclair Lewis, and a copy of the progressive magazine *In These Times* sit on his air mattress. He's trying to stay healthy, so he's switched to diet drinks, and there are maybe a half-dozen two-liter bottles scattered around: diet cranberry, Mountain Dew, Gatorade. Some sport a black-marker "X" on their twist top: they might contain rum or act as make-shift midnight latrines.

Gary is a straight-talking, wryly funny man with thinning white hair and Santa Claus–blue eyes. He smokes Pall Malls and shuffles through his meticulous paperwork, stored in clear Rubbermaid containers in his tent, while we talk. He has had a dozen careers: welder, mason, paralegal, door-to-door salesman, law student, and, most recently, document processor for a wholesale mortgage lender. He was laid off by his employer, GreenPoint Mortgage Funding, in the early 2000s, shortly before the collapse of the subprime mortgage industry. "I stayed there longer than anybody else—there was a lot of turnover. I was pretty much in charge of outsourcing my whole department," he says. "They found a place in India that would do the doc processing and email it across the planet." GreenPoint went on to make the Center for Public Integrity's "Subprime 25" list for their key role in causing the recession of 2007 and their intentional targeting of minority communities with predatory mortgage products.

Immediately after Gary was laid off, Hurricane Katrina hit the Gulf Coast. He had planned a vacation in New Orleans, so he canceled his flight and hotel reservations, and hooked up with a caravan that was traveling to Covington, Louisiana, to help with relief efforts. In the tiny city at the fork of the Bogue Falaya and Tchefuncte Rivers, Gary slept out in the makeshift "Camp Covington" while he helped the city rebuild. "It's still the best vacation I've ever had," he says.

When he returned to Orange County, he applied for unemployment and went back on the job market. He has a bachelor's degree and lots of experience with wholesale mortgages, but by that time the industry was collapsing. His housing in a sober living community near Disneyland became precarious when an unemployment check failed to arrive on time and he started "bumping heads with the housing manager." Before he lost his job, he had purchased a late-model used car. "I paid sixty-five hundred dollars cash for that car," he says. "It had low mileage, I kept it in good shape. That was my piggy bank. So I'm getting down to the last month for unemployment, thinking, 'No big deal.' Worst comes to worst, I can sell that, buy a thousand-dollar junker, and I've got a cushion. I was planning ahead. Doing what you're supposed to do."

Then, he got a ticket for leaving his vehicle in a public park—a charge Gary insists was unjustified and later challenged in court—and his car was towed and impounded. He couldn't afford to get it out of impound, and he couldn't sell it to free up some cash. "Basically," Gary says, "a cop stole my piggy bank."

He got kicked out of the sober living home when his unemployment ran out; he could no longer pay his rent. Homeless now, he headed to Santa Ana, where many of Orange County's social service agencies are concentrated. But Santa Ana was also the center of a police crackdown on unhoused people. A 1992 ordinance made camping in parks illegal. Police Chief Paul M. Walters was widely criticized for instigating weekly homeless "roundups" that corralled and ticketed unhoused people in what he characterized as an effort to "fight crime before it happens."

Gary started having regular run-ins with law enforcement. In five years, he racked up 25 separate tickets for crimes associated with homelessness: unlawfully entering or remaining in a park, failure to leave land as ordered by a peace officer, storage of personal property in public places, jaywalking, littering, and unauthorized removal of a shopping cart, among others.

Gary was facing jail time when a judge in Orange County Superior Court offered him a deal. He'd make all the tickets go away if Gary would leave Orange County and never come back. Gary took the deal and moved to Skid Row, 32 miles north.

Since moving to Skid Row, Gary has filled out the VI-SPDAT three times, and he's lost patience with the process. His first time, in April 2015, he took an hour-long bus ride to the office of the Volunteers of America on Lankershim Boulevard, 17 miles away. He tried to arrive by 5 or 6 a.m. so he could get in line before the doors opened at 8. He met with CES Navigator Dylan Wilde from L.A. Family Housing and took the survey. Wilde got him an appointment with Alpha Property Management, a private firm that oversees hundreds of low-income apartment units in California.

But the visit was a bust. No one told Gary that he would have to have a three-to-five-year verifiable rental history and a good credit history in order to qualify for their waiting list. "How is that all relevant to getting housing for the homeless?" he asks me, his voice rising. Gary also refused to go out of pocket to pay for a copy of his birth certificate, which Alpha Property Management required to qualify for their waitlist. "I played this game way too long to go out of pocket and spend *my* money to *not* get housing. I think [Wilde] was fairly new, a new hire. He was a young fellow. I don't think he realized what he was getting into. I tried to contact him for a follow-up, but he disappeared."

Gary took the VI-SPDAT the second time with a representative from Housing for Health, a division of the Los Angeles

County Department of Health Services focused on creating housing opportunities for those with "complex medical and behavioral health conditions." A caseworker asked for access to his mental health history, so Gary signed a consent form to release his psychiatric records from Orange County. "I did the survey, but I didn't have my social [security card] with me, so I went back up to the office and we worked on that. He knows where I'm at, but I haven't heard back."

The third time Gary took the VI-SPDAT, the police and the Bureau of Sanitation were on East 6th Avenue, where he had pitched his tent. A street outreach worker was with them, George Thomas from the Los Angeles Homeless Services Authority (LAHSA) Emergency Response Team. When Gary told him he had already taken the VI-SPDAT several times, Thomas responded that he could do the survey better than Housing for Health or L.A. Family Housing. "He said, 'Oh, no. I do it better than them,'" Gary recalls. "According to him, he had some way of cutting through the red tape. He was working with the police, talking to people about housing." Gary called at the time they had arranged for an appointment and left a message. Thomas called back and left a response on his cell phone, but spoke so quickly that Gary couldn't understand him. He returned the call, asking for clarification. He never heard back.

Gary doesn't think he scored very high on the VI-SPDAT. He's 64 and, other than a little high blood pressure and a hearing problem, mostly healthy. Though he's known by some as Commander Kush and keeps rum in a Mountain Dew bottle in his tent, his substance use doesn't seem abusive or debilitating. He's not sure what's in his mental health files from Orange County; no one has ever shared his diagnosis with him. In fact, it was a surprise when a judge for a hearing on his Santa Ana tickets said he had a psychiatric record.

He suspects that he is seen as difficult by caseworkers in the neighborhood. "I make it clear that bedbug amenities are unacceptable," he explains. "I learned to cope with them for a short period of time. But tenants cannot get rid of them. It's a landlord's job. And they don't do it." He was unable to take a place in a Salvation Army emergency shelter because he refused to give up his cell phone. "I need a telephone to get *into* the Salvation Army and then they want me to give it up? No." Fundamentally, Gary finds trading his self-determination and adult decision-making for access to a roof unacceptable. "I don't need a nanny," he says. "Don't tell me where to go and what to do and how to live my life. Any reasonable mature adult can't handle that. Nobody wants a nanny with their head up your ass." What is keeping him from housing, he guesses, is his "inability to bow down." "I've still got my personal integrity," he says. "And that's not for sale."

Skid Row has been ground zero for coordinated entry efforts in Los Angeles, and for good reason. Downtown Los Angeles has the largest number of homeless individuals—15,393 in 2017—and the most concentrated unhoused population. But just a few miles away lies a neighborhood with a nearly equal level of homelessness but far less attention: South Los Angeles. Coordinated entry is a very different experience for those who struggle with homelessness here in the shadow of the policy klieg light that shines downtown.

South Los Angeles is a 50-square mile area that drops below Highway 10, hugging midcity LA. It used to be known as South Central, but in 2003 the area was rebranded by the city council. Some say the current proliferation of "Sell your house for CA$H" signs and the expansion of the Expo and Crenshaw light-rail lines presage a wave of gentrification to come.

Taking the bus from Skid Row to South LA, I am reversing Monique Talley's daily commute from the Pathways shelter to the DWC. The two neighborhoods have a deeply entwined history. Alameda Street runs like an aorta from Union Station through downtown, along the eastern edge of Skid Row, under the freeway, and then south through Vernon, Watts, and eventually into Compton. The Alameda corridor was home to Los Angeles' defense and auto industries, which grew explosively after World War II.

The street also outlines one of Los Angeles' firmest racial boundaries. Before the Supreme Court found racially restrictive covenants unconstitutional in 1948, 80 percent of property in Los Angeles carried covenants barring Black families. To the east of Alameda Street were working-class white suburbs. To the west were South Central and Watts, two of the few areas where African American families were able to live.

After a period of rapid postwar economic advancement in South LA, declines in military spending and auto plant closures resulted in a stubborn unemployment rate of 14 percent, the highest in Los Angeles County. The neighborhood is home to the two largest public housing complexes in Los Angeles: Nickerson Gardens and Jordan Downs. Nevertheless, it has the most crowded housing in the United States.

Many working-age Black men in South LA who lost their jobs during the 1980s deindustrialization found their way to Skid Row. In the last decade, the trend has reversed. The rise in aggressive policing and gentrification pressures downtown have pushed many unhoused people into South LA. But the area has meager resources with which to respond. It has less than half as many shelter beds and one-seventh the number of permanent supportive housing beds as downtown. Yet, according to a 2008 report by Services for Groups, downtown and Skid Row received $1,132 in grants per homeless person per year while South LA received only $607.

The rise in local homelessness, influx of unhoused people from other neighborhoods, and extraordinarily limited resources in South LA have resulted in the creation of a massive open-air tent city. According to the 2017 homeless count for greater Los Angeles, 75 percent of the homeless in South LA are completely unsheltered. While 2,364 unhoused people find shelter beds or permanent supportive housing, another 6,879 live in the make-shift shelters that have become South LA's de facto source of low-income housing. Seventy percent of them are Black.

Quanetha Hunt is the former director of homeless services at Pathways to Home, the largest supplier of emergency shelter in South LA. The day I visit, in February 2016, her office is adorned with posters of civil rights figures and religious sayings and smells like vanilla. Her calendar proclaims, "My trust is not in money or things, my trust is in the Lord." But Hunt, born and raised in South LA, has a markedly secular way about her, and a nearly wicked sense of humor. She sports tall black leather boots and a perfect coral manicure. Tucked beneath the edge of her computer monitor is a tiny sign on a polka-dotted background which reads, "Fuck it: My new personal motto."

"South LA is like every other community," she says. "You have low-income, poverty, middle class, your very affluent. West over Crenshaw, that is Leimert Park: a middle-class African American community, homeowners. If you go further, you're in Windsor Hills, which is affluent. Southeast, you get to poverty-stricken areas. But we're all community. On my street, we all know each other. The people in South LA have the same desires: a decent meal, a roof over their head, their kids getting a quality education. South LA is very family oriented. My grandmother saw five generations here."

Surrounded by flatlands and low warehouses full of stitching garment workers, the shelter has a dramatic view of downtown, floating like a jeweled island three miles north. Pathways to Home is trying to bridge the gap between South LA's housing crisis and its thoroughly inadequate resources, offering beds to approximately 315 men and 115 women nightly. It is a low, large, beige building packed wall-to-wall with bunk beds with about two hand-spans of space between them. Despite the staff's attempts to make everyone feel welcome and to preserve clients' dignity, it feels like what it is: a warehouse for people.

Pathways follows a harm reduction, housing first philosophy, case manager Richard Renteria explains as he gives me a tour. This means that Pathways staff will do everything in their power to keep someone sheltered once they're in the door. If you're drunk, they'll get you a meal and put you to bed. If you're belligerent, they'll put you outside on the patio to cool off. They'll take "290s," sex offenders who have been released from prison and have nowhere else to go. Only those who persist in trying to start fights are put out to fend for themselves.

Renteria and other employees make sure to greet visitors warmly, to make eye contact, to engage. "Everybody has a story," he says, "Every single person has a different story with their own obstacles, goals, and dreams." But the shelter has only so much space, and the blocks nearby are strewn with mini-encampments: tents sit under the trees at the corner of Broadway and West 38th, and another handful, with sad irony, can be found on the corner of Broadway and Martin Luther King, Jr., Boulevard.

Pathways is officially a 90-day shelter, but getting people housed in three months is nearly impossible. There is "zero inventory of housing" in the area, says Hunt. Affordable housing is particularly difficult to find, she remarks, "And fair market value? Our population can't afford it." William Menjivar, Pathway's coordinated entry specialist, agrees. "We can't match a person to a unit here," he says. "There are no units accessible through CES to put somebody in."

Using coordinated entry in South LA is less like finding a date online and more like running an obstacle course. The first hurdle is the VI-SPDAT survey itself. Staff at Pathways regularly see clients who have been assessed elsewhere and scored very low. After spending some time getting to know case managers at Pathways, many open up more freely. One client Menjivar recalls was surveyed at another social service organization, and scored a 1 out of 17. He arrived at Pathways, was reassessed, and scored a 16. "I agree with data," says Hunt, "but data is only as good as the collector."

Pathways focuses on listening, using story-work to build trust. "Unless you have that human touch," says Renteria, "you can't truly assess where they're at. We have to gain their trust first in order to get them to open up." But in South LA, a high VI-SPDAT score is a catch-22. There is very little permanent supportive housing in the area, so Pathways clients have to go through a second interview with the housing authority to determine if they are able to live independently in private housing. A high VI-SPDAT score might qualify a Pathways client for a Section 8 voucher. But it can also be an indicator that he is too vulnerable to live on his own.

"The housing authority can be very, very tricky," says Menjivar. If a Pathways client scores a 16 on the VI-SPDAT, Menjivar explains, he should qualify for a shelter plus care voucher providing both rental assistance and supportive social services. "But then the housing authority says, 'You're not really capable of living independently. Go and get something from a doctor or psychiatrist letting us know that you won't put some water to boil and burn down the building.' It seems that the housing authority wants to interview you *out* of services," he says, "whereas I've interviewed you *into* services." So Pathways caseworkers counsel their clients to treat the interview at the housing authority like a court proceeding, to behave as if they are on trial. "We don't want to prime our clients, but we tell them, 'You answer what's being asked; don't divulge any additional information.'"

If case managers and clients successfully navigate the rocky shoals of the VI-SPDAT and the housing authority interview, they attain a coveted Section 8 voucher. But the voucher program relies on the private real estate market instead of permanent supportive housing like that built by nonprofits in Skid Row. Real estate capitalism, an ever-tightening rental market, and landlord bias are the last hurdles in the South LA coordinated entry obstacle course. There is no guarantee that Pathways clients will find housing from a private landlord, even with a Section 8 voucher in hand.

When Pathways staff take "vulnerable clients, who barely function day to day" to look for housing, says Renteria, "landlords will see the person, see the way they look, and assume the worst." Section 8 vouchers expire after six months, and the process starts all over again. "Clients are out there looking. They are getting frustrated," Renteria says, sighing. "A lot of clients just walk away." The units are not turning over nearly quickly enough to address need. "If [we] fill a unit," concludes Menjivar, "by the time that person decides to move, finds a job and lives independently, passes away or is evicted, we've already assessed another *thousand* people."

Those who can complete the VI-SPDAT, succeed in their HACLA interview, get their Section 8 voucher, and keep up a lengthy and taxing search may finally find housing through gumption, shoe leather, and a lot of support. But for many unhoused people, the unfulfilled promise of coordinated entry has been demoralizing. "We started to discover within the first three months that people were getting upset when we started to try to re-engage them," says Veronica Lewis of the Homeless Outreach Program Integrated Care System (HOPICS), also in South LA. "Like, 'Where's the housing?' There was a period of time, a lull of people being unresponsive to us. People were upset because—you come out here, you've been collecting information, what is the outcome?"

Their cynicism is not unwarranted. It is not the first time the homeless have been offered a magic-bullet solution to the seemingly intractable housing crisis in Los Angeles. "There's a lot of services out there where they will meet with you, ask you all of these questions, promise you something, and never come back," says Richard Renteria. "So, they got all this information to create this database, talk about how many thousands of people are homeless, [but] never come back to serve them."

For Monique Talley, coordinated entry was a gift from God. The system functions well, for some, if there is housing available. When Monique took the VI-SPDAT, the new Gateways Apartments complex was just about to open. Her name was chosen from among 500 applicants and her life changed for the better.

But in the absence of sufficient public investment in building or repurposing housing, coordinated entry is a system for managing homelessness, not solving it. At Lamp Community, Hazel Lopez spent most of 2015 encouraging her staff not to oversell the system. "It's definitely about managing expectations," she said. "When CES first started, people had this interpretation that [if] you put your person in, [they're] going to get matched to housing opportunities. Over time we've had to continuously create a message: We're not working with additional resources; we're just trying to target and utilize resources in a more efficient manner."

"Without increasing resources, we don't solve homelessness," said Molly Rysman, housing and homelessness deputy for Los Angeles County Supervisor Sheila Kuehl. "There is this pressure to stretch every dollar as far as you can, to make sure that you're being as absolutely efficient and effective as possible. Coordinated entry has made us much more efficient. But there's no chance of ending homelessness without resources." Chris Ko, architect of coordinated entry, agreed. "Coordinated entry is necessary but not sufficient," he said. "It's a tool to more efficiently use the resources fed into it. But we need permanent sources of subsidy."

In June 2015 Ko told me that he hoped that coordinated entry could provide more precise information about the county's housing crisis and contribute to progressive policy change. "For housing advocacy, we've never had such clear data on supply and demand," he said. "It can identify what kind of housing is needed by what kind of populations." By May 2017, it was beginning to look like his optimism and the community's hard work would pay off.

The current mayor of Los Angeles, Eric Garcetti, released the most comprehensive homeless strategy in the city's history in January 2016. It provides significant support for coordinated entry. It promotes rapid re-housing programs for those on the edge of homelessness, providing small amounts of money for expenses like deposits, rental assistance, moving costs, and case management. It supports converting existing commercial structures into short-term bridge housing and provides incentives to encourage landlords to accept Section 8 housing vouchers.

More recently, Los Angeles voters passed two ballot measures that provide increased funding for low-income housing and homeless services. Measure HHH authorized the city to issue $1.2 billion in bonds to buy, build, or remodel 13,000 units of housing, mental health–care facilities, medical clinics, and other services for the unhoused. It passed with an impressive 77 percent of the vote in November 2016. A second measure, Measure H, authorized a ten-year 0.25 percent county sales tax increase to fund homeless services and prevention. Measure H passed with 69 percent of the vote in March 2017.

Ko suggested that coordinated entry played a modest but important role in these unprecedented policy changes. The data collected by the system helped inform a preliminary budget gap analysis provided to the mayor's office by Home for Good. They used coordinated entry data to "dial in the ratios" of what kind of housing is needed: about 10,000 units of permanent supportive housing, plus new transitional housing beds and additional resources for rapid re-housing. Ko encouraged local coordinated entry partners to create "a dream budget" that included both housing and human resources—new units, but also caseworkers "to actually walk beside each person on their way home." They "spitballed" the cost of staffing at about $100 million. "It was something I did over the weekend," Ko said. "And somehow it got passed along to the mayor's office because that [number] popped up in a statement about what we need." The regional networks that grew out of the design and implementation of the coordinated entry system also helped solidify community support to pass Measures H and HHH.

But Ko believes that the measures really passed because of the sheer scale and visibility of the housing crisis in Los Angeles. Two court cases—*Jones v. City of Los Angeles* in 2006 and *Lavan v. City of Los Angeles* in 2012—reestablished unhoused people's right to life, liberty, and property. Los Angeles has one of the most restrictive antihomeless ordinances in the country, Los Angeles Municipal Code 41.18(d), which threatens six months' imprisonment and a fine for sleeping or sitting on the sidewalk. In *Jones*, the court declared that the sitting and sleeping ban, in the absence of available shelter beds, constitutes cruel and unusual punishment: it criminalizes the unhoused rather than confronting homelessness. The court required that the LAPD issue a policy directive stating that it would not enforce 41.18(d) between the hours of 9 p.m. and 6 a.m. until an additional 1,250 units of permanent supportive housing are constructed in the city of Los Angeles.

Until 2012 the LAPD also regularly confiscated and destroyed tents, tarps, sleeping bags, shopping carts, and other property of the unhoused without prior notice. Before the *Lavan* case, it was common for Skid Row residents to talk with a caseworker, shower, or grab a meal and return to find all their worldly possessions gone. The *Lavan* ruling barred city employees from seizing property unless it presents a threat to the public or is evidence of a crime, and required that any property collected as "abandoned" be held in a secure location for 90 days before it is destroyed. *Lavan* and *Jones* found that the Eighth, Fourth, and Fourteenth amendments apply to the unhoused as well as the housed, and that the government cannot arbitrarily imprison the homeless, invade their privacy, or seize their property.

These two rulings, in re-affirming the rights of the unhoused and suspending the most common practices used to harass and arrest them, virtually guaranteed the growth of semi-permanent tent encampments across the city. Measures H and HHH passed now, Ko believes, because *Jones* and *Lavan* "exploded the visibility of homelessness."

Ko pointed out that coordinated entry allowed members of the CES network to arrive at city council and board of supervisors meetings with impeccable regional numbers showing exactly what kinds of resources were needed in each community. But the real driver behind Angelenos' decision to take collective responsibility for the housing crisis was not better data. It was the spread of tent cities.

According to the LAHSA's 2017 homeless count, there are 57,794 unhoused people in Los Angeles County. Since 2014, the homeless services community has managed to survey 31,124 individuals with the VI-SPDAT, somewhere between 35 and 50 percent, assuming that many people cycled between homelessness and housing in the intervening three years. Of those, coordinated entry has managed to connect 9,627 people with housing or housing-related resources. Ko estimates that coordinated entry has cost approximately $11 million so far, if you include only the cost of technical resources, software, and extra personnel, not the cost of providing actual housing or services. CES eased the way to some kind of housing resource for 17 percent of the overall homeless population at a cost of approximately $1,140 per person. It is easy to argue that this is money well spent.

While the unhoused population of Los Angeles waits for Measure HHH's low-income housing units to be built, $10 million in emergency relief from the mayor has been earmarked for rapid re-housing. Rapid re-housing helps homeless individuals and families exit shelters and get into permanent housing quickly by providing financial assistance for housing-related expenses such as back rent payments and moving costs. A 2015 report by the Urban Institute found that rapid re-housing helps families exit homeless shelters quickly. But it also suggests that the subsidies may be too small and too time-limited—lasting six months to two years—to create permanent change. "Rapid re-housing, does not . . . solve long-term housing affordability problems," wrote the report's authors, Mary Cunningham, Sarah Gillespie, and Jacqueline Anderson. "After families exit rapid re-housing, they experience high rates of residential instability."[7]

Home for Good counts both permanent supportive housing and rapid re-housing as a "match" in the coordinated entry system. Chris Ko told me via email in May 2017 that they do not differentiate between these two vastly different kinds of interventions in their data. And while Ko estimates that 80 to 90 percent of those matched stay in their new housing, Home for Good would not release any retention data. "Retention is always an afterthought," said Hazel Lopez from Lamp Community in 2015. "There really is no mechanism to follow up." So it is impossible to know how many of the 9,627 people matched by coordinated entry received a place to call home, how many received assistance finding an apartment or a few hundred dollars to help with a rental deposit, and how many received assistance but since became homeless again.

Rapid re-housing is aimed at the crisis homeless. Coordinated entry in Los Angeles, which initially focused on getting the most vulnerable unhoused people into permanent supportive housing, now aims to match the newly homeless with short-term support. That leaves those in the middle—too healthy to qualify for a rare unit of permanent supportive housing but out on the street far too long to make a major change with the limited resources of rapid re-housing—out in the cold.

For Gary Boatwright and tens of thousands of others who have not been matched with any services, coordinated entry seems to collect increasingly sensitive, intrusive data to track their movements and behavior, but doesn't offer anything in return. When I asked T.C. Alexander about his experience with coordinated entry, he scoffed, "Coordinated entry system? The system that's supposed to be helping the homeless? It's *halting* the homeless. You put all the homeless people in the system, but they have nowhere for them to go. Entry into the system but with no action."

Some suspect that all that data is being held for other purposes entirely: to surveil and criminalize the unhoused. As of this writing, the protected personal information of 21,500 of Los Angeles' most vulnerable people remains in a database that may never connect them with life-saving services. It is possible to revoke your consent to be included in coordinated entry and HMIS, but the process is complicated. Even after expungement, some data stays in the system. No one I spoke to during my reporting, not even those who had been successfully housed, had requested that their coordinated entry record be expunged.

In the pilot phase of coordinated entry, there were more rigorous procedures for protecting personal data and providing alternate routes to resources. The original database, kept in an enormous Google spreadsheet, used a unique client identifier rather than a social security number to protect respondents' confidentiality. A certain percentage of services were set aside for those who did not want to go through the coordinated entry process, for whatever reason: perhaps the VI-SPDAT questions were too intrusive, or the individual was fleeing intimate violence and wanted to remain anonymous. Protecting the identities of the unhoused was the pilot system's default.

But then coordinated entry migrated to HMIS, which requires social security numbers. In theory, it is still possible to access resources while refusing to supply protected personal information, but the United Way concedes that they are "not sure how many people use this option." It is hard to imagine that many unhoused people compromise their chances at housing by refusing to supply a social security number. Protected personal information is now collected by default; the system requires the unhoused to "opt in" to confidentiality.

The coordinated entry system now serves as the primary passage point for all homeless services in Los Angeles. "It is now formally the service delivery system for the city and the county," Chris Ko told me in 2017. In other words, there is virtually no other path to homeless services in Los Angeles County except through coordinated entry.

According to federal data standards, service providers may disclose protected personal information in HMIS to law enforcement "in response to . . . [an] oral request for the purpose of identifying or locating a suspect, fugitive, material witness or missing person."[8] The information that the LAPD can access is limited to name, address, date and place of birth, social security number, and distinguishing physical characteristics. But there is no mandatory review or approval process for oral requests. There is no requirement that the information released be limited in scope or specific to an ongoing case. There is no warrant process, no departmental oversight, no judge involved to make sure the request is constitutional. Writing about lax data protection in HMIS, legal scholar J. C. O'Brien concludes, "This relaxed standard for disclosures based upon oral requests serves no purpose other than to make information more easily accessible to law enforcement."[9]

There is a long history of social services and the police collaborating to criminalize the poor in the United States. The most direct parallel is Operation Talon, a joint effort of the Office of Inspector General and local welfare offices that mined food stamp data to identify those with outstanding warrants, and then lured them to appointments regarding their benefits. When targeted recipients arrived at the welfare office, they were arrested.

According to Kaaryn Gustafson's 2009 article "The Criminalization of Poverty," before the 1996 welfare reforms, public assistance records were only available to law enforcement through legal channels. But today, she writes, "Welfare records are available to law enforcement officers simply upon request—without probable cause, suspicion, or judicial process of any kind."[10] Operation Talon and other initiatives like it use administrative data to turn social service offices into extensions of the criminal justice system.

In the absence of strong data protection rules, it seems likely that coordinated entry's electronic registry of the unhoused will be used for similar purposes. Outstanding warrants for status crimes provide justification for dragnet searches. Mobile and integrated administrative data can turn any street corner, any tent encampment, or any service provider into a site for a sting operation.

This kind of blanket access to deeply personal information makes little sense outside of a system that equates poverty and homelessness with criminality. As a point of contrast, it is difficult to imagine those receiving federal dollars through mortgage tax deductions or federally subsidized student loans undergoing such thorough scrutiny, or having their personal information available for access by law enforcement without a warrant. Moreover, the pattern of increased data collection, sharing, and surveillance reinforces the criminalization of the unhoused, if only because so many of the basic conditions of being homeless—having nowhere to sleep, nowhere to put your stuff, and nowhere to go to the bathroom—are also officially crimes. If sleeping in a public park, leaving your possessions on the sidewalk, or urinating in a stairwell are met with a ticket, the great majority of the unhoused have no way to pay resulting fines. The tickets turn into warrants, and then law enforcement has further reason to search the databases to find "fugitives." Thus, data collection, storage, and sharing in homeless service programs are often starting points in a process that criminalizes the poor.

The great majority of unhoused people in Los Angeles exist somewhere between the categories of chronic and crisis homelessness. Coordinated entry follows the resources: permanent supportive housing on one side of the spectrum and rapid re-housing on the other. Barring a financial intervention that is an order of magnitude larger than Measures H and HHH, coordinated entry will fail the tens of thousands of unhoused who fall somewhere in the middle.

Some have been incarcerated, or have drug or alcohol problems. Some are unable to find jobs that sustain the basic material requirements of living; others have been traumatized by violence and abuse. All who go unsheltered face severe and ongoing stresses that can lead to disability. "A lot of people like me, who are somewhat higher functioning, are not getting housing," said Gary Boatwright. "[Coordinated entry] is another way of kicking the can down the road."

Before the *Jones* and *Lavan* injunctions, Skid Row was one of the most policed neighborhoods in the world. William Bratton, the architect of the New York City Police Department's CompStat (Computerized Statistics) program, became the LAPD chief in October 2002. In 2006, Bratton and Mayor Antonio Villaraigosa launched the Safer City Initiative (SCI), which earmarked $6 million annually to target status crimes associated with homelessness: sitting on the sidewalk, jaywalking, littering, camping, and panhandling.

According to urban sociologist Forrest Stuart, LAPD officers made roughly 9,000 arrests and issued 12,000 citations in the first year of the initiative, in an area with only 12,000 to 15,000 residents. An assessment of SCI by Skid Row social justice organization Los Angeles Community Action Network showed that more than half of the 200 Skid Row residents they surveyed—both housed and unhoused—had been arrested in a single year. A 2008 analysis showed that the Safer City Initiative produced no statistically significant drop in serious crime, except for a small decline in burglaries.[11]

I visited Skid Row's police station—the Central Division—in January 2015 to talk with Senior Lead Officer Deon Joseph, who has worked for the LAPD for two decades, 18 of them on Skid Row. Officer Joseph is emblematic of the new approaches to community policing that attempt to reconnect police officers with the neighborhoods in which they work. He considers himself a homeless advocate and markets himself as an inspirational speaker. He started a Ladies' Night program to provide Skid Row women with information about their legal rights and basic self-defense training. He is well known for passing out hygiene kits to the unhoused. He is genuinely beloved by many in the community.

In many neighborhoods, community policing is preferable to reactive, incident-driven law enforcement. But it also raises troubling questions. Community policing casts officers as social service or treatment professionals, roles for which they rarely have appropriate training. It pulls social service agencies into relationships with police that compromise their ability to serve the most marginalized people, who often have good reason to avoid law enforcement. Police presence at a social service organization is sufficient to turn away the most vulnerable unhoused, who might have outstanding warrants for status crime tickets associated with being homeless.

Officer Joseph attends coordinated entry meetings at Lamp Community, participates in street cleaning campaigns with the Health Department, and, he said, "shows these social service providers where the most chronically homeless are." He sees community policing, integration into the community's social service networks, and surveillance as mutually reinforcing. "I'll go out, walk a foot beat, go right into the missions, into the courtyard where people are sleeping, tell them about what is happening in the area," he said. "I'll sit on the rooftops and watch the drug activity, so I can know who the ringleaders are. I'll go and do consensual encounters to meet people, talk to them to gather information, if they are willing to give it to me." The relationships he develops through community policing bring him intelligence: informants seek him out, the missions and other social service agencies share their surveillance camera footage. He believes in community policing, he says, because "it helps me solve crimes. It helps me improve the quality of life. It helps me get cooperation from individuals that normally wouldn't cooperate with the police."

Further integrating programs aimed at providing economic security and those focused on crime control threatens to turn routine survival strategies of those living in extreme poverty into crimes. The constant data collection from a vast array of high-tech tools wielded by homeless services, business improvement districts, and law enforcement create what Skid Row residents perceive as a net of constraint that influences their every decision. Daily, they feel encouraged to self-deport or self-imprison. Those living outdoors in encampments feel pressured to constantly be on the move. Those housed in SROs or permanent supportive housing feel equally intense pressure to stay inside and out of the public eye.

The experience of General Dogon, human rights defender with the Los Angeles Community Action Network, is emblematic. After spending 90 days on the street, he finally found housing in the Sanborn, an SRO. After being in the building for a few days, he went outside to smoke a cigarette. A private security guard working for the Business Improvement District approached him on what looked like a police bicycle. He asked, "How long you going to be standing out here?" General Dogon replied, "Well, I don't know." The security guard asked, "Is someone coming by? Are you going to meet somebody? You can't be just standing outside. You're loitering."

"I am?" Dogon asked. "I thought loitering was hanging out with criminal intent." The security guard replied, "Well, yeah, technically. But we want to keep people moving. Can you walk and smoke?"

It got so bad, Dogon explained, that everyone who lived in his SRO hid inside the building all day. "People in my hotel, they are so scared and shook up, that one day they was drawing straws to see who's going to make the store run," he said. "Leaving the house was like going to Vietnam or something. You wasn't sure you was gonna come back."

The over-concentration of police in the Central District leads to more officers responding to calls, people being over-ticketed, and excessive use of force. Tickets turn into warrants and then arrests. Because Skid Row residents can't afford bail, many of those arrested remain incarcerated waiting for their day in court. Charges for crimes associated with homelessness are often dismissed when cases come to trial, but in the meantime Skid Row residents might spend three or four months locked up. As a result, they lose their housing, their documents, their few possessions, and are passed over for social services. "It's like the guy that's homeless on this block is just being recycled," said Dogon. "He's got to do all that nonsense again."

Key to the neighborhood's survival was the strategic grassroots plan to "keep Skid Row scary." In the face of gentrification and intensified surveillance and policing, that strategy is beginning to fail. With the creative class attempting to claim downtown Los Angeles, pressure to recuperate Skid Row for the wealthy means increased pressure to make its poor inhabitants manageable. Coordinated entry and other high-tech tools make the behavior of the unhoused more visible, trackable, and predictable. If this subtle discipline fails, Skid Row's poor face incarceration.

The unhoused in Los Angeles are thus faced with a difficult trade-off: admitting risky, or even illegal, behavior on the VI-SPDAT can snag you a higher ranking on the priority list for permanent supportive housing. But it can also open you up to law enforcement scrutiny. Coordinated entry is not just a system for managing information or matching demand to supply. It is a surveillance system for sorting and criminalizing the poor.

To understand coordinated entry as a system of surveillance, it is crucial to differentiate between "old" and "new" surveillance.[12] Older analog systems of surveillance required individualized attention: a small number of law enforcement or intelligence personnel would compile a dossier by identifying a target, tracking her, and recording her movements and activities. The targets of older forms of surveillance were often chosen because of their group membership: COINTELPRO (the COunter INTELligence PROgram of the FBI), for example, focused on civil rights activists for both their race and their political activism. But wiretaps, photography, tailing, and other techniques of old surveillance were individualized and focused. The target had to be identified before the watcher could surveil.

In contrast, in new data-based surveillance, the *target often emerges from the data*. The targeting comes after the data collection, not before. Massive amounts of information are collected on a wide variety of individuals and groups. Then, the data is mined, analyzed, and searched in order to identify possible targets for more thorough scrutiny. Sometimes this involves old-school, in-person watching and tracking. But increasingly, it only requires finer sifting of data that already exists. If the old surveillance was an eye in the sky, the new surveillance is a spider in a digital web, testing each connected strand for suspicious vibrations.

Surveillance is not only a means of watching or tracking, it is also a mechanism for social sorting. Coordinated entry collects data tied to individual behavior, assesses vulnerability, and assigns different interventions based on that valuation. "Coordinated entry is triage," said Molly Rysman, the Housing and Homeless deputy for LA's Third District. "All of us have thought about it like a natural disaster. We have extraordinary need and can't meet all of that need at once. So you've got to figure out: How do we get folks who are going to bleed to death access to a doctor, and folks who have the flu to wait? It's unfortunate to have to do that, but it is the reality of what we're stuck with."

In his prescient 1993 book, *The Panoptic Sort*, communication scholar Oscar Gandy of the University of Pennsylvania also suggests that automated sorting of digital personal information is a kind of triage. But he pushes further, pointing out that the term is derived from the French *trier*, which means to pick over, cull, or grade marketable produce. "Although some metaphors speak for themselves, let me be clear," he writes. In digital triage, "individuals and groups of people are being sorted according to their presumed economic or political value. The poor, especially poor people of color, are increasingly being treated as broken material or damaged goods to be discarded."[13]

If homelessness is inevitable—like a disease or a natural disaster—then it is perfectly reasonable to use triage-oriented solutions that prioritize unhoused people for a chance at limited housing resources. But if homelessness is a human tragedy created by policy decisions and professional middle-class apathy, coordinated entry allows us to distance ourselves from the human impacts of our choice to not act decisively. As a system of moral valuation, coordinated entry is a machine for producing rationalization, for helping us convince ourselves that only the most deserving people are getting help. Those judged "too risky" are coded for criminalization. Those who fall through the cracks face prisons, institutions, or death.

Despite the successes of Measures H and HHH, the faith that faster, more accurate data will succeed in building the units Los Angeles needs may be naïve. Angelenos voted to pay a bit more in sales and property taxes in order to house the homeless. But will the housed let the homeless move into their neighborhoods?

Evidence suggests that building new low-income housing or repurposing older buildings to house the homeless will prove challenging. Two recent proposals to build storage units for the unhoused's *belongings* erupted into community-wide protest. In fall 2016 a proposal to build a storage facility in the beachside community of Venice led to an acrimonious series of community meetings and a homeowner lawsuit to stop the project. A similar storage center planned for San Pedro was scuttled when the housed community organized to stop it. As the perception of increased resources for the homeless rises, the city's fragile tolerance for homeless encampments may unravel. Shortly before voters committed to providing new resources to shelter the unhoused, the city council rewrote a municipal ordinance to reauthorize the kind of aggressive sweeps of tent encampments that were common before the *Jones* and *Lavan* rulings.

Like the public housing that was supposed to replace the boardinghouses and SRO hotels demolished during urban renewal in the 1950s, new affordable housing development may founder in the face of active obstruction by professional middle-class and wealthy Angelenos. The problem is not that the city lacks adequate data on what kind of housing is needed to address the homelessness problem. Rather, poor and working-class people and their allies may not be able to overcome explicit political resistance from organized elites.

The proponents of the coordinated entry system, like many who seek to harness computational power for social justice, tend to find affinity with systems engineering approaches to social problems. These perspectives assume that complex controversies can be solved by getting correct information where it needs to go as efficiently as possible. In this model, political conflict arises primarily from a lack of information. If we just gather all the facts, systems engineers assume, the correct answers to intractable policy problems like homelessness will be simple, uncontroversial, and widely shared.

But, for better or worse, this is not how politics work. Political contests are more than informational; they are about values, group membership, and balancing conflicting interests. The poor and working-class residents of Skid Row and South LA want affordable housing and available services. The Downtown Central Business Improvement District wants tourist-friendly streets. The new urban pioneers want both edgy grit and a Whole Foods. The city wants to clear the streets of encampments. While Los Angeles residents have agreed to pay a little more to address the problem, many don't want unhoused people moving next door. And they don't want to spend the kind of money it would take to really solve the housing crisis. These are deeply conflicting visions for the future of Los Angeles. Having more information won't necessarily resolve them.

Systems engineering can help manage big, complex social problems. But it doesn't build houses, and it may not prove sufficient to overcome deep-seated prejudice against the poor, especially poor people of color. "Algorithms are intrinsically stupid," said public interest lawyer, homeless advocate, and emeritus professor of law at UCLA Gary Blasi. "You can't build any algorithm that can handle as many variables, and levels of nuance, and complexity as human beings present." While coordinated entry may minimize some of the implicit bias of individual homeless service providers, Blasi reflected, that doesn't mean it is a good idea. "My objection to [coordinated entry] is that it has drawn resources and attention from other aspects of the problem. For 30 years, I've seen this notion, especially among well-educated people, that it's just a question of information. Homeless people just don't have the information."

"Fraud is too strong a word," said Blasi. "But homelessness is not a systems engineering problem. It's a carpentry problem."

The last time I saw Gary Boatwright, in October 2016, he looked less healthy, wilder, and his mental health seemed to be deteriorating. He was furious with a street sweeper he believed had stolen possessions from his tent. Later that month, he was asked to remove himself from his tent site in front of the LA CAN offices on East 6th Street after conflicts with other community members. Because LA CAN has been such a staunch defender of the rights of the unhoused, the block in front of their building serves as a sanctuary space, where the LAPD refrains from ticketing and arresting the homeless for status crimes. Boatwright moved his tent to Spring Street. A few weeks later, on December 2, he was arrested.

When he called from Men's Central Jail in January 2017, he told me that he had been charged with breaking the window of a bus with a plastic broom he bought at a 99 Cent Store. "Defying the laws of physics!" he asserted. "They showed up [to court] with a photograph of a bus with a broken window, and I suggested that the DA was withholding evidence that's exculpatory. Next thing, they came at me with a deal. It's impossible that they don't have video. Public buses have at least a half-dozen video cameras, don't they?" He was optimistic that he'd only spend a few months in jail before release. After his release in 2017, he faced all the struggles General Dogon described: he lost his tent, all of his possessions, his meticulously filed paperwork, and his social network. He had to start back at square one.

And the next time he takes the VI-SPDAT, he will likely score *lower*. The model counts prison as housing. The system will see him as less vulnerable, and his prioritization score will slip even lower. He'll stay trapped, too vigorous for intervention and too marginal to make a go of it without support. "I'm a criminal," he said, "just for existing on the face of the earth."

4

THE ALLEGHENY ALGORITHM

It's a week before Thanksgiving, and I'm squeezed into the far corner of a long row of gray cubicles in the call center for the Allegheny County Office of Children, Youth and Families (CYF) child neglect and abuse hotline. I'm sharing a desk and a tiny purple footstool with intake screener Pat Gordon. We're both studying the Key Information and Demographics System (KIDS), a blue screen filled with case notes, demographic data, and program statistics. We are focused on the records of two families: both are white, living in the city of Pittsburgh, one has two children, the other has three. Both were referred to CYF by a "mandated reporter," a professional who is legally required to report any suspicion that a child may be at risk of harm from their caregiver. Pat and I are competing to see if we can guess how a new predictive risk model the county is using to forecast child abuse and neglect, called the Allegheny Family Screening Tool (AFST), will score them.

Pat Gordon is the kind of woman who keeps pictures of other people's children in her cubicle. Gordon, a Pittsburgh native and

Pirates fan, wears a telephone headset that pushes back her ear-length bob. She will say only that she is "over forty." Six lines are busy on her phone as she stands to greet me. Her long-sleeved pink t-shirt complements her warm brown skin, and her mischievous laugh quickly transitions to quiet seriousness when we talk about the kids she serves.

In the noisy glassed-in room, intake screeners like Pat interview callers who have phoned the hotline to report suspicions of child abuse or neglect. Mostly female and about evenly split between African American and white, intake screeners search for information about families in a vast system of interconnected county databases. They have records from Drug and Alcohol Services, Head Start, Mental Health Services, the Housing Authority, the Allegheny County Jail, the state's Department of Public Welfare, Medicaid, the Pittsburgh Public Schools, and more than a dozen other programs and agencies at their fingertips.

Pat hands me a double-sided piece of paper called the "Risk/Severity Continuum." It took her a minute to find it, protected by a clear plastic envelope and tucked in a stack of papers near the back of her desk. She's worked in call screening for five years, and, she says, "Most workers, you get this committed to memory. You just know."

But I need the extra help. I am intimidated by the weight of this decision, even though I am only observing. From its cramped columns of tiny text, I learn that kids under five are at highest risk of neglect and abuse, that substantiated prior reports increase the chance that a family will be investigated, and that parent hostility toward CYF investigators is considered high-risk behavior. I take my time, cross-checking information in KIDS against the risk/severity handout while Gordon rolls her eyes at me, teasing, threatening to click the big blue button that runs the risk model.

The first child is a six-year-old boy I'll call Stephen. Stephen's mom, seeking mental health–care for anxiety, disclosed to her county-funded therapist that someone—she didn't know who—put Stephen out on the porch of their home on an early November day. She found him crying outside and brought him in. That week he began to act out, and she was concerned that something bad had happened to him. She confessed to her therapist that she suspected he might have been abused. Her therapist reported her to the state child abuse hotline.

But leaving a crying child on a porch isn't abuse or neglect as the state of Pennsylvania defines it. So the intake worker screened out the call. Even though the report was unsubstantiated, a record of the call and the call screener's notes remain in the KIDS system. A week later, an employee of a homeless services agency reported Stephen to a hotline again: he was wearing dirty clothes, had poor hygiene, and there were rumors that his mother was abusing drugs. Other than these two reports, the family had no prior record with CYF.

The second child is a 14-year-old I'll call Krzysztof. On a community health home visit in early November, a case manager with a large nonprofit found a window and a door broken and the house cold. Krzysztof was wearing several layers of clothes. The caseworker reported that the house smelled like pet urine. The family sleeps in the living room, Krzysztof on the couch and his mom on the floor. The case manager found the room "cluttered." It is unclear whether these conditions actually meet the definition of child neglect in Pennsylvania, but the family has a long history with county programs.

No one wants children to suffer, but the appropriate role of government in keeping kids safe is complicated. States derive their authority to prevent, investigate, and prosecute child abuse and neglect from the Child Abuse Prevention and Treatment Act, signed into law by President Richard Nixon in 1974. The law defines child abuse and neglect as the "physical or mental injury, sexual abuse, negligent treatment, or maltreatment of a child . . . by a person who is responsible for the child's welfare under circumstances which indicate that the child's health or welfare is harmed or threatened."

Even with recent clarifications that the harm must be "serious," there is considerable room for subjectivity in what exactly constitutes neglect or abuse. Is spanking abusive? Or is the line drawn at striking a child with a closed hand? Is letting your children walk to a park down the block alone neglectful? Even if you can see them from the window? The first screen of the list of conditions classified as maltreatment in KIDS illustrates just how much latitude call screeners have to classify parenting behaviors as abusive or neglectful. It includes: abandoned infant; abandonment; adoption disruption or dissolution; caretaker's inability to cope; child sexually acting out; child substance abuse; conduct by parent that places child at risk; corporal punishment; delayed/denied health care; delinquent act by a child under 10 years of age; domestic violence; educational neglect; environmental toxic substance; exposure to hazards; expulsion from home; failure to protect; homelessness; inadequate clothing, hygiene, physical care, or provision of food; inappropriate caregivers or discipline; injury caused by another person; and isolation. The list scrolls on for several more screens.

Three-quarters of child welfare investigations involve neglect rather than physical, sexual, or emotional abuse. Where the line is drawn between the routine conditions of poverty and child neglect is particularly vexing. Many struggles common among poor families are officially defined as child maltreatment, including not having enough food, having inadequate or unsafe housing, lacking medical care, or leaving a child alone while you work. Unhoused families face particularly difficult challenges holding on to their children, as the very condition of being homeless is judged neglectful.

In reality, most child welfare caseworkers aren't looking to put children into foster care simply because their parents are poor; investigators are often reluctant to define as "neglect" conditions that parents have little control over. On the contrary, child welfare workers sometimes use threats of putting a child in foster care to secure resources to keep a family safe. They may call the public assistance office to help a family get food stamps, force a landlord to make needed repairs, or offer a struggling parent counseling or community supports.

In Pennsylvania, abuse and neglect are relatively narrowly defined. Abuse requires bodily injury resulting in impairment or substantial pain, sexual abuse or exploitation, causing mental injury, or imminent risk of any of these things. Neglect must be a "prolonged or repeated lack of supervision" serious enough that it "endangers a child's life or development or impairs the child's functioning." So, as Pat Gordon and I run down the risk/severity matrix, I think both Stephen and Krzysztof should score pretty low.

In neither case are there reported injuries, substantiated prior abuse, a record of serious emotional harm, or verified drug use. I'm concerned about the inadequate heat in teenaged Krzysztof's house, but I wouldn't say that he is in imminent danger. Pat is concerned that there have been two calls in two weeks on six-year-old Stephen. "We literally shut the door behind us and then there was another call," she sighs. It might suggest a pattern of neglect or abuse developing—or that the family is in crisis. The call from a homeless service agency suggests that conditions at home deteriorated so quickly that Stephen and his mom found themselves on the street. But we agree that for both boys, there seems to be low risk of immediate harm and few threats to their physical safety.

On a scale of 1 to 20, with 1 being the lowest level of risk and 20 being the highest, I guess that Stephen will be a 4, and Krzysztof a

6. Gordon smirks and hits the button. The numbers come up exactly as she predicted. Stephen gets a 5. Krzysztof? A 14.

I have come to Pittsburgh to explore the impacts of the Allegheny Family Screening Tool (AFST) on poor and working-class families. The stakes are high. According to the U.S. Centers for Disease Control and Prevention, approximately 1 in 4 children will experience some form of abuse or neglect in their lifetimes. The agency's Adverse Childhood Experience Study concluded that the experience of abuse or neglect has "tremendous, lifelong impact on our health and the quality of our lives," including increased occurrences of drug and alcohol abuse, suicide attempts, and depression.[1]

The administrative offices of the Allegheny County CYF are just a stone's throw from where the Allegheny, Monongahela, and Ohio Rivers come together at the center of the city of Pittsburgh. Allegheny County has been a working-class stronghold with conservative Democratic leanings and a history of revolt against government interference since the Whiskey Rebellion started here in 1791. At the turn of the last century, it was home to the world's first billion-dollar corporation: J.P. Morgan and Andrew Carnegie's United States Steel Corporation.

Several decades of post-industrial economic disinvestment and population decline followed the abrupt closure of US Steel plants throughout the county in the mid-1980s. But in the last decade, Pittsburgh has seen a wave of young college graduates flocking to the region for jobs in the health professions, higher education, technology, and the arts. What was once Steel City now houses an estimated 1,600 technology companies, including a 450-employee office of Google and Uber's robotic self-driving car division.

Marc Cherna, director of the Allegheny County Department of Human Services, arrived in February 1996 to run what was then known as Children and Youth Services (CYS) in the wake of two very public scandals. In the first, known as the "Baby Byron" case, a white foster family, the Derzacks, refused to return an African American toddler, Byron Griffin, to the agency so he could be reunited with his mother. Then-director Mary Freeland, upholding standard policies of the time that discouraged foster parents from adopting children in their care and restricted transracial adoption, traveled to the Derzack family home with a police escort to remove Byron on December 27, 1993. After Byron was returned to his mother, LaShawn Jeffrey, the Derzacks made the rounds of national talk shows, characterizing themselves as the infant's thwarted saviors, and wrote a tell-all book about their experience.

Then, in March 1994, the body of two-year-old Shawntee Ford was found in a Pittsburgh motel. The chief forensic pathologist concluded that the toddler had been beaten to death, just weeks after being placed in the care of her father. CYS caseworkers had removed Shawntee from her mother, Mable Ford, while she underwent drug treatment. The two were later reunited. But when they were discovered living in a car in Buffalo, New York, Shawntee was removed again and her father, Maurice Booker, Sr., petitioned for custody.

During the hearing, a CYS worker told the judge that Booker had been investigated and that the agency didn't have any concerns about his caretaking. The caseworkers failed to mention that Booker had a record of arrests for drunk driving and reckless endangerment. In February, after the custody hearing but before Shawntee's death, Booker was also charged with holding his girlfriend and two other children hostage in a New Year's Eve standoff with police. Shortly after Shawntee died, the state Department of Public Welfare denied CYS a full license, citing 72 violations of regulations, including failure to complete timely criminal background checks on parents. Within a year, Mary Freeland, under pressure to resign, accepted a new post overseeing a children's commission in Florida.

"When I came here to run Children and Youth, it was a national disgrace," said Marc Cherna. When he arrived in 1996, there were 1,600 children waiting to be adopted, and the agency was only managing to process 60 adoptions a year. Caseworkers made 35 percent less than caseworkers in neighboring Erie County. Most did not have a degree in social work. They were burdened with excessive caseloads, serving 30 or more families at a time. A blue-ribbon commission characterized the agency's relationship to Pittsburgh's African American community as one of "severe antagonism."[2] Seventy percent of children in the foster care system were Black, though African Americans made up only 11 percent of the population of Allegheny County. The agency struggled to recruit and retain people of color as adoptive families, caseworkers, and administrators.

Around the time Marc Cherna was hired, a commission called ComPAC21 convened to study the county's political structure. It recommended shrinking county government by merging 30 distinct departments into nine large agencies. They combined the offices of aging, children and youth services, intellectual disability, behavioral health, and community services. They named the resulting agency the Department of Human Services (DHS) and appointed Cherna to lead it.

Formerly assistant director of the New Jersey Division of Youth and Family Services, Cherna is a ruddy-faced cheerful man who often sports a signature Save the Children necktie: kids' drawings of multiethnic toddlers on a brown background. He is deeply proud that he's managed to stay in his position 20 years, an impressive tenure for the leader of such a challenging agency. Today, DHS serves 200,000 people, employs 940 county workers, manages 417 contracting agencies, and operates with an $867 million annual budget.

Early in his tenure, Cherna proposed the creation of a data warehouse, a central repository that would pull together information collected by DHS, other county agencies, and state public assistance programs. With $2.8 million from a collection of local foundations, Cherna built the data warehouse in 1999. Today, it lives on two servers in DHS headquarters and holds more than one billion electronic records, an average of 800 records for every person in Allegheny County.

Twenty-nine different programs—including adult probation, the bureau of drug and alcohol services, the housing authority, the county jail, the juvenile probation office, the Allegheny County police department, the state office of income maintenance, the office of mental health and substance abuse services, the office of unemployment compensation, and almost 20 local school districts—send regular data extracts. The extracts include client names, social security numbers, dates of birth, addresses, and the type and amount of services they've received. The annual cost of the data warehouse, managed primarily through a contract with the multinational consulting firm Deloitte Touche Tohmatsu Ltd., tops $15 million a year, about 2 percent of DHS's annual budget.

Marc Cherna and Erin Dalton, his deputy director of Data Analysis, Research and Evaluation, see the data warehouse as a tool to increase agency communication and accountability, provide wraparound services for clients, and cut costs. The department can match internal to external data, verify a client's identity, establish eligibility for program resources, and keep a watchful eye on client behavior across all interactions with public services.

But the administration hasn't just focused on collecting and analyzing data. Early in his tenure, Cherna reached out to foster, adoptive, and birth parents; service providers; child advocates; lawyers; and judges. In a case study of his administration written by Stewards of Change, a management consulting firm, Cherna explained, "The goal is for the child welfare agency to be viewed in the community as a friend, not a foe."

"Marc has really solid relationships with private funders in this town. He has really positive relationships with the agencies," said Laurie Mulvey of the University of Pittsburgh's Office of Child Development. "He's clear that it's all about relationships. He's honest, and straightforward, and works hard." Nearly every community member I spoke to in my travels to Pittsburgh agreed with Mulvey, praising Cherna's team for their participatory approach, clear communication, and high ethical standards. Today's CYF is more diverse, more responsive, more transparent. It invites community input and leadership. Over the past 20 years, Cherna has earned the community's trust and goodwill.

In 2012, the Pennsylvania General Assembly reduced its human services allocations by 10 percent, cutting about $12 million from DHS. The budget reduction sharpened a crisis already created by steadily declining county revenues and increased demand for services following the 2007 recession. Rich in data but poor in material resources, Cherna and his team put together an RFP to "design and implement decision support tools and predictive analytics in human services." DHS offered up to one million dollars—provided by a Richard King Mellon Foundation grant—to build an automated triage system that would help them focus resources where they would do the most good.

The proposal they chose was submitted by a team from New Zealand's Auckland University of Technology, led by economist Rhema Vaithianathan and Emily Putnam-Hornstein, director of the Children's Data Network at the University of Southern California. They proposed to design, develop, and implement a decision-making tool that would mine Cherna's warehoused data to make predictions about which Allegheny County children might be at greatest risk for abuse and neglect.

Rhema Vaithianathan and Emily Putnam-Hornstein met because they share an ambition to predict child maltreatment at the moment of birth, or even before. A 2011 paper by Putnam-Hornstein and Barbara Needell concluded that a prenatal maltreatment-predicting algorithm was theoretically possible: "A risk assessment tool that could be used on the day of birth to identify those children at greatest risk of maltreatment holds great value," they wrote. "[P]renatal risk assessments could be used to identify children at risk . . . while still in the womb."[3] On the other side of the world, Rhema Vaithianathan, associate professor of economics at the University of Auckland, was on a team developing just such a tool.

As part of a larger program of welfare reforms led by conservative Paula Bennett, the New Zealand Ministry of Social Development (MSD) commissioned the Vaithianathan team to create a statistical model to sift information on parents interacting with the public benefits, child protective, and criminal justice systems to predict which children were most likely to be abused or neglected. Vaithianathan reached out to Putnam-Hornstein to collaborate. "It was such an exciting opportunity to partner with Rhema's team around this potential real-time use of data to target children," said Putnam-Hornstein.

Vaithianathan's team developed a predictive model using 132 variables—including length of time on public benefits, past involvement with the child welfare system, mother's age, whether or not the child was born to a single parent, mental health, and correctional history—to rate the maltreatment risk of children in the MSD's historical data. They found that their algorithm could predict with "fair, approaching good" accuracy whether these children would have a "substantiated finding of maltreatment" by the time they turned five. In a paper released in September 2013, the team suggested that the ministry, after performing a feasibility study and an ethical review, deploy the model to generate risk scores that would trigger targeted, voluntary early intervention programs "with the aim of preventing maltreatment."[4]

When the New Zealand public learned of the project in 2014, they responded with concern. Academic researchers warned that the model might not be as accurate as the team claimed: it was wrong about nearly 70 percent of the children it identified as at highest risk of harm in the historical data.[5] Others cautioned that the model was primarily a tool of surveillance of the poor.[6] Project reviewers raised concerns that the special needs of Māori families, which face child removal at dramatically disproportionate rates, were not adequately considered.[7]

In 2015, Social Development Minister Anne Tolley, who had replaced Bennett the year before, halted a plan to launch an observational experiment that would risk-rate 60,000 newborns to test the accuracy of the Vaithianathan team's tool. In the margin of a project briefing that was later leaked to the press, she wrote, "Not on my watch! These are children not lab rats." The experiment collapsed in the face of public resistance. But by that time, the Vaithianathan team had won the contract to create a similar predictive risk model in Allegheny County.

Back in the call center, Pat Gordon and I consider Stephen and Krzysztof's scores. As 4 p.m. rolls around, the noise level in the call center rises steeply. From cubicles all around us, I overhear the questions of other intake screeners: "What kind of drugs is she on?" "Do you have any kind of support systems right now? Even like good friends that help you out in these kinds of situations?" "How do you spell Duquan?" In the next cubicle, a caseworker is scrolling through custody documents from the Allegheny County Court of Common Pleas. Another is using

Facebook to try to identify a family who has been reported by a caller who only knows the mother's first name and phone number. The banter between intake workers gets saltier as the stress peaks.

Screeners like Pat Gordon take phone calls for the county's child abuse and neglect hotline and receive electronic reports from Pennsylvania's state hotline, called ChildLine. For each report, they collect information: the nature of the caller's concern, circumstances of the incident, and demographic information on the child and any other involved person, including names, ages, location, and addresses. They also collect history on all the people associated with the allegation of neglect or abuse. Intake screeners have high-level access to ClientView, the DHS's application for searching the data warehouse. They also search publicly accessible sources: court records, divorce filings, birth records, social media.

Krzysztof's case came over ChildLine, the state system. The report Gordon receives reads: "[Name redacted], Case manager with Diversified Care Management, reported that the window in the house is messed up and a door is broke. When its cold outside, the house ends up being very cold. C[hild] ends up wearing several layers of clothing. The house smells of urine from the cats and dogs. There has been feces on the floor. There's a lot of clutter in the living room. C[hild] sleeps in the living room on a couch by choice. M[other] sleeps on the floor in the living room."

Because there is an ongoing case on Krzysztof, Pat Gordon won't be deciding whether or not to screen the family in for investigation. She will simply document this report and try to provide Krzysztof's caseworker with a sense of the urgency of the allegation. If she had to make a decision whether to screen this case in or out, Gordon says, "There's tons of questions that I would ask [the case manager]: When is the last time you were in the home? How long have you been working with this family? What brings you to work with the family? Does the family know that you're making a report to us?"

Pat explains that, though the AFST has been getting a lot of attention lately, it's only the final step in a three-part intake process that determines if a family will be screened in for investigation. Intake screeners consider the nature of an allegation: Does it rise to Pennsylvania's legal definition of maltreatment? Is it within CYF's jurisdiction? They then consider the immediate risk to the child: Is there impending danger? Present danger? Finally, intake screeners search through all available data sources to determine a family history. The AFST supplements a call screener's work in developing that history.

The pairing of the human discretion of intake screeners like Pat Gordon with the ability to dive deep into historical data provided by the predictive risk model is the most important fail-safe of the system. "This is the place where we have the least information," said Erin Dalton. "The callers don't know that much. We know a lot about these families. There's so much history [in the data]. We can make a more informed recommendation."

Pat walks me through Krzysztof's case. "This kiddo is older," she says, "So his vulnerability is going to be low. There's no real injury or anything like that. Prior abuse and neglect? Well, there is an open GPS [General Protective Services] case on the family already. I don't get a mental health for the parents or the kiddo in this allegation." She chooses "Low" for the severity of the allegation. Then she considers the immediate safety of the child. A broken window and door is uncomfortable, she says, but "it's certainly not impending danger, it doesn't sound like present danger." Then, she clicks the button that runs the AFST. Krzysztof's score appears on her screen in a graphic that looks like a thermometer: it's green down at the bottom and progresses up through yellow shades to a vibrant red at the top. Krzysztof's 14 is at the bottom of the red section, in the "Emergency!" part of the scale.

I'm shocked that Krzysztof received a score nearly three times as high as Stephen's. Krzysztof is in his teens, while Stephen is only 6. The hotline report shows no harm beyond the crowded conditions and poor housing stock common to being poor. Why was he rated so highly? Pat tries to explain. His family's record with public services stretches back to when his mother was a child. So though the allegation is not severe and Krzysztof seems safe, the family's AFST score is high.

Though the screen that displays the AFST score states clearly that the system "is not intended to make investigative or other child welfare decisions," an ethical review released in May 2016 by Tim Dare from the University of Auckland and Eileen Gambrill from University of California, Berkeley, cautions that the AFST risk score might be compelling enough to make intake workers question their own judgment. Rhema Vaithianathan insists that the model is built in such a way that intake screeners will question its predictive accuracy and defer to their own judgment. "It sounds contradictory, but I want the model to be slightly undermined by the call screeners," she said. "I want them to be able to say, this [screening score] is a twenty, but this allegation is so minimal that [all] this model is telling me is that there's history."

But from what I saw in the call center during my visit, the model is already subtly changing how some intake screeners do their jobs. "The score comes at the end of the report, after we've already done all this research," said intake manager Jessie Schemm. "If you get a report and you do all the research, and then you run the score and your research doesn't match the score, typically, there's something you're missing. You have to back-piece the puzzle."

We all tend to defer to machines, which can seem more neutral, more objective. But it is troubling that managers believe that if the intake screener and the computer's assessments conflict, the human should learn from the model. The AFST, like all risk models, offers only probabilities, not perfect prediction. Though it might be able to identify patterns and trends, it is routinely wrong about individual cases. According to Vaithianathan and Putnam-Hornstein, intake screeners have asked for the ability to go back and change their risk assessments after they see the AFST score, suggesting that they believe that the model is less fallible than human screeners. So far, Cherna and Dalton have resisted. Intake screeners' risk and safety assessments are locked in and can't be changed after the AFST is run, except by a manager.

In the face of the seeming authority and objectivity of a computerized score, risk aversion, or an understandable excess of caution with children's lives at stake, it is easy to see how a flashing red number might short-circuit an intake screener's professional judgment. The AFST is supposed to support, not supplant, human decision-making in the call center. And yet, in practice, the algorithm seems to be training the intake workers.

What's more, if a family's AFST risk score is over 20, *the system automatically triggers an investigation* unless a supervisor overrides it. "Once the algorithm is run and the wheels start to turn," says Bruce Noel, regional intake manager of Allegheny County CYF, "one of the possibilities is that the model says you *must* screen this in."

A 14-year-old living in a cold and dirty house gets a risk score almost three times as high as a 6-year-old whose mother suspects he may have been abused and who may now be homeless. In these cases, the model does not seem to meet a commonsense standard for providing information useful enough to guide call screeners' decision-making. Why might that be?

Data scientist Cathy O'Neil has written that "models are

opinions embedded in mathematics."[8] Models are useful because they let us strip out extraneous information and focus only on what is most critical to the outcomes we are trying to predict. But they are also abstractions. Choices about what goes into them reflect the priorities and preoccupations of their creators. Human decision-making is reflected in three key components of the AFST: outcome variables, predictive variables, and validation data.

Outcome variables are what you measure to indicate the phenomenon you are trying to predict. In the case of the AFST, Allegheny County is concerned with child abuse, especially potential fatalities. But the number of child maltreatment–related fatalities and near fatalities in Allegheny County is very low—luckily, only a handful a year. A statistically meaningful model cannot be constructed with such sparse data.

Failing that, it might seem logical to use child maltreatment as substantiated by CYF caseworkers to stand in for actual child maltreatment. But substantiation is an imprecise metric: it simply means that CYF believes there is enough evidence that a child *may* be harmed to accept a family for services. Caseworkers will substantiate a case in order to get a family access to needed resources like food stamps or affordable housing. Some will substantiate because, though they don't have credible evidence, they have a strong suspicion that something's going on with a child. Other cases will be substantiated because frightened parents admit abuse or neglect they didn't actually commit. Substantiation is not clear-cut, so it can't be used as an outcome variable, either.

Though it would be best to use a more direct measure, the AFST uses two related variables—called proxies—as stand-ins for child maltreatment. The first proxy is *community re-referral*, when a call to the hotline about a child was initially screened out, but CYF receives another call on the same child within two years.

The second proxy is *child placement*, when a call to the hotline about a child is screened in and results in the child being placed in foster care within two years. So the AFST actually predicts decisions made by the community (which families will be reported to the hotline) and by the agency and the family courts (which children will be removed from their families), not which children will be harmed.

Predictive modeling requires clear, unambiguous measures with lots of associated data in order to function accurately. But that means that the model has to test what's available. "We don't have a perfect outcome variable," said Erin Dalton. "We don't think there are perfect proxies for harm."

Predictive variables are the bits of data within a data set that are correlated with the outcome variables. To find the predictive variables for the AFST, the Vaithianathan team ran a statistical procedure called a stepwise probit regression, a common, but somewhat controversial, data mining process. This computerized method knocks out variables that are not highly correlated enough with the outcome variables to reach statistical significance. In other words, it searches through all available information to pluck out any variables that vary along with the thing you are trying to measure—which leads to charges that the method is a kind of "data dredging," or a statistical fishing expedition.

For the AFST, the Vaithianathan team tested 287 variables available in Cherna's data warehouse. The regression knocked out 156 of them, leaving 131 factors that the team believes predict child harm.[9]

Even if a regression finds factors that predictably rise and fall together, correlation is not causation. In a classic example, shark attacks and ice cream consumption are highly correlated. But that doesn't mean that eating ice cream makes swimmers too slow to avoid aquatic predators, or that sharks are attracted to soft-serve. There is a third variable that influences both shark attacks and ice cream consumption: summer. Both ice cream eating and shark attacks go up when the weather is warmer.

Validation data is used to see how well your model performs. In Allegheny County, the model was tested on 76,964 referrals received by CYF between April 2010 and April 2014.[10] Vaithianathan and her team split the referrals into two stacks: 70 percent of them were used to determine the weights of the predictor variables (how important each variable is to the outcomes they are trying to predict). Then, the resulting model, with its 131 predictive variables properly weighted, was run against the other 30 percent of the cases to see if the model could reliably predict the actual outcomes of children in the historical data.

A perfectly predictive model would have what's called 100 percent fit in the area under the receiver operating characteristic (ROC) curve. A model that has no degree of predictive ability—its chances of being right are about the same as the chances of guessing heads or tails in a coin toss—would have a 50 percent fit under the ROC curve. The AFST's initial fit in the area under the ROC curve is 76 percent, about the same as the predictive accuracy of a yearly mammogram.[11]

Seventy-six percent might sound pretty good, but it's only halfway between a coin toss and perfect prediction. And while the mammogram comparison is persuasive, it's also important to remember that in 2009, the U.S. Preventative Services Task Force stopped recommending mammograms for women in their 40s, and recommended fewer mammograms for women over 50, due to concerns about the impacts of false positives, false negatives, and yearly radiation.[12] In 2016, there were 15,139 reports of abuse and neglect in Allegheny County. At its current rate of accuracy, the AFST would have produced 3,633 incorrect predictions.

To sum up: the AFST has inherent design flaws that limit its accuracy. It predicts referrals to the child abuse and neglect hotline and removal of children from their families—hypothetical proxies for child harm—not actual child maltreatment. The data set it utilizes contains only information about families who access public services, so it may be missing key factors that influence abuse and neglect. Finally, its accuracy is only average. It is guaranteed to produce thousands of false negatives and positives annually.

A model's predictive ability is compromised when outcome variables are subjective. Was a parent re-referred to the hotline because she neglects her children? Or because someone in the neighborhood was mad that she had a party last week? Did caseworkers and judges put a child in foster care because his life was in danger? Or because they held culturally specific ideas about what a good parent looks like, or feared the consequences if they didn't play it safe?

In the call center, I mention to Pat Gordon that I've been talking to parents in the CYF system about how the AFST might impact them. Most parents, I tell her, are concerned about false positives: the model rating their child at high risk of abuse or neglect when little risk actually exists. I see how Krzysztof's mother might feel this way if she was given access to her family's score.

But Pat reminds me that I should be concerned with false negatives as well—when the AFST scores a child at low risk though the allegation or immediate risk to the child might be severe. "Let's say they don't have a significant history. They're not active with us. But [the allegation] is something that's very egregious. [CYF] gives us leeway to think for ourselves. But I can't stop feeling concerned that . . . say the child has a broken growth plate, which is very, very highly consistent with maltreatment . . . there's only one or two ways that you can break it. And then [the score] comes in low!"

Allegheny County has an extraordinary amount of information about the use of *public* programs stored in its data warehouse.

But the county has no access to data about people who do not use public services. Parents accessing private drug treatment, mental health counseling, or financial support are not represented in DHS data. Because variables describing their behavior have not been defined or included in the regression, crucial pieces of the child maltreatment puzzle might be omitted from the AFST. It could be missing the crucial "summer" variable that links ice cream and shark attacks.

Geographical isolation might be an important factor in child maltreatment, for example, but it won't be represented in the data set because most families accessing public services in Allegheny County live in dense urban neighborhoods. I ask Pat Gordon if she is concerned with those cases in which a family lives in the suburbs and no one's ever called a hotline on them before, or a caregiver accesses private services for mental health or addiction so he's not in the system. "Exactly," she replies. "I wonder if people downtown really get that. I mean, we're not looking for this to do our job. We're really not. I hope they get that."

I met Angel Shepherd and Patrick Grzyb at the Duquesne Family Support Center, one of 26 community hubs where families attend programs, access resources, and connect with others. I was speaking with members of the organization's Parent Council on a crisp autumn day in 2016. It was a rollicking, wide-ranging, often heated conversation. The atmosphere in the conference room swung wildly from exasperated contempt to tearful appreciation to shocked dread as parents spoke about their experiences with the Allegheny County CYF.

Angel and Patrick didn't stand out right away because their experience is so utterly average, characteristic of the routine, mundane indignities experienced by the white working class. Since moving in together in 2002, they've worked a variety of service jobs, from clerking at Dollar General to providing armed security for a high school to catering. Patrick was born in nearby Munhall two decades before its primary employer, the Homestead Steel Works, closed in 1986. He left school after the ninth grade. He describes himself as "a slow learner," but is smart and diligent enough to raise three children, mostly on his own, while working full time. Angel took an audacious risk, boarding a bus from California to join Patrick after a two-year online courtship. More recently, Angel gambled again when she decided to pursue a college degree in cybersecurity. But this time, she wasn't as lucky. The for-profit online university left her deeply in student loan debt with no clear path to employment.

They are a blended, multigenerational family. Tabatha, one of Patrick's adult daughters, lives with them in their small rented duplex with her own daughter, an expansive and eager-to-please redheaded six-year-old charmer named Deseraye. Harriette, Angel's daughter, is a precocious, energetic, nine-year-old whirlwind of mocha skin and wavy black hair. She loves Scholastic's *I Survived* series of books with their covers featuring young people fleeing fires, tornados, volcanic eruptions, or Nazi invasion. During my November 2016 visit to their home, Harriette showed me her current favorite, *I Survived Hurricane Katrina*.

Patrick and Angel are creative, involved parents. When the two girls bicker, they put them in the "Get-Along Shirt," one of Patrick's roomy button-downs, together. Each girl puts one arm through a sleeve and one arm around the waist of the other. They stay in the Get-Along Shirt until they stop fighting. "Even if they got to go to the bathroom," Patrick explains, laughing, hazel eyes flashing.

Despite the St. Francis of Assisi blessing on the door of their brown asphalt-shingled home, the family has been touched by all the usual traumas of being working class in America: health crises, stretches of unemployment, and physical disability. Nevertheless, they remain remarkably resilient, funny, and generous.

Angel tends to smack Patrick while they're talking, for empha-sis, while he remains placid, like a Buddhist ex-biker, broad shoulders relaxed and elaborate facial hair twitching. He calls her "my Angel," beaming at her in unguarded moments. Now that Patrick's diabetes has cost him three toes and Angel is unem-ployed, they spend most of their time volunteering at the Family Support Center. Patrick works with the "Ready Freddy" pro-gram during the summers, helping prepare young children to enter kindergarten. Angel helps around the office with adminis-trative tasks and takes minutes at all the meetings.

Angel and Patrick have racked up a lifetime of interactions with CYF. Patrick was investigated for medical neglect in the early 2000s when he was unable to afford his daughter Tabatha's antibiotic prescription after an emergency room visit. When her condition worsened and he took her back to the ER the next day, a nurse threatened to call CYF on him. Frightened and angry, Patrick picked his daughter up and walked out. An investigation was opened. "They came late at night," he remembers. "It was like 11 or 12 o'clock, my kids were already asleep. They came up with the police, told us why they were there, came in, looked at the house, looked where the girls were sleeping. And then two or three days later I received a letter saying I'm going to be on file for child neglect until she's eighteen."

The CYF has been in Harriette's life since birth. Angel placed Harriette in foster care the day she was born, but fought to bring her back home when she began to suspect that the foster family was mistreating her. She asked for and received parenting classes and counseling from the agency, and her experience regaining custody was largely positive. Her caseworker even found an elec-trical problem in the nursery after Harriette came home and called Angel's landlord, threatening to pull the family from the house unless he sent a certified electrician out to repair it.

When Harriette was five, someone phoned in a string of reports to the child abuse and neglect hotline. The anonymous tipster explained that Harriette was running around the neighborhood unsupervised. "The most she has ever been unsupervised is two minutes," Angel counters, "but we had some people on the street who would call and [they] said all this stuff." CYF examiners opened an investigation on Harriette and came out to the house to interview the family and their neighbors. The investigator took Harriette by the hand and tried to walk her down the street, away from her mother, to talk. "To our pride, and my daughter's self-preservation," Angel remembers, "she said, 'I'm not allowed to go there. It's against the rules. I'm out of bounds.'" The worker instead took Harriette to the back porch and exiled Angel to the front.

After speaking to Harriette, the caseworker took Angel aside and said, "Wow. That's a pretty obedient child." Angel told her, "You have no idea what it took to get her like that." She explained the family's approach to discipline, and gave an example: they drew a stop sign on the sidewalk, writing the word "Stop" inside. If Harriette goes past the sign, she has to sit on the porch steps in a time-out. The investigator closed the case.

Another call was made to the hotline, reporting that Harriette was down the block teasing a dog. Angel knew that Harriette had been sneaking out of the yard when she went to the bathroom, throwing food just out of the dog's reach, barking at it. Angel tried everything to address the behavior. She explained that she might get hurt if she kept it up. She took away cartoons for the day. She made her go up the street to the dog's owner and apologize. "Which I made her do the day before CPS got called!" Angel says, shrugging. "I told the lady, 'I'm not going to lie to you. She's been caught teasing this dog multiple times. I'm working with her to resolve the situation.'" But the investigator wasn't convinced that Harriette was safe. "That could be child neglect,"

Angel remembers her saying. When Angel explained to a super-visor that she could see Harriette at all times, even from the bathroom, CYF closed the case.

Another series of calls to the hotline was made, claiming that Harriette wasn't being properly clothed, fed, or bathed and that she wasn't getting her anti-seizure medication. Angel and Patrick explained to the investigating caseworker that her neurologist had canceled two appointments in a row and then withheld a pre-scription because it had been more than a year since she had been examined. The medical device she was wearing on her head to measure her epilepsy made washing her hair difficult. But she wasn't running around in the cold barefoot, as the caller had claimed, and they were working on finding a new neurologist. Angel signed a waiver so CYF could access Harriette's medical file. After seeing that their story checked out, CYF closed the case.

Patrick and Angel suspect a neighbor or family member was placing nuisance calls to harass them. Angel wants to press charges, but there is little she can do. Voluntary callers to child abuse and neglect hotlines can remain anonymous if they choose, and mandated reporters have immunity from civil or criminal liability if they report in good faith. "It seemed like every other week they were coming out," Angel explains, frustrated. "They haven't found anything—our cases are closed. But every now and then I feel like they drive by just to see."

The lesson Patrick learned from his experience with CYF is this: always act deferential. Comply with everything CYF asks, even if you think you are being treated unfairly. "I didn't think it was fair, but I wasn't going to fight it," he says. "I thought maybe if I fought it they would actually come and take her." The deck is always stacked in the agency's favor, he explains. "It's scary. I'm thinking, 'They're coming to take my kids.' That's the first thing you think: CYF takes your kids away. It's a very sick feeling in the stomach, especially with the police there. I'll never forget it."

Angel Shepherd and Patrick Grzyb, like all the CYF-involved parents I spoke to, have deeply mixed feelings about their experiences with the agency. While they describe frightening, frustrating experiences, they are also grateful for the support and resources they received. They hope that their time volunteering at the Family Support Center helps other families keep their kids safe, but they also suspect that any interaction with CYF might drive up their AFST score.

Most parents reacted with fear and exasperation when I asked them about the AFST. Some think the system unfairly targets them for surveillance. Some find having their entire history as parents summed up in a single number dehumanizing. Some believe the model will make it even more difficult to exert the limited rights they have in the system.

This was particularly true for African American parents. Janine, who asked that I refer to her only by her first name for fear of CYF retribution, is an outspoken advocate for poor families from Rankin, PA. When I asked her what she thought about the predictive model, she shot back decisively, "That's going to fail. There's too many risks. Everybody is a risk."

When Janine says that "everybody is a risk," she doesn't mean that anyone might hit their child. She means that every parent in her community could be profiled by the AFST, simply for being poor and Black. According to statistics gathered by the National Council of Juvenile and Family Court Judges, in 37 states, the Dominican Republic, and Puerto Rico, African American and Native American children are removed from their homes at rates that significantly exceed their representation in the general population. For example, in 2011, 51 percent of children in foster care in Alaska were Native American, though Native Americans make up only 17 percent of the youth population. In Illinois, 53 percent of the children in foster care were African American, though African Americans make up only 16 percent of the youth population.

In 2016, 48 percent of children in foster care in Allegheny County were African American, though they made up only 18 percent of the county's children and youth. In other words, African American children are more than two and a half times as likely to end up in foster care than they should be, given their proportion of the population. Cherna and Dalton see the AFST as a tool to take the guesswork out of intake, hoping it will provide data that will uncover patterns of bias in intake screener decision-making. "I see a lot of variability now," said Dalton, "I would not go so far as to say that [the AFST] can correct disproportionality. But we can at least observe it more clearly." By mining the wealth of data in the warehouse, she suggested, the AFST can help subjective intake screeners make more objective recommendations.

But a 2010 study of racial disproportionality in Allegheny County CYF found that the great majority of disproportionality in the county's child welfare services arises from *referral bias*, not screening bias.[13] The community calls child abuse and neglect hotlines about Black and biracial families more often than they call about white families from Rankin, PA. Though there were three and a half times as many white children as African American and biracial children in Allegheny County in 2006, there were equal numbers of reports—roughly 3,500—submitted to CYF for each group.

The study found that disproportionate referrals were often made based on mandated reporters' misunderstandings of CYF's mission and role, perceptions of problems in neighborhoods where people of color live, and class-inflected expectations of parenting. "I'll never forget one I got," said one of their interviewees,

"I finally got a hold of this kid's therapist and I'm like what's going on here? This kid can go home. And the therapist, no lie, said it's a bad environment for the kid. You know, community violence in the neighborhood." Another reported that a clinic routinely called CYF to report parents for missing children's medical appointments, even if they made the appointments up at a later time.

The study showed that once children were referred to CYF, screener discretion didn't make much difference in disproportionality. Intake workers were only slightly more likely to screen Black and biracial children in for investigation than white children. They chose to screen-in 69 percent of cases focused on Black and biracial children, and 65 percent of cases focused on white children. For those screened in for investigation, roughly equal proportions were substantiated: 71 percent of cases involving Black or biracial children and 72 percent of those involving white children.

The AFST focuses all its predictive power and computational might on call screening, the step it can experimentally control, rather than concentrating on referral, the step where racial disproportionality is actually entering the system. Behind the scenes, the AFST produces two scores: the likelihood that another call will be made to the hotline about the child, and the likelihood of that child being placed in foster care. The AFST does not average the two, which might use the professional judgment of CYF investigators' and family court judges to mitigate some of the disproportionality coming from community referral. The model simply uses whichever number is higher.

Nuisance calls like those experienced by Angel and Patrick introduce contaminated data into the model and further compromise its accuracy. Feuding neighbors, estranged spouses seeking custody, landlords, and family members with interpersonal axes to grind routinely call CYF as punishment or retribution. While there is little research on the subject, a study of data from the 1998 Canadian Incidence Study of Reported Child Abuse and Neglect found that approximately 4 percent of reports of child maltreatment were intentionally false. Of the 15,139 total reports of child abuse and neglect Allegheny County received in 2016, we can conservatively estimate that 605 were intentionally false. It is illegal to call a malicious report into a child abuse and neglect hotline. But Pennsylvania currently accepts reports from anonymous callers, so there is little a parent can do if a neighbor, relative, or acquaintance decides to harass or intimidate them in this way. The AFST has no way of recognizing or screening out nuisance calls.

Call referral is a deeply problematic proxy for maltreatment. It can be easily manipulated. CYF's own research shows that it creates nearly all the racial disproportionality in the county's child protective system. In other words, the activity that introduces the most racial bias into the system is *the very way the model defines maltreatment*. This easily gameable, discriminatory variable threatens to reverse all of the extraordinary work Cherna and his team have done.

"We don't control the calls," said Marc Cherna. "How the folks respond when they get questioned in the emergency room, cultural factors, and all that other stuff . . . that's something we don't control." But the county does control what data it collects and which variables it chooses.

The overwhelming majority of families involved with CYF in Allegheny County, Black and white, are working class or poor. Though only 27 percent of Pittsburgh children receive public assistance, 80 percent of children placed in foster care in 2015 were removed from families relying on Temporary Assistance for Needy Families (TANF) or the Supplemental Nutrition Assistance

Program (SNAP). That is, in Allegheny County, class-based disproportionality is worse than racial disproportionality. But unlike other historically disadvantaged groups, the poor are not widely recognized as a legally protected class, so the disproportionate and discriminatory attention paid to poor families by child welfare offices goes largely unchallenged.

The AFST sees the use of public services as a risk to children. A quarter of the predictive variables in the AFST are direct measures of poverty: they track use of means-tested programs such as TANF, Supplemental Security Income, SNAP, and county medical assistance. Another quarter measure interaction with juvenile probation and CYF itself, systems that are disproportionately focused on poor and working-class communities, especially communities of color. The juvenile justice system struggles with many of the same racial and class inequities as the adult criminal justice system.[14] A family's interaction with CYF is highly dependent on social class: professional middle-class families have more privacy, interact with fewer mandated reporters, and enjoy more cultural approval of their parenting than poor or working-class families.[15]

The overwhelming majority of child welfare investigations in the United States involve neglect, not abuse. According to the U.S. Department of Health and Human Services Administration for Children and Families, of the 3.4 million children involved in child welfare investigations in 2015, 75 percent were investigated for neglect, while only a quarter were investigated for physical, emotional, or sexual abuse.[16]

Defining neglect requires more subjective judgment than physical or sexual abuse. "Neglect is so wide," said Tanya Hankins from the Family Support Center in East Liberty, a mostly African American neighborhood of Pittsburgh. "I've had a situation where two people are arguing and mom runs out the door and the baby is in the house and somebody calls CYF. I had a mom, when CYF knocked on the door, she didn't answer. She was petrified. So they didn't get a chance to see the baby, and put in for the baby to be removed."

Nearly all of the indicators of child neglect are also indicators of poverty: lack of food, inadequate housing, unlicensed childcare, unreliable transportation, utility shutoffs, homelessness, lack of health care. "The vast, vast majority of cases are neglect, stem[ming] from people who have difficult, unsafe neighborhoods to live in," said Catherine Volponi, director of the Juvenile Court Project, which provides *pro bono* legal support for parents facing CYF investigation or termination of their parental rights. "We have housing issues, we have inadequate medical care, we have drugs and alcohol. It's poverty. The reality is that most children [investigated by CYF] are not physically or sexually abused."

Child welfare services are not means-tested; you don't have to be low-income to access them. CYF can offer parents a multitude of useful resources: respite care for a new mom who needs an hour off to do some laundry, early childhood education and development programs, even a visiting home aid to help with household chores. But professional middle-class families rely instead on private sources for family support, so their interactions with helping professionals are not tracked or represented in the data warehouse.

It is interesting to imagine the response if Allegheny County proposed including data from nannies, babysitters, private therapists, Alcoholics Anonymous, and luxury rehabilitation centers to predict child abuse among wealthier families. "We really hope to get private insurance data. We'd love to have it," says Erin Dalton. But, as she herself admits, getting private data is likely impossible. The professional middle class will not stand for such intrusive data gathering.

Families avoid CYF if they can afford to, because the agency mixes two distinct and contradictory roles: provider of family support and investigator of maltreatment. Accepting resources means accepting the agency's authority to remove your children. This is an invasive, terrifying trade-off that parents with other options are not likely to choose. Poor and working-class families feel forced to trade their rights to privacy, protection from unreasonable searches, and due process for a chance at the resources and services they need to keep their children safe.

Poverty *is* incontrovertibly harmful to children. It is also harmful to their parents. But by relying on data that is only collected on families using public resources, the AFST unfairly targets the poor for child welfare scrutiny. "We definitely oversample the poor," said Dalton. "All of the data systems we have are biased. We still think this data can be helpful in protecting kids."

We might call this *poverty profiling*. Like racial profiling, poverty profiling targets individuals for extra scrutiny based not on their behavior but rather on a personal characteristic: living in poverty. Because the model confuses parenting while poor with poor parenting, the AFST views parents who reach out to public programs as risks to their children.

Janine and I are sitting in a bus shelter behind a CVS pharmacy in a small borough just east of Pittsburgh on a warm September day in 2016. A middle-class suburb for most of its existence, Wilkinsburg lost about half its population in the last five decades, reeling from the closure of the Homestead Steel Works. The Kentucky Fried Chicken is celebrating its Day of Giving by distributing 10,000 free meals, and Janine and her friends are using the opportunity to register people to vote. In her late 40s, Janine wears a white tank top and a black rubber bracelet for the Poise Foundation, an African American community foundation "focused on building sustainable black communities and strengthening black families."

I found it surprising that someone who has lost a child to the foster care system now volunteers for a CYF-funded organization.

But Janine acknowledges that she needed help with her son, Jeremiah, more than a decade ago. She had insecure housing, struggled with transportation to get to work, and was managing health problems. Jeremiah started skipping school and disappearing, and someone called the hotline on her.

From Janine's perspective, the system's support requires heart-wrenching choices. Caseworkers opened an investigation when a call came in about her son's truancy, she said, but closed it before she could access any services. Eventually, the agency required her to give up her son to access the basic material resources that would have allowed her to care for him effectively herself. "Instead of giving me help, they were like, 'Put [Jeremiah] in foster care and we'll help you,'" she explains. "You've got to put your kid in." Her son went into foster care. She got help finding stable housing and medical care. Although she is still in touch with him today—Jeremiah's now 22 and enrolled in college—she never regained custody.

And yet, she does not hesitate to call the abuse and neglect hotline if she believes someone is endangering a child. "It's not being mean," she explains. "You just have to understand that if something happened, I'm not going to feel bad, [thinking], 'Why didn't you call? You should have called!' I'm not trying to do no harm, but to protect kids. One thing's for sure and two's for certain, I am a mother and I love all kids."

While we talk on the bus stop bench, Sarah, a dark-haired white woman in her late 20s, jumps into the conversation unprompted to share her own story. Sarah is raising her daughter after fighting to get her back from seven years in foster care. It is her only day off from work that week, she says. She is running from appointment to appointment, trying to fulfill CYF's expectations. Getting support for your parenting is great, she agrees. But the agency's services often feel more like barriers than benefits, adding a frustrating new layer of responsibility on top of work and single motherhood. "People who have never been in the system don't understand," she says. "They don't know what it's like. Drug and Alcohol come to my house [for drug screenings] once a week. I go to court every three months. I have to go to therapy for me, and therapy for my kids."

Every organization that Sarah, Janine, Angel, and Patrick access for help with their parenting is staffed by mandated reporters. In 2015, in the wake of the Jerry Sandusky scandal—the ex–Penn State football coach is currently serving 30 to 60 years for molesting ten boys—Pennsylvania lowered the standard for what constitutes child abuse. The state also created 15 categories of mandated reporters, including health-care and school employees, volunteers, clergy, and librarians. Under the law, mandated reporters *must* report any suspicion of child neglect or abuse, whether they learned about it through direct experience or heard about it secondhand. Mandated reporters do not have to identify how they learned about alleged abuse or neglect. They have immunity from legal prosecution. They are protected if they breach mental health or medical confidentiality. In fact, they can face legal prosecution, fines, and even jail time if they *fail* to report their suspicions. In the year after the changes, calls to abuse and neglect hotlines increased 40 percent.

The people most likely to offer poor parents help and support are all mandated reporters: teachers, doctors and nurses, psychiatrists and therapists, childcare providers, priests, volunteers at afterschool programs, employees of social service agencies. The pressure in the face of such invasive scrutiny and the cost of failing to meet the agency's expectations are immense. The pressure often overwhelms parents who are already struggling.

Sarah is puzzled that so many caseworkers don't seem to understand why a mom might lose her temper with them: "They're like, 'Why are you so angry?' Because I'm tired of you being here! Leave me alone. I'm trying to get you to go away. We want you to go away." I give her my card and Janine tells her to drop in at a

Family Support Center. Then, spying her bus, Sarah dashes off to her next appointment.

If a child abuse and neglect investigation was a benign act, it might not matter that the AFST is imperfectly predictive. If a child abuse and neglect investigation inevitably resulted in adequate, culturally appropriate, and nonpunitive resources being offered to families, it wouldn't matter that the system overrepresents poor and working-class people. But CYF resources come with increased surveillance and strict behavioral compliance requirements. For many, a child abuse and neglect investigation is an intrusive, frightening event with lasting negative impacts.

The price of help from CYF can be high. Janine argues that you have to "put your kid in" to foster care before you get support. Sarah's schedule is filled with appointments with helping professionals she needs to please with displays of servility. Twenty years after he was accused of medical neglect, Patrick Grzyb still remembers feeling watched, monitored, and judged. "When they come to your house, they are looking around, watching your every move," he explained. "It was like I was under a microscope. Every time one of my kids got sick, I had to take them to the emergency room. You walk in there and it's like all these eyes [on you]. 'Hey, he's the one. We had to call on him.' I felt like that for a long time."

Many poor and working-class parents in Allegheny County are thankful that the data warehouse and other changes at DHS have narrowed resource gaps and eased the often cumbersome process of applying for multiple services. But there are others who feel that, once they are in "the system," microscopic scrutiny ups the ante on their parenting, raising the stakes so high that they are bound to lose. "We try to comply," said Janine. "But look, we can't do it all. You're opening up a door for ten other things I've got to do. It's just a downward spiral."

Parenting while poor means parenting in public. The state of Pennsylvania's goal for child safety, "being free from immediate physical or emotional harm," can be difficult to reach, even for well-resourced families. Each stage of the process introduces the potential for subjectivity, bias, and the luck of the draw. "You never know exactly what's going to happen," said Catherine Volponi in her office at Pittsburgh's Juvenile Court Project. "Let's say there was a call because the kids were home alone. Then they're doing their investigation with mom, and she admits marijuana use. Now you get in front of a judge who, perhaps, views marijuana as a gateway to hell. When the door opens, something that we would not have even been concerned about can just mushroom into this big problem."

At the end of each child neglect or abuse investigation, a written safety plan is developed with the family, identifying immediate steps that must be followed and long-term goals. But each safety action is also a compliance requirement, and parents' responses are carefully monitored. Sometimes, factors outside parents' control make it difficult for them to implement their plan. Contractors who provide services to CYF-involved families fail to follow through. Public transportation is unreliable. Overloaded caseworkers don't always manage to arrange promised resources. Sometimes parents resist CYF's dictates, resenting government intrusion into their family.

Failing to meet safety goals increases the likelihood that a child will be removed. "We don't try to return CYF families to the level at which they were operating before," said Volponi, "We raise the standard on their parenting, and then we don't have enough resources to keep them up there. It results in epic failures too much of the time."

A report of abuse or neglect that is found credible has profound impact on a parent's life for decades. Most jobs and volunteer positions that involve interaction with children in the state of Pennsylvania require that applicants submit a child abuse history certification. If the applicant is listed in the state's ChildLine Abuse Registry as a perpetrator of abuse or neglect, she cannot apply for a job working with children. If she already has a job working with children, she will lose it. She can't be a Girl Scout troop leader, softball coach, or volunteer at her child's school.

"You [have to] change the way you support your family," says Amanda Green Hawkins, a Pittsburgh attorney who argued a *pro bono* CYF expungement case in 2015. A child abuse record "can keep you from getting employment in a lot of areas—anything having to do with kids. You can't be a teacher anymore. You can't be program manager . . . at the Boys and Girls Club anymore. How those people get their lives back—that can be very tricky."

Parents who go through a CYF investigation and a family court hearing and are found guilty of child maltreatment—the agency term for this is "indicated" or "founded"—receive notice that they have been included in the ChildLine registry. Within 90 days, they can request an administrative review to amend or expunge their record. At the hearing, the county presents the evidence it used to prove abuse or neglect, and the parent rebuts it. Sometimes, when poor families challenge the child welfare system, they win. But not many dare to take CYF on in court.

Tracey McCants Lewis, attorney and *pro bono* program coordinator for Duquesne University School of Law, told me that she's never represented a client in a CYF expungement case, in part because it is a "much more extensive process than criminal expungement." Amanda Green Hawkins agrees that such challenges are vanishingly rare. "[CYF] expungements are very difficult," she said. "You are going up against the government. It's like David taking on Goliath." While Allegheny County has a nonprofit organization that will represent parents when they go to court in child protection matters, there is no public defender for those seeking to expunge their record. They must find an attorney willing to work for free or they have to represent themselves. If a "founded" or "indicated" ruling is not promptly expunged, the parent remains in the state abuse registry until the child who is the subject of the investigation turns 23.

The expungement process applies only to those reported to Pennsylvania's ChildLine Abuse Registry for grievous neglect or abuse. Any allegations that involve "non-serious injury or neglect" are referred to General Protective Services (GPS). GPS data is kept in the Allegheny County DHS data warehouse indefinitely. So the multiple calls on Harriette, Angel's feisty but mostly obedient daughter? There is no way to expunge them, even though they were clearly nuisance calls. When and if Harriette becomes a mom, she'll start out with a higher AFST score, because she had interactions with the child protective system as a kid. The assumption might be that she had a bad mother, and so she had no mental model of how to parent, and the county needs to keep an eye on her. No one will know about the chalked stop sign on the sidewalk, the vocabulary games played on the living room floor, or the obvious pride that shines in Angel's eyes when she looks at her daughter.

Marc Cherna and Erin Dalton argue that allowing parents to expunge hotline reports, no matter how spurious, would rob CYF of critical data they need to identify and prevent abuse. "The stuff stays in the system," said Cherna. "A lot of times where there's smoke there's fire." Dalton agreed. "I personally am sympathetic to the idea of redemption," she said, "but getting rid of data that might predict abuse and neglect is like taking away the biggest tool we have in preventing future abuse."

Amanda Green Hawkins is not convinced that data's potential predictive power outweighs parents' constitutional rights. "Everyone is entitled to due process in our system," she said. "That process will determine whether or not [CYF is] able to keep a report on someone for the rest of their life. That no one should be entitled to due process to do anything about it? That runs afoul of our Constitution. That's pitiful."

Marc Cherna and his team hope that the AFST will provide better, more timely information to help target CYF interventions to the families who need them most. They see little downside to data collection because they understand the agency's role as primarily supportive, not punitive. Even if a family is screened in for investigation, Cherna and Dalton explained to me, most will be offered services rather than have their children removed. But the social stigma that comes from being involved with CYF is significant, and the level of intrusion is intense.

Having your child rearing choices constantly watched, monitored, and corrected can heighten parents' perceptions that they are being targeted and trapped. "There's so many women walking around here who don't have their children," said Carmen Alexander, senior operations manager of New Voices Pittsburgh, a grassroots organization dedicated to the complete well-being of Black women and girls. "It's almost like you can't even sneeze the wrong way around your children. You have to keep quiet. It builds a culture of distrust."

When a CYF investigation is launched, parents have only two meaningful options: either resist the agency's dictates and risk losing their children, or defer to the agency's authority completely. Research by University of Denver sociologist Jennifer Reich shows that, like police officers, many child welfare caseworkers see resistance as an indicator of guilt. The risk/severity document that Pat Gordon showed me underscores her point. If a parent is "appropriately responsive to requirements" of CYF, "acknowledges problems," and "initiates contact with Caseworker [to] seek additional services," she is considered a minimal risk to her children. If she "actively resists any agency contact or involvement . . . will not permit investigation to occur" or "denies problems," she is considered high risk. But a mother who is falsely accused of abuse or neglect may resist agency contact and involvement. And parents who fight for their children may also fight CYF.

"If we are painting with a really broad brush, there are two types of clients that come to my door. One comes in, gets in my face, yells at me, and tells me I'm part of the problem," said Catherine Volponi. "The other comes in and assumes the position to be kicked again. I would much rather have the one who got in my face, because they are still in it. These are the people who will eventually prevail."

Professional middle-class families reach out for support all the time: to therapists, private drug and alcohol rehabilitation, nannies, babysitters, afterschool programs, summer camps, tutors, and family doctors. But because it is all privately funded, none of those requests ends up in Allegheny County's data warehouse. The same willingness to reach out for support by poor and working-class families, because they are asking for public resources, labels them a risk to their children in the AFST, even though CYF sees requesting resources as a positive attribute of parents.[17] "If a mom has accessed county mental health services in the past, why does that hurt her? Or drug and alcohol services?" asked Pittsburgh civil rights attorney and Duquesne University law professor Tiffany Sizemore-Thompson. "Shouldn't that show that she's actually a responsible person who went and got services that she felt she needed?"

CYF-involved families acknowledge the fallibility of human decision-making. They understand perfectly well that the call screeners, caseworkers, administrators, and judges who decide who will be investigated, what kind of services they will receive, which children will be removed, and how quickly children in foster care are reunited with their birth families have biases that influence their work. Nevertheless, they'd rather have an imperfect person making decisions about their families than a flawless computer. "You can teach people how you want to be treated," said Pamela Simmons, staffing the voter registration table across the street from the Kentucky Fried Chicken in Wilkinsburg. "They come with their own opinions but sometimes you can change their opinion. There's opportunity to fix it with a person. You can't fix that number."

Human bias has been a problem in child welfare since the field's inception. In its earliest days, Charles Loring Brace's orphan trains carried away so many Catholic sons and daughters that the religious minority had to create an entirely parallel system of child welfare organizations. Scientific charity workers had religious biases that tended to skew their decision-making. They believed that the children of Protestants could be redeemed by their families, but Catholics were incorrigible and had to be sent to labor on (mostly Protestant) farms in the Midwest. Today, racial disproportionality shatters the bonds of too many Black and Native American families. Some of that disproportion can certainly be traced to human discretion in child welfare decision-making.

But human bias is a built-in feature of the predictive risk model, too.

The outcome variables are proxies for child harm; they don't reflect actual neglect and abuse. The choice of proxy variables, even the choice to use proxies at all, reflects human discretion.

The predictive variables are drawn from a limited universe of data that includes only information on public resources. The choice to accept such limited data reflects the human discretion embedded in the model—and an assumption that middle-class families deserve more privacy than poor families.

The model's validation data is a record of decisions made by human caseworkers, investigators, and judges, bearing all the traces of their humanity.

Once the big blue button is clicked and the AFST runs, it

manifests a thousand invisible human choices. But it does so under a cloak of evidence-based objectivity and infallibility. Intake screeners reflect a variety of experiences and life paths, from the suburban white Penn State postgraduate to an African American Pittsburgh native, like Pat Gordon, with over a decade of experience. The automated discretion of predictive models is the discretion of the few. Human discretion is the discretion of the many. Flawed and fallible, yes. But also fixable.

Parents in Allegheny County helped me articulate an inchoate idea that had been echoing in my head since I started my research. In Indiana, Los Angeles, and Allegheny County, technologists and administrators explained to me that new high-tech tools in public services increase transparency and decrease discrimination. They claimed that there is no way to know what is going on in the head of a welfare caseworker, a homeless service provider, or an intake call screener without using big data to identify patterns in their decision-making.

I find the philosophy that sees human beings as unknowable black boxes and machines as transparent deeply troubling. It seems to me a worldview that surrenders any attempt at empathy and forecloses the possibility of ethical development. The presumption that human decision-making is opaque and inaccessible is an admission that we have abandoned a social commitment to try to understand each other. Poor and working-class people in Allegheny County want and deserve more: a recognition of their humanity, an understanding of their context, and the potential for connection and community.

"A computer is only what a person puts in it," Janine reflected. "I trust the caseworker more. . . . You can talk, and be like, 'You don't see the bigger problems?'"

Like the Indiana automated eligibility system, the AFST interprets the use of public resources as a sign of weakness, deficiency, even villainy. Marc Cherna spent the greater part of his career creating a culture of strength-based practice, open community communication, and peer support in the CYF. Unfortunately, he has commissioned an automated tool that sees parents using public programs as a danger to their children.

Targeting "high-risk" families might lead them to withdraw from networks that provide services, support, and community. According to the US Centers for Disease Control's Division of Violence Prevention, the largest risk factors for the perpetration of child abuse and neglect include social isolation, material deprivation, and parenting stress, all of which increase when parents feel watched all the time, lose resources they need, suffer stigma, or are afraid to reach out to public programs for help. A horrible irony is that the AFST might create the very abuse it seeks to prevent.

It is difficult to say a predictive model works if it produces the outcome it is trying to measure. A family scored as high risk by the AFST will undergo more scrutiny than other families. Ordinary behaviors that might raise no eyebrows before a high AFST score become confirmation for the decision to screen them in for investigation. A parent is now more likely to be re-referred to a hotline because the neighbors saw child protective services at her door last week. Thanks in part to the higher risk score, the parent is targeted for more punitive treatment, must fulfill more agency expectations, and faces a tougher judge. If she loses her children, the risk model can claim another successful prediction.

The AFST went live on August 1, 2016, three and a half months before my visit with Pat Gordon. In the model's first nine months, the intake center received more than 7,000 calls. Data released by the Office of Data Analysis, Research and Evaluation (DARE) in May 2017 show that slightly more calls (6 percent) were screened in for investigation by intake workers using the AFST than by those working without the model the previous year. However, the number of screened-in calls that went on to be investigated and substantiated jumped by nearly a quarter (22 percent). Calls scored more highly by the AFST, on average, were more likely to be substantiated: 48 percent of calls receiving an AFST score between 16 and 20, 43 percent of those between 11 and 15, 42 percent of those between 6 and 10, and 28 percent of those between 1 and 5. DARE's admittedly preliminary analysis concludes that referrals scored more highly by intake screeners using the AFST were substantiated and accepted for services by child welfare investigators at higher rates. Because only intake screeners, not child welfare investigators, receive the AFST scores, DARE believes that these early results "perhaps validat[e] the real risk differences the tool has identified."

But if you look closer at the data, some troubling idiosyncrasies emerge. Of the 333 calls the AFST scored above 20, thereby triggering a mandatory investigation, 94 (28 percent) were overridden by a manager and dismissed out of hand. Only half (51 percent) of the remaining mandatory screen-ins resulted in substantiation. In other words, only 37 percent of calls that triggered a mandatory investigation were found to have merit. And there are other discrepancies. Intake workers screened in about the same number of calls scoring 20 as they did calls scoring 12. Roughly the same number of 9's were substantiated by later investigation as 19's. That the number of screen-ins has not changed much while the number of substantiated investigations has risen could suggest that the AFST is simply modeling the agency's own decision-making.

A few days after I visited the intake call center, on November 29, 2016, the Vaithianathan team implemented a major data fix to the AFST. Twenty percent of the families reported to the hotline in the months after the AFST launched received no score. "We weren't scoring cases where only the parents had human services experience," said Erin Dalton. "The most vulnerable kids tend to be young; infants don't have social services history. [The AFST was] not generating a score for these infants where I have Jack the Ripper for the father and his bride for the mother." The updated model now evaluates the entire household—paramours, uncles, cousins, grandmothers, housemates, and every single child living together—and the AFST rating is based on the child who receives the highest score, even if she was not the child reported to the hotline. The AFST now produces a score for more than 90 percent of families reported to the hotline, and it is returning many more scores of 18 and above.

In many ways, the AFST is the best-case scenario for predictive risk modeling in child welfare. The design of the tool was open, participatory, and transparent. Elsewhere, child welfare prediction systems have been designed and implemented by private companies with very little input or discussion from the public. Implementation in Allegheny County has been thoughtful and slow. The goals of the AFST are intentionally limited and modest. The tool is meant to support human decision-making, not replace it.

Nevertheless, Allegheny County's experiment in predicting child maltreatment is worth watching with a skeptical eye. It is an early adopter in a nationwide algorithmic experiment in child welfare: similar systems have been implemented recently in Florida, Los Angeles, New York City, Oklahoma, and Oregon.

As this book goes to press, Cherna and Dalton continue to experiment with data analytics. The next iteration of the AFST will employ machine learning rather than traditional statistical modeling. They also plan to introduce a second predictive model, one that will not rely on reports to the hotline at all. Instead, the planned model "would be run on a daily or weekly basis on all babies born in Allegheny County the prior day or week," according to a September 2017 email from Dalton. Running a model that relies on the public to make calls to a hotline does not capture the whole population of potential abusers and neglecters;

at-birth models are much more accurate. But the primary goal is not to use a more precise model, insists Dalton. "We aren't considering this because it is more accurate," she wrote, "but because we have the potential to prevent abuse and neglect."

Nevertheless, using a model to risk-rate every child born to families using county resources raises vexing questions about how the results will be used. "We have a home-visiting hotline and home-visiting services. If we have limited resources, do we prioritize higher-risk populations with those services?" asks Erin Dalton. "It feels to me like that might be ethical and there might be community acceptance for that sort of thing. Another step beyond that is, let's say somebody walks into a family support center and requests services and wants to get engaged. Do you get a flag that doesn't necessarily say high risk, but says something like 'Really try to engage, keep them engaged?'" Marc Cherna insists that CYF is "not about to knock on your door and say 'You're at high risk of abusing your kid.'" But this is exactly how other risk models, such as the algorithm that produces the Chicago Police Department's violent crime "heat list," have been implemented.

Cherna's administration wants to identify those families who could use help earlier, when interventions could make the most difference. But community members wonder if data collected with the best of intentions might be used against them in the future. "People have concerns about what happens when Marc and Erin leave," said Laurie Mulvey from the Office of Child Development. The DHS held a series of meetings introducing local agencies, funders, and community members to the predictive model. At those meetings, explained Mulvey, people were saying, "We trust you, Erin. We trust you, Marc. What happens when you're gone?"

Under the right conditions—fiscal austerity, a governor looking to downsize public agencies, or a rash of child deaths—the AFST could easily become a machine for automatically removing children from their homes. It wouldn't even require reprogramming the model. Today, if a family's risk score exceeds 20, CYF must open an investigation. Tomorrow, a score of 20 might trigger an emergency removal. Or a score of 10 ... or of 5.

When I asked the AFST's designer Rhema Vaithianathan if she worries about possible abuses of the model, she offered me a hypothetical solution. "The one thing that we could do is say [in our contract], 'If we feel that it ever gets used unethically, we have the right to say something about that.'" But the assumption that academics speaking out against the way their research is used will have a significant impact on public policy or agency practice is naïve.

If a neighbor or an emergency room nurse calls the hotline about Angel and Patrick's family again, they will undoubtedly receive a high AFST score. One of the children in the household is six. There are multiple caregivers, and while they are a tight-knit family, not all of them are biologically related. The household has a long history with public assistance. Angel is seeing a counselor and taking medication for PTSD. They have been involved with CYF for decades, though for the last nine years their relationship with CYF has largely consisted of their volunteer service and Angel requesting parenting classes, hands-on help, and respite care.

Near the end of our interview, Angel reflected on the double bind she faces. "I know I'm not the only one that has had positive experiences with CYF," she said, "reaching out to them saying, 'Hey, I need your help here.' [But] I do have a history because of my daughter. I've also used county services. They would plug me high for that reason. [The AFST] would flag me big time."

Patrick and Angel live in fear that there will be another call on their family and that the AFST will target their daughter or granddaughter for investigation, and possibly for removal to foster care. "My daughter is now nine," said Angel, "and I'm still afraid that they are going to come up one day and see her out by herself, pick her up, and say, 'You can't have her anymore.'"

5

THE DIGITAL POORHOUSE

It is a warm April day in 2017, and I am walking to the public library to find pictures of the Los Angeles County Poor Farm, known today as Rancho Los Amigos. A middle-aged African American man in a pink baseball cap and a grimy hoodie stands on the sidewalk near the corner of 5th and South Grand. He moves as if buffeted by winds, arms swimming in front of him as he turns in tortured circles. He is keening: a high, surprisingly gentle sound, halfway between singing and sobbing, with no words. Dozens of people—white, Black, Latino, tourist and local, rich and poor—walk around him without even turning their heads. As we pass his swaying figure, we look away from each other, our mouths set in grim lines. No one stops to ask if he needs help.

In the United States, wealth and privation exist side by side. The contrast is particularly stark in downtown Los Angeles, where everyday urban professionals drink lattes and check their smartphones within arm's reach of the utterly destitute. But the invisible membrane between those who struggle to meet their basic daily needs and those who do not exists in every American city, town, and village. I saw it in Muncie, Indiana, and in Munhall, Pennsylvania. I see it in my hometown.

Poverty in America is not invisible. We see it, and then we look away.

Our denial runs deep. It is the only way to explain a basic fact about the United States: in the world's largest economy, the majority of us will experience poverty. According to Mark Rank's groundbreaking life-course research, 51 percent of Americans will spend at least a year below the poverty line between the ages of 20 and 65. Two-thirds of them will access a means-tested public benefit: TANF, General Assistance, Supplemental Security Income, Housing Assistance, SNAP, or Medicaid.[1] And yet we pretend that poverty is a puzzling aberration that happens only to a tiny minority of pathological people.

Our relationship to poverty in the United States has always been characterized by what sociologist Stanley Cohen calls "cultural denial." Cultural denial is the process that allows us to know about cruelty, discrimination, and repression, but never openly acknowledge it. It is how we come to know what not to know. Cultural denial is not simply a personal or psychological attribute of individuals; it is a social process organized and supported by schooling, government, religion, media, and other institutions.

When we passed the anguished man near the Los Angeles Public Library and did not ask him if he needed help, it was because we have collectively convinced ourselves that there is nothing we can do for him. When we failed to meet *each others'* eyes as we passed, we signaled that, deep down, we know better. We could not make eye contact because we were enacting a cultural ritual of not-seeing, a semiconscious renunciation of our responsibility to each other. Our guilt, kindled because we perceived suffering and yet did nothing about it, made us look away. That is what the denial of poverty does to us as a nation. We avoid not only the man on the corner, but each other.

Denial is exhausting and expensive. It is uncomfortable for individuals who must endure the cognitive dissonance required to both see and not-see reality. It contorts our physical geography, as we build infrastructure—suburbs, highways, private schools, and prisons—that allow the professional middle class to actively avoid sharing the lives of poor and working-class people. It weakens our social bonds as a political community; people who cannot meet each others' eyes will find it very difficult to collectively govern.

Poverty in America is actively denied by the way we define it: as falling below an arbitrary income line at a single moment in time. The official poverty line makes poverty look like a regrettable anomaly that can be explained away by poor decisions, individual behavior, and cultural pathology. In fact, poverty is an often-temporary state experienced cyclically by a huge number of people from wildly different backgrounds displaying a nearly infinite range of behaviors.

Our public policy fixates on attributing blame for poverty rather than remedying its effects or abolishing its causes. The obsession with "personal responsibility" makes our social safety net conditional on being morally blameless. As political theorist Yascha Mounk argues in his 2017 book, *The Age of Responsibility*, our vast and expensive public service bureaucracy primarily functions to investigate whether individuals' suffering might be their own fault.

Poverty is denied by the media and political commentators, who portray the poor as a pathologically dependent minority dangerous to professional middle-class society. This is true from both conservative and liberal perspectives: voices from the Right tend to decry the poor as parasitic while voices from the Left paternalistically hand-wring about the poor's inability to exert agency in their own lives. The framing of poor people and communities as without hope or value is so profoundly limiting that most of us, even those who experience poverty directly, downplay or deny it in our life stories.

Our habits of denial are so vigorous that poverty is only acknowledged when poor and working-class people build grassroots movements that directly challenge the status quo through disruptive protest. As Frances Fox Piven and Richard Cloward famously pointed out in their classic texts *Poor People's Movements* and *Regulating the Poor*, when poor people organize and fight for their rights and survival, they win. But the institutions of poverty management—the poorhouse, scientific charity, the public welfare system—are remarkably adaptable and durable. The push to divert, contain, police, and punish the poor persists, though the shape of institutions that regulate poverty shift over time.

For example, the Great Railroad Strike of 1877 dramatized not just the suffering of the poor but also their immense political power. Poor and working people's activism terrified elites and won significant accommodations: a return to a poor-relief system focused on distributing cash and goods and a move away from institutionalization. But almost immediately, scientific charity rose to take its place. The techniques changed—scientific casework focused on investigation and policing rather than containing the poor in quasi-prisons—but the results were the same. Tens of thousands of people were denied access to public resources, families were torn apart, and the lives of the poor were scrutinized, controlled, and imperiled.

The pattern repeated during the Great Depression and again during the backlash against welfare rights in the 1970s. It is happening again now.

In short, when poor and working people in the United States become a politically viable force, relief institutions and their technologies of control shift to better facilitate cultural denial and to rationalize a brutal return to subserviency. Relief institutions are machines for undermining the collective power of poor and working-class people, and for producing indifference in everyone else.

When we talk about the technologies that mediate our interactions with public agencies today, we tend to focus on their innovative qualities, the ways they break with convention. Their biggest fans call them "disruptors," arguing that they shake up old relations of power, producing government that is more transparent, responsive, efficient, even inherently more democratic.

This myopic focus on what's new leads us to miss the important ways that digital tools are embedded in old systems of power and privilege. While the automated eligibility system in Indiana, the coordinated entry system in Los Angeles, and the predictive risk model in Allegheny County may be cutting-edge, they are also part of a deep-rooted and disturbing history. The poorhouse preceded the Constitution as an American institution by 125 years. It is mere fantasy to think that a statistical model or a ranking algorithm will magically upend culture, policies, and institutions built over centuries.

Like the brick-and-mortar poorhouse, the digital poorhouse diverts the poor from public resources. Like scientific charity, it investigates, classifies, and criminalizes. Like the tools birthed during the backlash against welfare rights, it uses integrated databases to target, track, and punish.

In earlier chapters, I provided an on-the-ground view of how new high-tech tools are operating in social service programs across the country. It's crucial to listen to those who are their primary targets; the stories they tell are different than those told from the perspective of administrators and analysts. Now, I will zoom out to give a bird's-eye view of how these tools work together to create a shadow institution for regulating the poor.

Divert the poor from public resources: Indiana.

The digital poorhouse raises barriers for poor and working-class people attempting to access shared resources. In Indiana, the combination of eligibility automation and privatization achieved striking reductions in the welfare rolls. Cumbersome administrative processes and unreasonable expectations kept people from accessing the benefits they were entitled to and deserved. Brittle rules and poorly designed performance metrics meant that when mistakes were made, they were always interpreted as the fault of the applicant, not the state or the contractor. The assumption that automated decision-making tools were infallible meant that computerized decisions trumped procedures intended to provide applicants with procedural fairness. The result was a million benefit denials.

But unequivocal diversion can only ever have limited success. In Indiana, the visible and seemingly haphazard suffering caused by benefit denials stoked outrage, creating vigorous resistance. Those denied benefits told their stories. Advocates gathered their allies. Lawsuits were launched. And ordinary Hoosiers won . . . to a degree. While Governor Mitch Daniels canceled IBM's contract and the FSSA launched the hybrid system, TANF receipt is still at a historic low in the state.

The eligibility experiment in Indiana collapsed because it failed to create a convincing story about "unworthiness." The Daniels administration's hostility to the poor was indiscriminate. The automation's effects touched six-year-old girls, nuns, and grandmothers hospitalized for heart failure. Advocates argued that these were blameless victims, and the plan could not stand up against Hoosiers' natural inclination toward charity and compassion.

While automated social exclusion is growing across the country, it has key weaknesses as a strategy of class-based oppression. So, when direct diversion fails, the digital poorhouse creates something more insidious: a moral narrative that criminalizes *most* of the poor while providing life-saving resources to a lucky handful.

Classify and criminalize the poor: Los Angeles.

Homeless service providers in Los Angeles County want to use resources efficiently, to collaborate more effectively, and, perhaps, to outsource the heartbreaking choice of who among 60,000 unhoused people should receive help.

According to its designers, the county's coordinated entry system matches the greatest need to the most appropriate resource. But there is another way to see the ranking function of the coordinated entry system: as a cost-benefit analysis. It is cheaper to provide the most vulnerable, chronically unhoused with permanent supportive housing than it is to leave them to emergency rooms, mental health facilities, and prisons. It is cheaper to provide the least vulnerable unhoused with the small, time-limited investments of rapid re-housing than to let them become chronically homeless. This social sorting works out well for those at the top and the bottom of the rankings. But if, like Gary Boatwright, the cost of your survival exceeds potential taxpayer savings, your life is de-prioritized.

The data of unhoused Angelenos who receive no resources at all—21,500 people as of this writing—stay in the Homeless Management Information System for seven years. There are few safeguards to protect personal information, and the Los Angeles Police Department can access it without a warrant. This is a recipe for law enforcement fishing expeditions. The integration of policing and homeless services blurs the boundary between the maintenance of economic security and the investigation of crime, between poverty and criminality, tightening a net of constraint that tracks and traps the unhoused. This net requires data-based infrastructure to surround and systems of moral classification to sift.

The data collected by coordinated entry also creates a new story about homelessness in Los Angeles. This story can develop in one of two ways. In the optimistic version, more nuanced data helps the county, and the nation, face its cataclysmic failure to care for our unhoused neighbors. In the pessimistic version, the very act of classifying homeless individuals on a scale of vulnerability erodes public support for the unhoused as a group. It leaves professional middle-class people with the impression that those who are truly in need are getting help, and that those who fail to secure resources are fundamentally unmanageable or criminal.

When the digital poorhouse simply bars access to public benefits, as in Indiana, it is fairly easy to confront. But classification and criminalization work by *including* poor and working-class people in systems that limit their rights and deny their basic human needs. The digital poorhouse doesn't just exclude, it sweeps millions of people into a system of control that compromises their humanity and their self-determination.

Predict the future behavior of the poor: Allegheny County.

Assessing tens of thousands of unhoused people in Los Angeles to produce a moral classification system is laborious and expensive. Prediction promises to produce hierarchies of worth and deservingness using statistics and existing data instead of engaging human beings with clinical methods. When diversion fails and classification is too costly, the digital poorhouse uses statistical methods to infer. Surveys such as Los Angeles' VI-SPDAT ask what action a person has already taken. Predictive systems such as Allegheny County's AFST speculate what action someone is *likely to take* in the future, based on behavioral patterns of similar people in the past.

Classification measures the behavior of individuals to group like with like. Prediction is aimed instead at networks. The AFST is run on every member of a household, not only on the parent or child reported to the hotline. Under the new regime of prediction, you are impacted not only by your own actions, but by the actions of your lovers, housemates, relatives, and neighbors.

Prediction, unlike classification, is intergenerational. Angel and Patrick's actions will affect Harriette's future AFST score. Their use of public resources drives Harriette's score up. Patrick's run-ins with CYF when Tabatha was a child will raise Harriette's score as an adult. Angel and Patrick's actions today may limit Harriette's future, and her children's future.

The impacts of predictive models are thus exponential. Because prediction relies on networks and spans generations, its harm has the potential to spread like a contagion, from the initial point of contact to relatives and friends, to friends' networks, rushing through whole communities like a virus.

No poverty regulation system in history has concentrated so much effort on trying to guess how its targets *might* behave. This is because we, collectively, care less about the actual suffering of those living in poverty and more about the potential threat they might pose to others.

The AFST responds to a genuine and significant problem. Caregivers sometimes do terrible things to children, and it is appropriate for the state to step in to protect those who cannot protect themselves. But even the possibility of extraordinary harm cannot rationalize unchecked experimentation on the families of the poor. The professional middle class would never tolerate the AFST evaluating their parenting. That it is deployed against those who have no choice but to comply is discriminatory, undemocratic, and unforgivable.

In the nineteenth century, the growing desire for cadavers for medical school dissection led to a rash of grave-robbing and strict laws against the theft of bodies. Poorhouse burial grounds quickly became favorite targets for the now-illegal body trade. In response to escalating pressure from hospitals and doctors for cheaper cadavers, states passed legislation legalizing the black market in poor corpses: unclaimed bodies of poorhouse and prison inmates could be given to medical schools for dissection. What was unimaginable treatment for the bodies of the middle class was seen as a way that the poor could contribute to science.

Forensic anthropologists still routinely find skeletons in poorhouse burying grounds that show evidence of being tampered with: saw marks on femurs and pelvic bones, skulls with tops that lift off like lids.[2] Yesterday, we experimented on the corpses of the poor; today, we tinker with their futures.

A dangerous form of magical thinking often accompanies new technological developments, a curious assurance that a revolution in our tools inevitably wipes the slate of the past clean. The metaphor of the digital poorhouse is meant to resist the erasure of history and context when we talk about technology and inequality.

The parallels between the county poorhouse and the digital poorhouse are striking. Both divert the poor from public benefits, contain their mobility, enforce work, split up families, lead to a loss of political rights, use the poor as experimental subjects, criminalize survival, construct suspect moral classifications, create ethical distance for the middle class, and reproduce racist and classist hierarchies of human value and worth.

However, there are ways that the analogy between high-tech tools in public services and the brick-and-mortar poorhouse falls short. Just as the county poorhouse was suited to the Industrial Revolution, and scientific charity was uniquely appropriate for the Progressive Era, the digital poorhouse is adapted to the particular circumstances of our time. The county poorhouse responded to middle-class fears about growing industrial unemployment: it kept discarded workers out of sight but nearby, in case their labor was needed. Scientific charity responded to native elites' fear of immigrants, African Americans, and poor whites by creating a hierarchy of worth that controlled access to both resources and social inclusion.

Today, the digital poorhouse responds to what Barbara Ehrenreich has described as a "fear of falling" in the professional middle class. Desperate to preserve their status in the face of the collapse of the working class below them, the grotesque expansion of wealth above them, and the increasing demographic diversity of the country, Ehrenreich writes, the white professional middle class has largely abandoned ideals of justice, equity, and fairness.[3] Until the election of Donald Trump, their increasing illiberalism was somewhat moderated in public. It was a kind of "dog whistle" cruelty: turning fire hoses on Black schoolchildren would not be tolerated, but the fatal encounters of Michael Brown, Freddie Gray, Natasha McKenna, Ezell Ford, and Sandra Bland with law enforcement wouldn't be condemned. Involuntary sterilization of the poor was a nonstarter, but welfare reforms that punish, starve, and criminalize poor families were tacitly approved. The digital poorhouse is born of, and perfectly attuned to, this political moment.

While they are close kin, the differences between the poorhouse of yesterday and the digital poorhouse today are significant. Containment in the physical institution of a county poorhouse had the unintentional result of creating class solidarity across race, gender, and national origin. When we sit at a common table, we might see similarities in our experiences, even if we are forced to eat gruel. Surveillance and digital social sorting drive us apart as smaller and smaller microgroups are targeted for different kinds of aggression and control. When we inhabit an invisible poorhouse, we become more and more isolated, cut off from those around us, even if they share our suffering.

What else is new about the digital poorhouse?

The digital poorhouse is hard to understand. The software, algorithms, and models that power it are complex and often secret. Sometimes they are protected business processes, as in the case of the IBM and ACS software that denied needy Hoosiers access to cash benefits, food, and health care. Sometimes operational details of a high-tech tool are kept secret so its targets can't game the algorithm. In Los Angeles, for example, a "Dos and Don'ts" document for workers in homeless services suggested: "*Don't* give a client a copy of the VI-SPDAT. *Don't* mention that people will receive a score. [W]e do not want to alert clients [and] render the tool useless." Sometimes the results of a model are kept secret to protect its targets. Marc Cherna and Erin Dalton don't want the AFST risk score to become a metric shared with judges or investigating caseworkers, subtly influencing their decision-making.

Nevertheless, transparency is crucial to democracy. Being denied a public service because you earn too much to qualify for a particular program can be frustrating and feel unfair. Being denied because you "failed to cooperate" sends another message altogether. Being denied benefits to which you know you are entitled and not being told why says, "You are worth so little that we will withhold life-saving support just because we feel like it."

Openness in political decision-making matters. It is key to maintaining confidence in public institutions and to achieving fairness and due process.

The digital poorhouse is massively scalable. High-tech tools like automated decision-making systems, matching algorithms, and predictive risk models have the potential to spread very quickly. The ACS call centers in Indiana rejected welfare applications at a speed never before imaginable, partly because the call centers' employees required less time-consuming human connection than public caseworkers. The coordinated entry system went from a privately funded pilot project in a single neighborhood to the government-supported front door for all homeless services in

Los Angeles County—and its 10 million residents—in less than four years. And while the AFST is being held to modest initial goals by a thoughtful human services administration, similar child abuse risk models are proliferating rapidly, from New York City to Los Angeles and Oklahoma to Oregon.

In the 1820s, supporters argued that there should be a poorhouse in every county in the United States. But it was expensive and time-consuming to build so many prisons for the poor. Though we still ended up with more than a thousand of them across the country, county poorhouses were difficult to scale. Eugenicist Harry Laughlin proposed ending poverty by involuntarily sterilizing the "lowest one-tenth" of the nation's population, approximately 15 million people. But Laughlin's science of racial cleansing only scaled in Nazi Germany, and his plan for widespread sterilization of the "unfit" fell out of favor after World War II.[4]

The digital poorhouse has much lower barriers to rapid expansion.

The digital poorhouse is persistent. Once they scale up, digital systems can be remarkably hard to decommission. Think, for example, about what might happen if the world learned about a gross violation of trust at a large data company like Google. For the sake of argument, say that the company was selling calendar data to an international syndicate of car thieves. There would be a widespread and immediate outcry that the policy is unfair, dangerous, and probably illegal. Users would rush to find other services for email, appointments, document storage, video conferencing, and web search.

But it would take some time for us to disentangle our electronic lives from the grasp of Google. You'd have to forward your Gmail to a new email account for a while, otherwise no one would be able to find you. A Google calendar might be the only one that works with your Android phone. Google's infrastructure has been integrated into so many systems that it has an internal momentum that is hard to arrest.

Similarly, once you break caseworkers' duties into discrete and interchangeable tasks, install a ranking algorithm and a Homeless Management Information System, or integrate all your public service information in a data warehouse, it is nearly impossible to reverse course. New hires encourage new sets of skills, attitudes, and competencies. Multimillion-dollar contracts give corporations interests to protect. A score that promises to predict the abuse of children quickly becomes impossible to ignore. Now that the AFST is launched, fear of the consequences of *not* using it will cement its central and permanent place in the system.

New technologies develop momentum as they are integrated into institutions. As they mature, they become increasingly difficult to challenge, redirect, or uproot.

The digital poorhouse is eternal. Data in the digital poorhouse will last a very, very long time. Obsolescence was built in to the age of paper records, because their very physicality created constraints on their storage. The digital poorhouse promises, instead, an eternal record.

Past decisions that hurt others should have consequences. But being followed for life by a mental health diagnosis, an accusation of child neglect, or a criminal record diminishes life chances, limits autonomy, and damages self-determination. Additionally, retaining public service data *ad infinitum* intensifies the risk of inappropriate disclosure and data breaches. The eternal record is punishment and retribution, not justice.

Forty years ago, the French National Commission on Informatics and Liberties established the principle of a "right to be forgotten" within data systems. As David Flaherty reports in *Protecting Privacy in Surveillance Societies*, the commission believed that data should not be stored indefinitely in public systems by default. Instead, electronic information should be preserved only if it serves a necessary purpose, especially when it poses significant risk if disclosed.

The idea has provoked much resistance in the United States. But justice requires the possibility of redemption and the ability to start over. It requires that we find ways to encourage our data collection systems to forget. No one's past should entirely delimit their future.

We all live in the digital poorhouse. We have all always lived in the world we built for the poor. We create a society that has no use for the disabled or the elderly, and then are cast aside when we are hurt or grow old. We measure human worth based only on the ability to earn a wage, and suffer in a world that undervalues care and community. We base our economy on exploiting the labor of racial and ethnic minorities, and watch lasting inequities snuff out human potential. We see the world as inevitably riven by bloody competition and are left unable to recognize the many ways we cooperate and lift each other up.

But only the poor lived in the common dorms of the county poorhouse. Only the poor were put under the diagnostic microscope of scientific charity. Today, we *all* live among the digital traps we have laid for the destitute.

Think of the digital poorhouse as an invisible spider web woven of fiber optic strands. Each strand functions as a microphone, a camera, a fingerprint scanner, a GPS tracker, an alarm trip wire, and a crystal ball. Some of the strands are sticky. They are interconnected, creating a network that moves petabytes of data. Our movements vibrate the web, disclosing our location and direction. Each of these filaments can be switched on or off. They reach back into history and forward into the future. They connect us in networks of association to those we know and love. As you go down the socioeconomic scale, the strands are woven more densely and more of them are switched on.

Together, we spun the digital poorhouse. We are all entangled in it. But many of us in the professional middle class only brush against it briefly, up where the holes in the web are wider and fewer of the strands are activated. We may have to pause a moment to extricate ourselves from its gummy grasp, but its impacts don't linger.

When my family was red-flagged for a health-care fraud investigation, we only had to wrestle one strand at a time. We weren't also tangled in threads emerging from the criminal justice system, Medicaid, and child protective services. We weren't knotted up in the histories of our parents or the patterns of our neighbors. We challenged a single delicate strand of the digital poorhouse and we prevailed. If we survived our encounter, so can many of the people currently reading this book. So why should professional middle-class Americans care about an invisible network that mostly acts to criminalize the poor?

IT IS IN OUR SELF-INTEREST

At the most ignoble level, the professional middle class should care about the digital poorhouse because it is in our self-interest to do so. We may very well end up in the stickier, denser part of the web. As the working class hollows out and the economic ladder gets more crowded at the very top and bottom, the professional middle class becomes ever more likely to fall into poverty. Even if we don't cross the official poverty line, we are likely to use a means-tested program for support at some point.

The programs we encounter will be shaped by the contempt we held for their initial targets: the chronically poor. We will endure invasive and complicated procedures meant to divert us from accessing public resources. Vast amounts of our data will be collected, mined, analyzed, and shared. Our worthiness, behavior, and network of associations will be investigated, our missteps criminalized. Once we fall into the stickier levels of the digital poorhouse, its web of threads will make it difficult for us to recover from the bad luck or poor choices that put us there.

Or, the system may come to us. The strands at the top of the web are only widely spaced and switched off *for now*. As Dorothy Allen, the mom in Troy, reminded me almost 20 years ago, technological tools tested on the poor will eventually be used on everyone. A national catastrophe or a political regime change might justify the deployment of the digital poorhouse's full surveillance capability across the class spectrum. Because the digital poorhouse is networked, whole areas of professional middle-class life might suddenly be "switched on" for scrutiny. Because the digital poorhouse persists, a behavior that is perfectly legal today but becomes criminal in the future can be used to persecute retroactively.

AUTOMATED INEQUALITY HURTS US ALL

Taking a step back from narrow self-interest, we should all care about the digital poorhouse because it intensifies discrimination and creates an unjust world. Key to understanding how the digital poorhouse automates inequality is University of Pennsylvania communications scholar Oscar Gandy's concept of "rational discrimination."[5] Rational discrimination does not require class or racial hatred, or even unconscious bias, to operate. It only requires ignoring bias that already exists. When automated decision-making tools are not built to explicitly dismantle structural inequities, their speed and scale intensify them.

For example, from 1935 to 1968, the Federal Home Loan Bank Board and the Home Owners' Loan Corporation collected data to draw boundaries around African American neighborhoods, characterizing them as high-risk investments. Both public and private lenders then refused loans in these areas. Real estate redlining was based in blatant racial hostility and greed. As Douglas S. Massey and Nancy A. Denton explain in their 1993 classic *American Apartheid: Segregation and the Making of the Underclass*, racial hostility was exploited through practices like blockbusting, where realtors would select working-class white neighborhoods for racial turnover, acquire a few homes, and quietly sell them to Black families. They would then go door-to-door stoking racist fears of an "invasion" and offering to purchase white homes at cut-rate prices. Redlining had such a profound impact on the shape of our cities that zip codes still serve as remarkably effective proxies for race.

But as openly discriminatory practices became politically unacceptable, facially race-neutral practices took their place. Today, data-based "reverse" redlining has replaced earlier forms of housing discrimination. According to Seeta Peña Gangadharan of the London School of Economics and Political Science, financial institutions use metadata purchased from data brokers to split the real estate market into increasingly sophisticated micropopulations like "Rural and Barely Making It" and "X-tra Needy." While the algorithms that drive this target-marketing don't explicitly use race to make decisions—a practice outlawed by the Fair Housing Act of 1968—a category like "Ethnic Second-City Strugglers" is clearly a proxy for both race and class.[6] Disadvantaged communities are then targeted for subprime lending, payday loans, or other exploitative financial products.

Reverse redlining is rational discrimination. It is not discriminatory in the sense that it relies on hostile choices being made by racist or classist individuals. In fact, it is often characterized as inclusionary: it provides access to financial products in "underbanked" neighborhoods. But its outwardly neutral classifications mask discriminatory outcomes that rob whole communities of wealth, compounding cumulative disadvantage.

The digital poorhouse replaces the sometimes-biased decision-making of frontline social workers with the rational discrimination of high-tech tools. Administrators and data scientists focus public attention on the bias that enters decision-making systems through caseworkers, property managers, service providers, and intake center workers. They obliquely accuse their subordinates, often working-class people, of being the primary source of racist and classist outcomes in their organizations. Then, managers and technocrats hire economists and engineers to build more "objective" systems to root out the human foibles of their economic inferiors. The classism and racism of elites are mathwashed, neutralized by technological mystification and data-based hocus-pocus.

I spent much of my November 2016 trip to Pittsburgh trying to spy one of Uber's famous driverless cars. I didn't have any luck because the cars are found mostly downtown and in the Strip District, neighborhoods that are gentrifying quickly. I spent my time in Duquesne, Wilkinsburg, the Hill District, and Homestead. I didn't see a single one.

The autonomous cars use a vast store of geospatial data collected from Uber's human drivers and a two-person team of onboard engineers to learn how to get around the city and interact with other vehicles, bikes, and pedestrians. Asked by Julia Carrie Wong of *The Guardian* how he felt about his role in Uber's future, Rob Judge, who had been driving for the company for three months, said, "It feels like we're just rentals. We're kind of like placeholders until the technology comes out."[7]

I asked Bruce Noel, the regional office director in Allegheny County, if he's concerned that the intake workers he manages might be training an algorithm that will eventually replace them. "No," he insisted. "There will never be a replacement for that human being and that connection." But in a very real sense, humans have already been removed from the driver's seat of human services. In the past, during times of economic hardship, America's elite threw the poor under the bus. Today, they are handing the keys to alleviating poverty over to a robotic driver.

THE DIGITAL POORHOUSE COMPROMISES OUR NATIONAL VALUES

We should all care about the digital poorhouse because it is inconsistent with our most dearly held collective values: liberty, equity, and inclusion.

Americans have professed to cherish liberty since the nation's founding. It is an inalienable right named in the Declaration of Independence. The Fifth and Fourteenth Amendments assure that "no person . . . shall be deprived of life, liberty, or property, without due process of law." Schoolchildren pledge their allegiance to a republic promising "liberty and justice for all."

Conflict arises, though, when we stop talking in generalities and try to decide the best way to secure liberty for the greatest number of people in a diverse nation. Agreement about how to interpret liberty tends to accumulate around two poles. On one side liberty is *freedom from* government interference and the right to do what you want. Groups who want to decrease government regulation of business in order to lower barriers to competition, for example, are asking for *freedom from*. On the other side, liberty is *freedom to* act with self-determination and exert agency. Groups who want to provide federal student loans at below market rates, for example, argue that all students should have the *freedom to* pursue higher education without being crippled by a lifetime of debt.

The digital poorhouse restricts *both* kinds of liberty.

The digital poorhouse facilitates government interference, scrutiny, and surveillance, undermining *freedom from*. The rise of high-tech tools has increased the collection, storage, and sharing of data about the behavior and choices of poor and working-class people. Too often, this surveillance primarily serves to identify sanctionable offenses resulting in diversion and criminalization. No one could argue that the systems described in this book promote freedom from red tape and government interference.

The digital poorhouse also impairs the ability of poor and working-class people to exert self-determination and autonomy, undermining *freedom to*. The complexity of the digital poorhouse erodes targets' feelings of competence and proficiency. Too often, these tools simply grind down a person's resolve until she gives up things that are rightfully hers: resources, autonomy, respect, and dignity.

Americans have also reached broad consensus on equity as a key national value. The Declaration of Independence, though signed by slaveholders, famously proclaims "that all men are created equal; that they are endowed by their Creator with certain unalienable rights." But like liberty, there are many different ways to interpret equity.

On one hand, many understand equity as *equal treatment*. Those who argue for mandatory sentencing suggest that like crimes should incur like penalties, regardless of the characteristics of the perpetrator or the circumstances of the crime. On the other hand, many believe that equity is only achieved when different people and diverse groups are able to derive *equal value* from common goods and political membership. For this kind of equity to thrive, structural barriers to opportunity must be removed.

The digital poorhouse undercuts *both* kinds of equity.

The digital poorhouse reproduces cultural bias and weakens due process procedures, undermining equity as *equal treatment*. High-tech tools have a built-in authority and patina of objectivity that often lead us to believe that their decisions are less discriminatory than those made by humans. But bias is introduced through programming choices, data selection, and performance metrics. The digital poorhouse, in short, does not treat like cases alike.

The digital poorhouse also weakens poor and working-class people's ability to derive *equal value* from public resources and political membership. It redefines social work as information processing, and then replaces social workers with computers. Humans that remain become extensions of algorithms.

But casework is not information processing. As Supreme Court Justice William J. Brennan, Jr., famously said when reflecting on his decision in *Goldberg v. Kelly*, equity in public assistance requires "the passion that understands the pulse of life beneath the official version of events."[8] At their best, caseworkers promote equity and inclusion by helping families navigate complex bureaucracies and by occasionally bending the rules in the name of higher justice.

The digital poorhouse also limits equity as *equal value* by freezing its targets in time, portraying them as aggregates of their most difficult choices. Equity requires the ability to develop and evolve. But as Cathy O'Neil has written, "Mathematical models, by their nature, are based on the past, and on the assumption that patterns will repeat."[9] The political pollsters and their models failed to anticipate Donald Trump's 2016 presidential victory because voters did not act in the ways statistical analysis of past voter behavior predicted. People change. Movements rise. Societies shift. Justice demands the ability to evolve, but the digital poorhouse locks us into patterns of the past.

Finally, Americans generally agree on a third national value of political and social inclusion. Inclusion requires participation in democratic institutions and decision-making—what Lincoln named at Gettysburg a government "of the people, by the people, for the people." Inclusion also requires social and cultural incorporation, a sense of belonging in the nation, of mutual obligation and shared responsibility for each other. This ideal persists in the *de facto* motto of the United States, *E Pluribus Unum* ("Out of many, one"), that appears on our passports and money.

Like liberty and equity, there are many ways to define inclusion. One of the most common is inclusion *as assimilation*, the notion that individuals and groups must conform to existing structures, values, and ways of life in order to belong in a society. Groups that believe US government materials should only be provided in English are promoting inclusion as assimilation. Another way to understand inclusion is by thinking of it as the ability to thrive *as your whole self* in community. Inclusion as your whole self demands that we shift social and political structures to support and respect the equal value of every child, woman, and man.

The digital poorhouse undercuts *both* kinds of inclusion.

The digital poorhouse undermines inclusion *as assimilation*. In the most egregious examples, such as the explosion of public assistance denials in Indiana, it simply acts to exclude people from government programs. More subtly, the digital poorhouse promotes social and political division through policy microtargeting. Data mining creates statistical social groupings, and then policy-makers create customized interventions for each precise segment of society. Bespoke, individualized governance will likely harden social divisions rather than promote inclusion. Customized government might serve some individuals very well, but it will increase intergroup hostility as perceptions of special treatment proliferate.

The digital poorhouse also limits the ability of its targets to achieve inclusion *as their whole selves*. Poor and working-class people learn lessons about their comparative social worth and value when they come under digital scrutiny. The Stipes family and Shelli Birden learned that their lives mattered less than those of their more well-off neighbors. Lindsay Kidwell and Patrick Gryzb learned that no one can win when they go up against government. Gary Boatwright and Angel Shepherd learned that someone is always watching, expecting shows of compliance and submission. These are terrible lessons in how to be a member of a just and democratic political system.

The digital poorhouse denies access to shared resources. It asks invasive and traumatizing questions. It makes it difficult to understand how government bureaucracy works, who has access to your information, and how they use it. It teaches us that we only belong in political community if we are perfect: never leave a "T" uncrossed, never forget an appointment, never make a mistake. It offers paltry carrots: 15 minutes with a county psychologist, a few dollars cash, a shot at rental assistance. It wields an enormous stick: child removal, loss of health care, incarceration. The digital poorhouse is a "gotcha" system of governance, an invisible bully with a lethally fast punch.

THE DIGITAL POORHOUSE PREEMPTS POLITICS

The digital poorhouse was created in the 1970s to quietly defuse the conflict between the political victories of the welfare rights movement and the professional middle-class revolt against public assistance. To accomplish this goal, its new high-tech tools had to be seen as embodying simple administrative upgrades, not consequential political decisions.

When the digital poorhouse was born, the nation was asking difficult questions: What is our obligation to each other in conditions of inequality? How do we reward caregiving? How do we face economic changes wrought by automation and computerization? The digital poorhouse reframed these big political dilemmas as mundane issues of efficiency and systems engineering: How do we best match need to resource? How do we eliminate fraud and divert the ineligible? How do we do the most with the least money? The digital poorhouse allowed us to drop the bigger, more crucial conversation.

Today, we are reaping the harvest of that denial. In 2012, economic inequality in the United States reached its highest level since 1928. A new class of the extreme poor, who live on less than $2 per day, has emerged. Enormous accumulation of wealth at the top has led observers to describe our moment, without hyperbole, as a second Gilded Age.

And yet, all three systems described in this book share the unstated goals of downsizing government and of finding apolitical solutions to the country's problems. "By 2040, Big Data should have shrunk the public sector beyond recognition," AFST designer Rhema Vaithianathan wrote in a 2016 opinion piece for New Zealand's *Dominion Post*. "Once our data is up to the task, these jobs won't need to be done the old-fashioned way by armies of civil servants. The information and insights will be immediate, real time, bespoke and easy to compare over time. And, ideally, agreed by all to be perfectly apolitical."[10] Automated eligibility, coordinated entry, and the AFST all tell a similar story: once we perfect the algorithms, a free market and free information will guarantee the best results for the greatest number. We won't need government at all.

Troubling this vision of a government governing best by governing least is the fact that, historically, we have only made headway against persistent poverty when mass protest compelled substantial federal investment. Many of the programs of the Social Security Act, the GI Bill, and the War on Poverty suffered from fatal flaws: by excluding women and men of color from their programs, they limited their own equalizing potential. But they offered broadly social solutions to risk and acknowledged that prosperity should be widely shared.

The very existence of a social safety net is premised on an agreement to share the social costs of uncertainty. Welfare states distribute the consequences of bad luck more equally across society's members. They acknowledge that we, as a society, share collective responsibility for creating a system that produces winners *and* losers, inequity and opportunity. But the moral calculus of the digital poorhouse individualizes risk and shreds social commitment.

It would stand us all in good stead to remember that infatuation with high-tech social sorting emerges most aggressively in countries riven by severe inequality and governed by totalitarians. As Edwin Black reports in *IBM and the Holocaust*, thousands of Hollerith punch card systems—an early version of computer software—allowed the Nazi regime to more efficiently identify, track, and exploit Jews and other targeted populations. The appalling reality is that the serial numbers tattooed onto the forearms of inmates at Auschwitz began as punch card identification numbers.

The passbook system that controlled the movements, work opportunities, health care, and housing of 25 million Black South Africans was made possible by data mining the country's 1951 census to create a centralized population register assigning every person to one of four racial categories. In an amicus brief filed in 2015 on behalf of Black South Africans attempting to sue IBM for aiding and abetting apartheid, Cindy Cohn of the Electronic Frontier Foundation wrote, "The technological backbone for the South African national identification system ... enabled the apartheid regime to efficiently implement 'denationalization' of the country's black population: the identification, forced segregation, and ultimate oppression of South African blacks by the white-run government."[11]

Classifying and targeting marginalized groups for "special

attention" might offer helpful personalization. But it also leads to persecution. Which direction you think the high-tech tools of the digital poorhouse will pivot largely hinges on your faith—or lack of faith—that the US government will protect us all from such horrors.

We must not dismiss or downplay this disgraceful history. When a very efficient technology is deployed against a despised outgroup in the absence of strong human rights protections, there is enormous potential for atrocity. Currently, the digital poorhouse concentrates administrative power in the hands of a small elite. Its integrated data systems and digital surveillance infrastructure offer a degree of control unrivaled in history. Automated tools for classifying the poor, left on their own, will produce towering inequalities unless we make an explicit commitment to forge another path. And yet we act as if justice will take care of itself.

If there is to be an alternative, we must build it on purpose, brick by brick and byte by byte.

Conclusion

DISMANTLING THE DIGITAL POORHOUSE

On March 31, 1968, Dr. Martin Luther King, Jr., gave his last Sunday sermon, "Remaining Awake through a Great Revolution," in the National Cathedral in Washington, DC. King declared that the world was undergoing a triple revolution: a technological revolution sparked by automation and "cybernation," a revolution in warfare triggered by nuclear weapons, and a human rights revolution inspired by anticolonial struggles for freedom across the globe. Though technological innovation was bringing the world a sense of "geographical oneness," he preached, our ethical commitment to each other was not keeping pace. "Through our scientific and technological genius, we have made of this world a neighborhood and yet we have not had the ethical commitment to make of it a brotherhood," he said. "But somehow, and in some way, we have got to do this. . . . We are tied together in the single garment of destiny, caught in an inescapable network of mutuality."

In the twenty-first century, we have accomplished the geographical oneness King prophesized. But we continue to fall far short of achieving the ethical growth he envisioned. He called for the immediate eradication of the national disease of racial injustice. He called on us to "rid our nation and the world of poverty." He warned the complacent that social movements would soon be offering them a wake-up call for the revolution.

"We are coming to Washington in a Poor People's Campaign," he concluded. "We read one day, 'We hold these truths to be self-evident, that all men are created equal, that they are endowed by their Creator with certain inalienable Rights, that among these are Life, Liberty, and the pursuit of Happiness.' . . . We are coming to ask America to be true to the huge promissory note that it signed years ago."

King was assassinated four days later in Memphis, Tennessee, where he was supporting striking African American sanitation workers.

The Poor People's Campaign carried forward after King's death, but it did not have the outcomes he had anticipated. The campaign enjoyed a budget of one million dollars, the participation of a broad coalition of poor people's groups across color lines, and high profile supporters such as Coretta Scott King and Harry Belafonte. Nine major caravans from across the country—including New York, Los Angeles, Seattle, Selma, and most famously, a mule train that departed from Marks, Mississippi—arrived in Washington, DC, without major incident. They had a clear, if ambitious, agenda: to engage waves of America's poorest people in militant nonviolent action in the capitol until they secured a federal commitment to pass an economic and social Bill of Rights.

But the campaign also faced extraordinary challenges. King's assassination left the Southern Christian Leadership Conference (SCLC) riven with internecine fighting, and divided in its commitment to eradicating poverty. The urban insurrections taking place across the country in the wake of King's death intensified a siege mentality among professional middle-class whites, and the backlash against the civil rights movement intensified.

J. Edgar Hoover's FBI took particular interest in the campaign, mounting a counterinsurgency effort against the 3,000 poor people living in a "Resurrection City" they built on the National Mall. According to Gerald McKnight's 1998 book, *The Last Crusade*, the camp was subject to around-the-clock surveillance not only by the FBI, but by US Army Intelligence, Border Patrol, National Park Police, and the Metropolitan Police Department. Paid informants from the Interdivisional Intelligence Unit of the Justice Department and COINTELPRO agents infiltrated the encampment, fomenting violence and dissent. The tiny city's phones were tapped and its radio transmissions were intercepted to identify "criminals and terrorists."

The campaign was also undermined by SCLC leaders' unacknowledged gender and class prejudice. The group routinely de-emphasized the important role of welfare rights leaders—mostly poor Black women—in building the national network of organizations that made the campaign possible. Famously, this led Johnnie Tillmon to chastise Dr. King for asking for the National Welfare Rights Organization's support when he didn't know much about welfare issues.

As journalists Mary Lynn and Nick Kotz recount in their 1977 book, *A Passion for Equality*, when King seemed confused by pointed questions from welfare rights leaders in a 1968 Chicago planning meeting, Johnnie Tillmon gently said, "You know, Dr. King, if you don't know about these questions, you should say you don't know." To his credit, King replied, "You're right, Mrs. Tillmon. We don't know anything about welfare. We are here to learn."[1]

This attitude of humility didn't survive King's assassination. When SCLC leadership arrived in Washington, they stayed at a nearby motel rather than join protestors in Resurrection City. No cooking facilities were planned for the encampment. While SCLC staff ate hot meals, the rank and file had to make do with weeks of donuts, cereal, and baloney and cheese sandwiches. Sanitation and security were inadequate, and what they once called the City of Hope eventually sank under the weight of weeks of rain and mud, unmet material needs, and interpersonal violence. According to McKnight, SCLC leadership was relieved when the federal government bulldozed Resurrection City six weeks into the occupation.

The Poor People's Campaign is one of our nation's great unfinished journeys. Its aspirations are as pressing today as they were 50 years ago. But the digital poorhouse presents new challenges that King failed to envision. We are at a momentous crossroads. Across the country, the technological revolution King described is poised to gut the promise of the ethical revolution for which he yearned, organized, and fought.

Despite our unparalleled communications capabilities, we are in the midst of a violent retrenchment on equity and pluralism. Rather than achieving a basic standard of "jobs and income now" for all, we face economic inequity of history-shattering proportions. Our failure as a nation to rise to King's 1968 invitation to eradicate racism and eliminate poverty has produced a generation of astonishing, sophisticated technologies that automate discrimination and deepen inequality.

But there is nothing inevitable about this outcome. We can dismantle the digital poorhouse.

It will take more than high-tech tweaks to bring down the institutions we have built to profile, police, and punish the poor. It will take profound changes to culture, politics, and personal ethics.

The most important step in dismantling the digital poorhouse is changing how we think, talk, and feel about poverty. As counterintuitive as it may sound, the best cure for the misuse of big data is telling better stories. But our vision has been radically limited by the narrow frame that has evolved for talking about poor and working-class people. Journalist Monica Potts suggests that we can only tolerate illustrations of suffering, litanies of misery, or morality plays of bad choices and their consequences. It is as if telling stories of economic hardship allows only two lessons, she writes: " 'You should feel sorry for the poor' or 'You shouldn't.' "[2]

Further limiting our vision is the narrative that the poor are a people apart. The insistence that there is a "culture of poverty" takes on the character of a bizarre and delusional mantra when we understand that poverty is a majority experience in the United States. This is not to say that those who are born in poverty do not face special challenges in escaping it. They do. The best single predictor of adult poverty in America is if you were born poor, because poverty impacts the quality of your education, the resources in your neighborhood, your exposure to violence and trauma, and your health. This is also not to say that everyone experiences poverty in the same way. Racial inequality and discrimination, gendered expectations of caregiving, chronic health problems, mental illness, physical disability, and the extra hurdles faced by undocumented migrants and those with criminal records can combine to make poverty more likely and more difficult to escape.

But poverty is not an island; it is a borderland. There's quite a lot of movement in the economic fringes, especially across the fuzzy boundary between the poor and the working class. Those who live in the economic borderlands are pitted against one another by policies that squeeze every possible dime from the wallets of the working class at the same time that they cut social programs for the poor and absolve the professional middle class and wealthy of their social obligations. There is a lot of self-blame and horizontal violence in the borderlands, but there is also a lot of shared experience. The first challenge we face in dismantling the digital poorhouse is building empathy and understanding among poor and working-class people in order to forge winning political coalitions.

The good news is that this mission is already well under way. Broad-based inclusive movements to end poverty, led by the poor, have been on the rise in the United States for two decades. The Poor People's Economic Human Rights Campaign (PPEHRC), for example, was born out of a New Freedom Bus tour organized in June 1998 to showcase the devastating impacts of welfare reform. The organizations hosting the tour formed PPEHRC under the leadership of welfare rights activist Cheri Honkala a few months later. For PPEHRC, redefining poverty and expanding the union of those who see themselves as poor is central to its goal to "build a movement to unite the poor across color lines."

If you lack even one of the economic rights promised by the 1948 Universal Declaration of Human Rights—including health care, housing, a living-wage job, and quality education—PPEHRC counts you among the poor. The redefinition is tactical, an attempt to help poor and working-class people see themselves reflected in each others' experiences. The movement engages in a wide array of strategies, from building tent cities and reoccupying abandoned "human rights houses" to direct action marches and documenting economic human rights abuses. But storytelling is central to their work.

For example, in 2013, the PPEHRC held a World Court of Women on poverty in Philadelphia. The World Courts of Women are public hearings that draw attention to violence against women, including violations of our basic human rights. They create a space for ordinary people to deliver testimony over the course of several days, and a panel of jurors listens, reflects, and gathers evidence to hold governments and corporations accountable for human rights abuses.

Over three days, about 100 attendees from the eastern states shared space and told stories. "This is a sacred space, a place where we listen to people who have been made invisible, who have been disappeared, who have been made to feel worthless," Honkala said on the first day. "Listening to the voices of those who have been told to be quiet and to disappear is incredibly important, strategic, and vital. It's not just a nice thing to do. Or a morally correct thing to do. It's a winning thing to do. It's a transforming thing to do. It's a changing-the-world thing to do."

Such sustained, practiced empathy can change the "us/them" to a "we," without obscuring the real differences in our experiences and life chances. The righteous anger that wells up when we recognize our common suffering is an earthshaking, structure-tumbling, visionary force.

The PPEHRC was recently joined in their work by the New Poor People's Campaign, a coalition of religious, civil rights, and economic justice activists and organizers committed to addressing the massive human suffering and oppression caused by poverty and racism. Like PPEHRC, storytelling through Truth Commissions has been central to their strategy.

And yet, justice requires more than truth-telling. It requires mobilizing grassroots power to disrupt the status quo. Today's poor people's movement struggles to build a truly interracial, cross-class movement led by the poor themselves, just like the Poor People's Campaign 50 years ago. Those organizations genuinely led by poor and working people face unique difficulties attracting resources, because foundations rarely trust that the poor can manage money. They are often marginalized in progressive coalitions that include professional middle-class activists because their language and be-havior do not always fit prevailing norms of movement culture. Their actions and policy recommendations are rarely reported in the mainstream media. Those organizations led by the professional middle class on behalf of the poor, on the other hand, are more successful in attracting funding, progressive allies, and public attention. But they are often disconnected from the radical analysis and boundless energy of poor and working-class communities.

In February 1968, King and other members of the SCLC drafted a letter to President Johnson and the Congress making their demands for an economic and social Bill of Rights clear. "We do not come here to ask for charity," they wrote, "We demand justice.... We speak as black men and women on behalf of black men and women. But the rights we insist upon do not apply only to our own people. They are, as this nation has proclaimed, but not practiced ... the rights of all men." They then laid out six fundamental rights required for all Americans to achieve life, liberty, and the pursuit of happiness. These included:

1. The right of every employable citizen to a decent job.
2. The right of every citizen to a minimum income.
3. The right of a decent house and the free choice of neighborhood.
4. The right to an adequate education.
5. The right to participate in the decision-making process.
6. The right to the full benefits of modern science in health care.

To fund their ambitious agenda, the SCLC demanded that the Johnson administration immediately withdraw from Vietnam, create a domestic Marshall Plan dedicating 3 percent of the Gross National Product to building affordable housing, and pass a peacetime GI Bill to support higher education or vocational schooling for millions of poor youth.

"With these rights," they concluded, "the United States could, by the two hundredth anniversary of its Declaration of Independence, take giant steps towards redeeming the American dream." In a letter to supporters, King warned that the Poor People's Campaign was America's "last chance" to arouse its "conscience toward constructive democratic change."[3]

Instead, by 1976, the digital poorhouse had emerged and a movement to restrict the rights of poor families was sweeping the country. The combination of more restrictive rules, faster processing, less human discretion, and more complete surveillance shredded our already inadequate social safety net. The Congress used the cost of the war in Vietnam to rationalize dismantling War on Poverty programs. The peacetime GI Bill, public service jobs, and minimum guaranteed income called for by the Poor People's Campaign never materialized.

Today, these goals still sometimes feel hopelessly out of reach. But if we are serious about dismantling the digital poorhouse—and ending poverty—we could do worse than to start with this list of 50-year-old demands. Certainly, creating enough adequately paying jobs would eliminate much of the cyclical use of public programs that occurs when working-class people—and even some in the professional middle class—dip below the poverty line and into the densest web of the digital poorhouse. But, as Kathryn J. Edin and H. Luke Shaefer point out in *$2.00 a Day: Living on Almost Nothing in America*, work doesn't always work for everyone. "We need a program that can provide a temporary cash cushion," they write, "because no matter what strategies we implement, work . . . will sometimes fail."[4]

In the face of fears that automation promises a jobless future, a cash assistance plan, the universal basic income (UBI) is enjoying a resurgence. Experiments in UBI are currently being conducted in Finland and in Ontario, Canada. In May 2017, Hawaii adopted a bill declaring that "all families . . . deserve basic financial security" and began to explore instituting a UBI. High-tech entrepreneurs such as Mark Zuckerberg, CEO of Facebook, and Elon Musk, founder of Tesla Motors, believe that a UBI will provide a cushion allowing everyone to innovate and try new ideas.

UBI plans usually offer between $8,000 and $12,000 a year. In principle, a UBI would be truly universal—offered to every citizen—but in political practice, guaranteed adequate income programs tend to be offered to those who are unemployed or who fall below a minimum income line. They offer unconditional cash: those who receive a UBI are allowed to work, and can spend or save their allotment however they want. Supporters, who span political ideology, say that basic incomes compensate for wage stagnation, shrink welfare bureaucracies, protect against economic shocks, and allow low-wage workers to supplement their earnings. They also allow for basic human dignity: no drug testing, scrutiny of your parenting, or financial surveillance. Unconditional cash assumes that poor and working-class people know best how to spend their money and care for their families.

But, as the welfare rights movement learned when their adequate income plan went up against Nixon's Family Assistance Plan, a UBI is not a panacea. It can be seen as a bribe encouraging poor and working-class people to accept political, social, and workforce exclusion. The income in these plans is usually so low that, even combined with low-wage work, families would find it difficult to build financial stability for the next generation. It might weaken wages for others, or allow companies to engage in ever-more precarious and exploitative employment arrangements. It could be presented as a wholesale replacement or privatization of the social welfare state, making it more difficult to access subsidized housing, medical care, nutritional assistance, child-care, or job training.

Nevertheless, a UBI might be a great first step in dismantling the digital poorhouse. Freed from the mandate to find fraud, divert the "undeserving," produce sanctionable offenses, and perform triage in an atmosphere of constant scarcity, the punitive machinery of the digital poorhouse would certainly be seen for what it is: an overly elaborate technological infrastructure that wastes time, resources, and human potential.

Making public assistance less punitive and more generous would also ameliorate many of the problems in homeless services and child protective services that I've described. According to Gale Holland of the *Los Angeles Times*, 13,000 people on public assistance fall into homelessness *every month* in Los Angeles County because benefits are both inadequate and too hard to keep.[5] A guaranteed economic cushion would likely eliminate many of the 2.6 million child maltreatment cases that stem from neglect rather than abuse every year.

Many UBI advocates, including Martin Luther King, Jr., have argued that a guaranteed income is not a substitute for a vigorous social welfare state. A system of non-punitive cash assistance might help dismantle the digital poorhouse, but it will not end poverty.

Changing cultural understandings and political responses to poverty will be difficult, abiding work. It is unlikely that techno-logical development will slow down to wait for our new stories and visions to emerge. In the meantime, we need to develop basic technological design principles to minimize harm.

At lectures, conferences, and gatherings, I am often approached by engineers or data scientists who want to talk about the eco-nomic and social implications of their designs. I tell them to do a quick "gut check" by answering two questions:

Does the tool increase the self-determination and agency of the poor?

Would the tool be tolerated if it was targeted at non-poor people?

Not one of the technologies I describe in this book rises to this feeble standard. We must demand more.

As we create a new national narrative and politics of poverty, we must also begin dismantling the digital poorhouse. It will require flexing our imaginations and asking entirely different kinds of questions: How would a data-based system work if it was meant to encourage poor and working-class people to use resources to meet their needs in their own ways? What would decision-making systems that see poor people, families, and neighborhoods as infinitely valuable and innovative look like? It will also require sharpening our skills: high-tech tools that protect human rights and strengthen human capacity are more difficult to build than those that do not.

Think of the principles of non-harm, below, as a first draft of a Hippocratic oath for the data scientists, systems engineers, hackers, and administrative officials of the new millennium.

Oath of Non-Harm for an Age of Big Data

I swear to fulfill, to the best of my ability, the following covenant:

I will respect all people for their integrity and wisdom, understanding that they are experts in their own lives, and will gladly share with them all the benefits of my knowledge.

I will use my skills and resources to create bridges for human potential, not barriers. I will create tools that remove obstacles between resources and the people who need them.

I will not use my technical knowledge to compound the disadvantage created by historic patterns of racism, classism, able-ism, sexism, homophobia, xenophobia, transphobia, religious intolerance, and other forms of oppression.

I will design with history in mind. To ignore a four-century-long pattern of punishing the poor is to be complicit in the "unintended" but terribly predictable consequences that arise when equity and good intentions are assumed as initial conditions.

I will integrate systems for the needs of people, not data. I will choose system integration as a mechanism to attain human needs, not to facilitate ubiquitous surveillance.

I will not collect data for data's sake, nor keep it just because I can.

When informed consent and design convenience come into conflict, informed consent will always prevail.

I will design no data-based system that overturns an established legal right of the poor.

I will remember that the technologies I design are not aimed at data points, probabilities, or patterns, but at human beings.

It is possible that the digital poorhouse will prove so isolating and stigmatizing that it will undercut our common aspirations. But it could also have the opposite effect. The ubiquity of its high-tech tools could allow us to see how our struggles, hopes, and dreams are linked together. It might create unlikely allies, as it did in Indiana, when the automation experiment ravaged welfare recipients, state caseworkers, nonprofit organizations, and local governments alike. Its web could draw us together. But it won't happen by accident. As Dr. King reminds us, "Human progress never rolls in on the wheels of inevitability."[6] The digital poorhouse must be met with organized and visible resistance.

The most inspiring social movements of the past decade have begun to address classism and poverty, but they have failed to recognize the role of the digital poorhouse in perpetuating economic violence.

Occupy Wall Street brought crucial attention to the grotesque expansion of wealth among the 1 percent. But the big tent of the 99 percent obscured very real differences in the life chances of the professional middle class, the working class, and the poor. The movement built momentum for higher minimum wages and debt forgiveness but remained largely silent on public services. And while the unhoused often became part of Occupy encampments, the movement struggled to embrace their leadership and center their issues.

The affirmation of *all* Black lives at the heart of the Black Lives Matter movement has helped to bridge class divides and to mobilize an extraordinary cross-section of people to fight against police brutality, end mass incarceration, and build strong and loving communities. The movement's founders, Alicia Garza, Opal Tometi, and Patrisse Cullors, are clear that the movement condemns *all* state violence, not just police violence. As part of its reparations platform, The Movement for Black Lives—a collective of 50 organizations including the Black Lives Matter Network—calls for the establishment of an unconditional and guaranteed minimum livable income for all Black people.

But despite the expansive view of Black Lives Matter, the interventions that have attracted the most public attention have been those focused on violence committed against Black bodies, minds, and souls by the criminal justice system. Similar surveillance of brutality and dehumanization in public assistance, homeless services, and child protective services must take their rightful place at the center of our social justice work. As my colleague, Mariella Saba of the Stop LAPD Spying Coalition, always reminds me: it's vital to keep our eyes on the badge. But the culture of policing wears many uniforms.

And the state doesn't require a cop to kill a person.

The digital poorhouse kills people. The majority of them are women, children, the mentally ill, the disabled, and the elderly.

Many are poor and working-class people of color. Many others are poor and working-class whites. Addressing the digital poorhouse can help progressive social movements shift attention from "the police" to the processes of *policing*.

Policing is broader than law enforcement: it includes all the processes by which we maintain order, regulate lives, and press people into boxes so they will fit our unjust society. The county poorhouse was an extrajudicial institution, built to imprison those who were not guilty of any crime. Scientific charity policed the lives of poor and working-class people for two generations, with brutal results. Today, the digital poorhouse uses its high-tech tools to infer and predict: to police events that haven't even happened yet.

In my most pessimistic moments, I fear that we are winning the fight against mass incarceration at just the historical moment when the digital poorhouse makes the physical institution of the prison less necessary. Corporations already anticipate the immense cost savings of building a digital prison state without walls. A 2012 Deloitte Touche Tohmatsu report titled *Public Sector, Disrupted*, for example, sees "transforming criminal justice with electronic monitoring" as an "opportunity for disruptive innovation" in government services.

A graphic brings their point home. On the left side is a stick figure behind prison bars. In the middle, there is an equal sign. On the right, there are five and a half stick figures wearing electronic ankle bracelets. The violence of the digital poorhouse is less direct than police brutality, its operation harder to see. But we must resist its moralizing classifications. We must resist its erasure of history, context, and structure.

Exposing the violence of the digital poorhouse will require a great deal of courage. The poor and working class will have to stand in the truth of their experiences, recognizing commonalities and building on differences to create unshakable coalitions. Because race has for so many years been central to dividing us, a first order of business will be to expand and nurture the antiracist capacity of poor people's movements. But it will be equally important to confront the deep classism of many progressive organizations. A true revolution will start where people are. It will engage them in terms of their basic material needs: safety, shelter, wellness, food, and family. And it will honor poor and working-class people's deep knowledge, strength, and capacity for leadership.

At the same time, the professional middle class and wealthy will have to acknowledge the immense suffering economic inequity causes, recognize their culpability, and reassess their role in creating a more just world. This is doubly true for technology professionals who hold immense resources, including specialized knowledge, tools, time, and money. Though they may have been unwitting participants in its construction, they must bend their tools toward dismantling the digital poorhouse.

In his March 31, 1968, sermon, Dr. Martin Luther King, Jr., called those who would be "conscientious objector[s] in the war against poverty" to a moral reckoning. In his ringing voice, he stood in the nation's capitol and intoned,

> This is the question facing America. Ultimately a great nation is a compassionate nation. America has not met its obligations and its responsibilities to the poor.
>
> One day we will have to stand before the God of history and we will talk in terms of things we've done. Yes, we will be able to say we built gargantuan bridges to span the seas, we built gigantic buildings to kiss the skies. Yes, we made our submarines to penetrate oceanic depths. We brought into being many other things with our scientific and technological power.
>
> It seems that I can hear the God of history saying, "That was not enough! But I was hungry, and ye fed me not. I was naked, and ye clothed me not. I was devoid of a decent sanitary

house to live in, and ye provided no shelter for me. And consequently, you cannot enter the kingdom of greatness. If ye do it unto the least of these, my brethren, ye do it unto me." That's the question facing America today.

Fifty years later, King's question has become only more urgent. He did not foresee that the very technological wonders he extolled might be turned against the poor. Our ethical evolution still lags behind our technological revolutions. But more importantly, because the nation failed to address King's most crucial challenges—dismantling racism and ending poverty—the digital revolution has warped to fit the shape of our still-inequitable world.

We, too, will stand in the eyes of justice and talk of what we've done. We have programmed bots to converse like humans. We have built cars that drive themselves. We even have apps that allow us to document police abuse and mobilize protest.

The God of history is still saying, "That is not enough!"

ACKNOWLEDGMENTS

At the heart of this book are the stories of those who inhabit the digital poorhouse in Indiana, Los Angeles, and Allegheny County. Many of the people who agreed to talk about their experiences did so at enormous risk. They faced losing life-saving medical services, food, housing, and custody of their children. Reliving their experience was often traumatic, as well. I am awed by the courage of all those who agreed to share their stories. I hope I have captured their truths with the respect and accuracy they deserve.

Though many people gave me feedback and encouragement, a few deserve special mention. Nick Matulis read every word of the manuscript, sometimes multiple times, and gave invaluable editorial feedback. Fearless snark detector, he pushed me to pull the threads together and not lose track of the story's beating heart. Alethia Jones read on the subway, in stolen weekend minutes, and over late nights. Her fast, fierce readings held me to an ever-higher standard. Her integrity reminded me that a book can be an invitation to conversation and a call to action. Patricia Strach's feedback was both generous and penetrating. Our conversations made the book stronger and her rock-steady support helped me overcome doubts along the way. My words never sound better than they do coming out of Nadya Lawson's mouth. Thanks for being my Amen Corner.

Adrian Nicole LeBlanc stepped into the breach at a fraught moment, and has relentlessly championed the work.

My editor at St. Martin's, Elisabeth Dyssegaard, took a huge gamble on this book and its writer. I am grateful for her faith when I was starting, her flexibility when I was struggling, and her firmness when I needed to push the manuscript over the finish line. The rest of the team at St. Martin's—Laura Apperson, Alan Bradshaw, Laury Frieber, Sarah Becks and Danielle Prielipp—poked, prodded, and polished until the book was the best it could be.

My agent, Sam Stoloff, agreed to do everything backward with impeccably good humor. He is an advocate and staunch ally, an observant reader and trusted confidant.

My fact-checker, Stephanie McFeeters, is a hero with a fine-toothed comb who caught errors more often than I would like to admit.

Nina Baldwin, Carole Eubanks, Julie Novkov, Melissa Thorne, and the Diver Library Writers' Group of Schaghticoke, New York, also filled the margins of the manuscript with insight and my heart with courage. Jesse Stiles, Olivia Robinson, Lauren Allen, and Rich Pell made a home for me in Pittsburgh.

Throughout the writing of the manuscript, I cherished ongoing conversations with the Our Data Bodies team: Seeta Peña Gangadharan, Tamika Lewis, Tawana Petty, and Mariella Saba. Their commitment, humor, and insight continually raise the bar on who I want to be and what I want to accomplish.

This book could not have been written without the support of a Ford Academic Fellowship from New America, which funded a substantial proportion of my reporting in Indiana, Los Angeles, and Allegheny County. Thanks especially to Andres Martinez and Peter Bergen. In addition, the 2015 class of fellows and the staff at New America were important mentors and allies, especially Monica Potts, Andrea Elliott, Fuzz Hogan, Becky Schafer, Kristen Berg, Rachel Black, Aleta Sprague, Becky Shafer, Elizabeth Weingarten, Andrew Bolden, Christopher Leonard, Greta Byrum, Andy Gunn, Ryan Gerety, and Josh Breitbart. The TDM team at New America, especially Lisa Watson and Fanny McKeithen, came to my family's rescue in a very dark moment, and I'll always be grateful.

Automating Inequality also benefitted from two writing residencies that arrived at crucial moments. My thanks to Harriet Barlow, Ben Strader, Zohar Gitlis, and all the other staff and supporters of the Blue Mountain Center. Thanks, too, to fellow campers, especially Andrea Quijada, Mónica Hernández, Kathleen Sutcliffe, and Marin Watts, for supporting me when Jason was attacked and I was stranded in the woods.

The Carey Institute for Global Good provided a Logan Nonfiction Fellowship that provide respite and focus at a crucial moment. Thanks to Tim Weiner for his advocacy and for very generous critical readings of work-in-progress. Thanks to Carol Ash, Gareth Crawford, and Josh Friedman for building support and structure for this incredible resource, and to Tammy Cook, John Murray, and the rest of the staff that keep things running.

I am grateful to my employer, the University at Albany, SUNY. My students and colleagues in the Department of Women's, Gender, and Sexuality Studies provided me a vibrant, challenging home for 12 years. My colleagues in the Department of Political Science provided me with flexibility and support so I could develop this work.

And finally, my deepest debt of gratitude is to my partner, Jason Martin, who showed extraordinary grace, honesty, and courage over four years of risky change, catastrophe, and renewal. He somehow managed to help hold me up, even when he was falling down himself. Jason, there is no one I'd rather walk through Hell with.

SOURCES AND METHODS

The notes that follow are intended to give more precise information about sourcing, provide transparency about my process, and supply readers with a list of material that was crucial to my thinking but may not have been used directly. There is a growing body of exceptional work on automated decision-making, algorithmic accountability, and new forms of digital discrimination. I hope what follows helps readers find a path to a deeper understanding of the promise of the age of data and the perils of automating inequality.

I list below all of the interviews that I completed, both those that were explicitly quoted in the text, and those that were not. I deeply appreciate each person's generosity in speaking with me, and their contribution to my understanding was indispensable. The handful of sources who chose to stay off the record are, of course, not listed here.

I started my reporting in each location by reaching out to organizations working closely with families most directly impacted by the systems I explored. Indiana Legal Services, the

ACLU of Indiana, and the Generations Project connected me with those who lost their benefits during the eligibility modernization. The Los Angeles Community Action Network, the Downtown Women's Center, and the Pathways to Home shelter in South LA introduced me to unhoused individuals participating in coordinated entry. And a network of family support centers throughout Allegheny County introduced me to parents being ranked by the Allegheny Family Screening Tool.

My preference was to conduct interviews in person. I made two extended research trips to Indiana, the first in December 2014, and the second in March 2015. I took five research trips to Los Angeles, in January 2015, May–June 2015, December 2015, February 2016, and May 2016. I made four trips to Allegheny County, in July, August, September, and November of 2016. The shortest of these trips was six days, the longest close to a month. Some follow-up interviews took place over the telephone. Very rarely, I interviewed a source solely over the phone or on a video conference call.

Interviews used in the book were transcribed verbatim. A few were only partially transcribed because of length. Where interview material is used directly in the text, it appears in quotes. Quotes have occasionally been edited for clarity. Material attributed to an interviewee but not appearing in quotes is the source's recollection of an event in the past, or a paraphrase of a longer conversation derived from interview transcripts and my notes.

I used a pseudonym (Dorothy Allen) for one individual who participated in academic research many years ago on the condition of anonymity, and a first name only for another who requested that I do so. As noted in chapter 4, the names Stephen and Krzystof are also pseudonyms. Otherwise, all quoted individuals appear under their full names.

In the final stages of editing, I hired a professional fact-checker to verify the manuscript. Her insight, attentiveness, and hard work were crucial to the story I was able to tell. She checked my historical research. She spoke to sources, read interview transcripts, watched video of public hearings, read newspaper accounts, and pored over my reporting notes to verify identities and events.

INTRODUCTION: RED FLAGS

Interviews

Dorothy Allen

Published Literature

Federal Bureau of Investigations. "What We Investigate: Health Care Fraud." https://www.fbi.gov/investigate/white-collar-crime/health-care-fraud.

Moretto, Mario. "LePage Releases EBT Data Showing Transactions at Strip Clubs, Bars, Smoke Shops." *Bangor Daily News*, Jan. 7, 2014.

National Health Care Anti-Fraud Association. "The Challenge of Health Care Fraud." https://www.nhcaa.org/resources/health-care-anti-fraud-resources/the-challenge-of-health-care-fraud.aspx.

State of Maine. "EBT Transaction Data." 2014. https://docs.google.com/file/d/0B2MlKOvJIQRGRnItZGVzaXllY0U/edit. [Accessed Sept. 13, 2017.]

State of Maine House of Representatives. *Committee Amendment "A" to H.P. 725, L.D. 1030, Bill, "an Act to Require That Electronic Benefits Transfer System Cash Benefits Are Used for the Purpose for Which the Benefits Are Provided."* 126th Legislature, H.P. 725, L.D. 1030.

Tice, Lindsay. "Mainers Using EBT Cash in Unusual Places." *Bangor Daily News*, Jan. 19, 2014.

US Department of Health and Human Services. "Departments of Justice and Health and Human Services Announce over $27.8 Billion in Returns from Joint Efforts to Combat Health Care Fraud." News Release, Mar. 19, 2015. http://www.hhs.gov/about/news/2015/03/19/departments-of-justice-and-health-and-human-services-announce-over-27-point-8-billion-in-returns-from-joint-efforts-to-combat-health-care-fraud.html.

Xerox Corporation. "Public Welfare Agency Burdened by Paper Processes. Xerox Delivered Needed Relief." In *Case Study: Government*, nd. http://docushare.xerox.com/pdf/PADeprofPublicWelfare-CS.pdf. [Accessed May 5, 2015.]

1. FROM POORHOUSE TO DATABASE

Published Literature

Almy, Frederic. *Relief: A Primer for the Family Rehabilitation Work of the Buffalo Charity Organization Society.* New York: Charity Organization Dept. of the Russell Sage Foundation, 1910.

Ambrose, Jay. "Welfare Clients—Victims or Villains?" *Knickerbocker News*, Feb. 25, 1971, 1-A, 4-A.

Axelrod, Donald. "Memo to Richard L. Dunham: Welfare Requests for Your Discussion at Governor's Staff Meeting." Albany, NY: New York State Archives, 1971. Record 15000-88, Box 30: Welfare Programs: Welfare Administration Computerization Projects.

Bailis, Lawrence Neil. *Bread or Justice: Grassroots Organizing in the Welfare Rights Movement.* Lexington, MA: Lexington Books, 1974.

Bellesiles, Michael A. *1877: America's Year of Living Violently.* New York: New Press, 2010.

"Body Speculators in Troy." *New York Times*, Feb. 3, 1879, 1.

Bolton, Charles C. "Farmers without Land: The Plight of White Tenant Farmers and Sharecroppers." *Mississippi History Now*, 2004. http://www.mshistorynow.mdah.ms.gov/articles/228/farmers-without-land-the-plight-of-white-tenant-farmers-and-sharecroppers. [Accessed Sept. 13, 2017.]

"Children of the Poor House." *The Standard* (Syracuse, NY), Jan. 21, 1856.

Clement, Priscilla Ferguson. *Welfare and the Poor in the Nineteenth-Century City: Philadelphia, 1800–1854.* Rutherford, NJ: Fairleigh Dickinson University Press, 1985.

Crannell, Linda. "The Poorhouse Story." http://www.poorhousestory.com/.

Dawes, Sharon S. *New York's Welfare Management System: The Politics of Information.* Nelson A. Rockefeller Institute of Government, State University of New York, 1986.

Du Bois, W.E.B. *The Philadelphia Negro.* Publications of the University of

Pennsylvania, No. 14. Series in Political Economy and Public Law. Millwood, NY: Kraus-Thomson Organization Ltd., 1973.

Federal Government Information Technology: Electronic Record Systems and Individual Privacy. Congress of the United States, Office of Technology Assessment, 1986.

Gilens, Martin. "How the Poor Became Black: The Racialization of American Poverty in the Mass Media." In *Race and the Politics of Welfare Reform*, Sanford F. Schram, Joe Soss, and Richard C. Fording, eds. Ann Arbor: University of Michigan Press, 2003: 101–30.

Grauer, Anne L., Vanessa Lathrop, and Taylor Timoteo. "Exploring Evidence of Nineteenth Century Dissection in the Dunning Poorhouse Cemetery." In *The Bioarchaeology of Dissection and Autopsy in the United States*, Kenneth C. Nystrom, ed. Switzerland: Springer International Publishing, 2017: 301–13.

Green, Elna C. *This Business of Relief: Confronting Poverty in a Southern City, 1740–1940.* Athens, GA: University of Georgia Press, 2003.

Greenberg, David H., Wolf Douglas, and Jennifer Pfiester. *Using Computers to Combat Welfare Fraud: The Operation and Effectiveness of Wage Matching.* New York: Greenwood Press, 1986.

Gustafson, Kaaryn S. *Cheating Welfare: Public Assistance and the Criminalization of Poverty.* New York: New York University Press, 2011.

Holcomb, Charles. "Rocky to Thin 'Welfare Gravy.'" *Knickerbocker News*, Mar. 16, 1971, 1A, 5A.

In the Matter of an Inquiry into the Administration, Discipline, and Moral Welfare of the Rensselaer County Poorhouse. Albany, NY: New York State Archives, 1905.

Jackson, Larry R., and William A. Johnson. "Protest by the Poor: The Welfare Rights Movement in New York City." New York: RAND Institute, 1973.

Katz, Michael B. *In the Shadow of the Poorhouse: A Social History of Welfare in America.* New York: Basic Books, 1996.

———. *The Undeserving Poor: From the War on Poverty to the War on Welfare.* 1st ed. New York: Pantheon Books, 1990.

Katz, Michael B., and the Committee for Research on the Urban Underclass Social of the Science Research Council. *The "Underclass" Debate: Views from History.* Princeton, NJ: Princeton University Press, 1993.

Kennedy, Howard. "Policy Due on 'Night Raid' Checking of Welfare Cases," *LA Times*, Feb. 18, 1963, 1.

Killgrove, Kristina. "How Grave Robbers and Medical Students Helped Dehumanize 19th Century Blacks and the Poor." *Forbes*, July 13, 2015. https://www.forbes.com/sites/kristinakillgrove/2015/07/13/dissected -bodies-and-grave-robbing-evidence-of-unequal-treatment-of-19th -century-blacks-and-poor/#1c2632f66d12. [Accessed July 27, 2017.]

"Leasing the County Farm and Stone Quarry on the Same." *Troy Daily Whig*, Feb. 8, 1869, 1.

Lombardo, Paul. "Eugenics Sterilization Laws." Dolan DNA Learning Center, Cold Spring Harbor Laboratory. http://www.eugenicsarchive .org/html/eugenics/essay 8, fs.html. [Accessed June 23, 2017.]

Lombardo, Paul A. *Three Generations, No Imbeciles: Eugenics, the Supreme Court, and* Buck v. Bell. Baltimore: Johns Hopkins University Press, 2008.

Massachusetts General Court Committee on Paupers Laws and Josiah Quincy. *Commonwealth of Massachusetts: In the Year of Our Lord One Thousand Eight Hundred and Twenty One: The Committee, to Whom Was Referred, at the Last Session of the General Court, the Consideration of the Paupers Laws of This Commonwealth, with Directions to Report, Whether Any, and If Any, What Amendments, or Alterations May Be Made Therein, with Leave to Report by Bill, or Otherwise, Ask Leave to Report.* Boston: Russell & Gardner, 1821.

Mink, Gwendolyn. *The Wages of Motherhood: Inequality in the Welfare State, 1917–1942.* Ithaca, NY: Cornell University Press, 1995.

Nadasen, Premilla. *Rethinking the Welfare Rights Movement.* New York: Routledge, 2012.

———. *Welfare Warriors: The Welfare Rights Movement in the United States.* New York: Routledge, 2005.

Nadasen, Premilla, Jennifer Mittelstadt, and Marisa Chappell. *Welfare in the United States: A History with Documents, 1935–1996.* New York: Routledge, 2009.

New York Legislature, Senate Select Committee Appointed to Visit Charitable Institutions. *Report of Select Committee Appointed to Visit Charitable Institutions Supported by the State and All City and County Poor and Work Houses and Jails of the State of New York: Transmitted to the Legislature, January 9, 1857.* In Senate; 1857, No. 8; Senate Document (New York State). Albany, NY: C. Van Benthuysen, printer to the legislature, 1857.

New York State Department of Social Services. *Welfare Management*

System: A Proposed Design and Implementation Plan. Albany, NY: Department of Social Services, 1975.

Orwig, Timothy T. "Three Nineteenth-Century Massachusetts Almshouses and the Origins of American Poorhouse Architecture." Masters Thesis, Boston University, 2001.

"Our County Institutions." *Troy Daily Whig,* Feb. 6, 1857, 1.

Peel, Mark. "Charity Organization Society." In *Encyclopedia of American Urban History,* David R. Goldfield, ed. Thousand Oaks, CA: Sage Publications, 2007.

Piven, Frances Fox, and Richard A Cloward. *Regulating the Poor: The Functions of Public Welfare.* New York: Pantheon, 1971.

Quadagno, Jill S. *The Color of Welfare: How Racism Undermined the War on Poverty.* New York: Oxford University Press, 1994.

Reese, Ellen. *Backlash against Welfare Mothers: Past and Present.* Oakland, CA: University of California Press, 2005.

"Revelations Promised: Alleged Mismanagement of the Rensselaer County Poorhouse." *Albany Express,* Dec. 5, 1885, 1.

Rezneck, Samuel. "The Depression of 1819: A Social History." *American Historical Review* 39, 1 (1933): 30–31.

Richmond, Mary Ellen. *Social Diagnosis.* New York: Russell Sage Foundation, 1917.

Rockefeller, Nelson A. *Public Papers of Nelson A. Rockefeller, Fifty-Third Governor of the State of New York.* Albany, NY: New York State Archives, 1959.

Schneider, David M. *The History of Public Welfare in New York State.* Chicago: University of Chicago Press, 1938.

"Shot Himself: Financial Troubles Drove Calvin B. Dunham to End His Life with a Pistol Ball." *Illustrated Buffalo Express,* Jan. 19, 1896.

Smith, Bruce. "Poor Relief at the St. Joseph County Poor Asylum, 1877–1891." *Indiana Magazine of History* 86, 2 (1990): 178–96.

Trattner, Walter I. *From Poor Law to Welfare State: A History of Social Welfare in America,* 6th ed. New York: Free Press, 1999.

Wagner, David. *Ordinary People: In and Out of Poverty in the Gilded Age.* New York: Routledge, 2016.

Watkinson, James D. "Rogues, Vagabonds, and Fit Objects: The Treatment of the Poor in Antebellum Virginia." *Virginia Calvacade* 49, Winter 2000: 16–29.

Weise, Arthur James. *Troy's One Hundred Years: 1789–1889*. London: Forgotten Books, 2015.

Welfare Management System: A Proposed Design and Implementation Plan. Albany: New York Dept. of Social Services, 1975.

Wyman, George K. "Nationwide Demonstration Project Newsletter." Albany: New York State Dept. of Social Services, 1971.

Yates, John Van Ness. "Report of the Secretary of State in 1824 on the Relief and Settlement of the Poor." In *Annual Report for the Year 1900*, vol. 1, New York State Board of Charities, 937–1145. Albany, NY: 1824.

Unpublished Documents

Much of my research for the rise of the digital poorhouse in New York State came from the wonderful collection at the New York State Archives. Important resources included: Record 15000-88 Boxes 29 and 30: Welfare Programs: Welfare Administration Computerization Projects.

2. AUTOMATING ELIGIBILITY IN THE HEARTLAND

Interviews

Jamie Andree; Michelle Birden; Glenn Cardwell; John Cardwell; Karen Francisco; Dennis Frick; Fred Gilbert; Patty Goff; Jane Porter Gresham; Chris Holly; Denny Lanane; Senator Tim Lanane; Ruth Lawson; Gene Lushin; Marcia; Maria Martino; Adam Mueller; Kim Murphy; Ginny Nilles; Matt Pierce; Gavin Rose; Dan Skinner; Jeff Stewart; Kim and Kevin Stipes; Marilyn "Kay" Walker; Terry R. West; Myra Wilkie; Lindsay Williams (Kidwell); Kyle Wood

Published Literature

"Bill Would Slow FSSA Rollout." *South Bend Tribune*, Jan. 21, 2009.

Bradner, Eric. "Agency Tests a Nun's Faith (Indiana Welfare Agency in Disarray)." *Courier Press*, Mar. 20, 2009.

Burdick, Betsy. "Indiana State Government's Performance Report, July-December 2007." 2008.

Carr, Mike, and Rich Adams. "The Hybrid System." http://www.aphsa.org/content/dam/aphsa/pdfs/NWI/2012-07-Business-Model-for-Hybrid-System-Integration.pdf. [Accessed June 23, 2017.]

Cermak, Joe. "Local Representative Wants Legislators to Change Modernized Welfare." *NewsLink Indiana*, May 16, 2008.

Cole, Eric, and Sandra Ring. *Insider Threat: Protecting the Enterprise from Sabotage, Spying, and Theft.* Rockland, MA: Syngress, 2006.

Corbin, Bryan. "Bill Filed to Halt Further Expansion of Indiana's New Welfare Eligibility Program." *Indiana Economic Digest*, Jan. 19, 2009.

———. "Welfare Gripes Persist." *Evansville Courier Press*, Dec. 29, 2008.

Creek, Julie. "Losing the 'Human Factor': State Focuses on Technology in Privatizing Key Welfare Duties." *Fort Wayne Journal Gazette*, May 14, 2006, 13A.

Daniels, Mitch. "Editorial: FSSA Contract with IBM Is Obvious Answer to Obvious Need." *South Bend Tribune*, Jan. 3, 2007. http://articles.south bendtribune.com/2007-01-03/news/26769021_1_welfare-system -fssa-indiana-economy. [Accessed June 28, 2017.]

Davis, Martha F. *Brutal Need: Lawyers and the Welfare Rights Movement, 1960–1973.* New Haven, CT: Yale University Press, 1993.

Ernst, Rose, Linda Nguyen, and Kamilah C. Taylor. "Citizen Control: Race at the Welfare Office." *Social Science Quarterly* 94, no. 5 (2013): 1283–307.

"FSSA Releases Details of New Eligibility System—the Hybrid System." News release, Dec 14, 2009. http://blog.ihca.org/2009/12/fssa-releases -details-of-new.html. [Accessed Sept. 13, 2017.]

Greenhouse, Linda. "New Look at an 'Obscure' Ruling, 20 Years Later." *New York Times*, May 11, 1990.

Harvey, Roger. "Church Leaders Charged with Food Stamp Fraud." Channel 13 WTHR, May 9, 2006.

Herbers, John. "Reagan Called Warm to Welfare-Work Plan." *New York Times*, Feb. 23, 1987.

Higgins, Will. "Falling through Welfare's Cracks." *Indianapolis Star*, July 20, 2009, A1, A4.

Holtz, Maribeth. "Hundreds Line Up to Share Their FSSA Complaints." *Chronicle Tribune*, May 14, 2008.

Indiana Family and Social Services Administration (FSSA). Monthly Management Reports. http://www.stats.indiana.edu/fssa_m/index .html. [Accessed Aug. 3, 2017.]

Indiana Inter-Agency Review Committee. "Eligibility Modernization: An Indiana Solution." June 2005. http://www.in.gov/fssa/transformations

/pdf/Eligibility Modernization_ An Indiana Solution.pdf. [No longer accessible.]

Jarosz, Francesca, Heather Gillers, Tim Evans, and Bill Ruthhart. "Rollout of Welfare Changes Halted." *Indianapolis Star*, July 31, 2008, A1, A11.

Kusmer, Ken. "IBM Releases Plan for Fixing Indiana's Welfare Problems." *News and Tribune*, July 24, 2009. http://www.newsandtribune.com /news/local_news/ibm-releases-plan-for-fixing-indiana-s-welfare -problems/article_eb1cf1cf-fdd4-5b99-b14b-0c26fb175708.html. [Accessed July 27, 2017.]

Leadership Conference on Civil Rights. "Justice on Trial: Racial Disparities in the American Criminal Justice System." Washington, DC: 2000. https://web.archive.org/web/20161007113926/http://www.protect civilrights.org/pdf/reports/justice.pdf. [Accessed July 27, 2017.]

Linville, Erin, and Indiana Family & Social Services Administration. "Eligibility Modernization: The Need for Change." 2006.

"Mitch Daniels: The Right Stuff." *Economist*, Apr. 19, 2010.

Murray, John. "Disputed Welfare Practices Don't Hold up in Court." *Indianapolis Star*, Apr. 1, 2010.

"Numbers Don't Support State's Claim That All Is Well." *Star Press* (Muncie), May 18, 2008, 2D.

Overmyer, Beth. "Medicaid Enrollment & Modernization–What You Should Know!" Indiana Council of Community Mental Health Centers presentation, 2009.

Riecken, Rep. Gail. "FSSA Disclosure, Transparency, Evaluation Must Be Priorities." *Fort Wayne Journal Gazette*, May 21, 2010, 13A.

Rowe, Gretchen, Carolyn O'Brien, Sam Hall, Nancy Pindus, Lauren Eyster, Robin Koralek, and Alexandra Stanczyk. "Enhancing Supplemental Nutrition Assistance Program (SNAP) Certification: SNAP Modernization Efforts: Final Report." Alexandria, VA: US Department of Agriculture, Food and Nutrition Service, Office of Research and Analysis, 2010.

Roysdon, Keith. "Once-Mighty Borg-Warner Plant Sits Empty, Waiting in Muncie." *Indiana Economic Digest*, Mar. 23, 2015.

Schneider, Mary Beth. "Audit of FSSA Finds 185 Problems." *Indianapolis Star*, June 16, 2005.

Schneider, Mary Beth, and Tim Evans. "Shake-Up Pro Will Take Over the FSSA." *Indianapolis Star*, Dec. 8, 2004.

———. "Ex-Local Official to Head the FSSA." *Indianapolis Star,* Dec. 8, 2004, A1, A8

Schneider, Mary Beth, and Bill Ruthhart. "Daniels: Critics Were Right." *Indianapolis Star,* Oct. 16, 2009, A1, A15.

Sedgwick, Weston. "Governor Accepts Recommendation to Modernize FSSA Eligibility Processes." News release, Nov. 29, 2006.

Soss, Joe, Richard C. Fording, and Sanford Schram. *Disciplining the Poor: Neoliberal Paternalism and the Persistent Power of Race.* Chicago: University of Chicago Press, 2011.

State of Indiana. "Request for Proposals 6-58: Eligibility Determination Services." Department of Administration and Indiana Family and Social Service Administration. Indianapolis, IN: 2006.

Taylor, Steve. "Border Lawmakers: Cancellation of Accenture Contract Was Long Overdue." *Rio Granda Guardian,* Mar. 13, 2007.

Welch, Matt, Joshua Swain, and Jim Epstein. "Mitch Daniels on How to Cut Government & Improve Services." *Reason,* May 19, 2015.

"'Welfare Queen' Becomes Issue in Reagan Campaign," *New York Times,* Feb. 15, 1976, 51. Reprinted from the *Washington Star,* no author credited.

Werner, Nick. "Welfare Troubles Prompt Meeting." *Star Press,* Apr. 23, 2008, 3A.

Court Materials

Brief of Appellants: *Sheila Perdue v. Anne W. Murphy,* No. 49A02-1003-PL-00250 (Indiana Court of Appeals 2010).

Complaint for Damages and Declaratory Relief: *State of Indiana v. International Business Machines Corporation* (Marion County Court 2016).

Finding of Fact, Conclusions of Law, and Judgement for IBM, *State of Indiana v. International Business Machines Corporation* (Marion County Court, 2012).

Findings of Fact, Conclusion of Law, and Summary Judgment: *Sheila Perdue, et al. v. Anne W. Murphy,* No. 49D10-0803-PL-013340 (Marion Superior Court 2010).

Goldberg v. Kelly, No. 397 U.S. 254, 62 (United States District Court for the Southern District of New York 1970).

Plaintiff Complaint: *International Business Machines v. The State of Indiana* (Marion Circuit/Superior Court 2010).

Sheila Perdue, et al. v. Michael A. Gargano, et al., No. 49S02-1107-PL-437 (Indiana Supreme Court 2012).

State of Indiana v. International Business Machines Corporation, No. 49S02-1408-PL-00513 (Indiana Supreme Court 2016).

3. HIGH-TECH HOMELESSNESS IN THE CITY OF ANGELS

Interviews

Jose-Antonio Aguilar; T.C. Alexander; Gary Blasi; Gary Boatwright; Lou Contreras; Devin Desjarlais; General Dogon; Bob Fitzgerald; Kris Freed; Maria Funk; John Horn; Quanetha Hunt; Deon Joseph; Rachel Kasselbrock; Hamid Khan; Chris Ko; Veronica Lewis; Hazel Lopez; Tracy Malbrough; Patricia McHugh; William Menjivar; Christina Miller; Robert Mitchell; Ana Muñiz; Richard Renteria; Tiffany Russell; Molly Rysman; Al Sabo; James Smith; Monique Talley; Tanya Tull; Nathaniel VerGow; Danielle Wildkress; Jennifer Wolch

Published Literature

Aron, Hillel. "L.A.'s Culture War Over the Last True Skid Row in America." *LA Weekly*, July 24, 2014.

Barragan, Bianca. "Downtown LA Vacancy Rate Hits 17-year High," *Curbed Los Angeles*, Sept 15, 2017. https://la.curbed.com/2017/9/15/16316040/downtown-la-high-vacancy-rate-rent. [Accessed Sept. 21, 2017.]

———. "Historic South-Central Has the Most Crowded Housing in the US." *Los Angeles Curbed*, March 10, 2014.

Blasi, Gary, and Forrest Stuart. "Has the Safer Cities Initiative in Skid Row Reduced Serious Crime?" 2008. http://wraphome.org/wraparchives/downloads/safer_cities.pdf. [Accessed June 26, 2017.]

Boden, Paul. "The Devastating Impacts of Safer Cities Policing in Skid Row." *Huffington Post*, 2011. http://www.huffingtonpost.com/paul-boden/on-homeless-memorial-day-_1_b_811966.html. [Accessed Aug. 1, 2017.]

Boyle, Hal. "Skid Row: The West's Bowery." *Evening Independent*, June 14, 1947: 10.

Culhane, Dennis P. "We Can End Homelessness." *Penn Top Ten*, 2016. http://www.penntopten.com/wp-content/uploads/2016/05/Top-10-Homelessness-Essay.pdf. [Accessed June 26, 2017.]

Cunningham, Mary, Sarah Gillespie, and Jacqueline Anderson. "Rapid Re-Housing: What the Research Says." New York: Urban Institute, 2015. http://www.urban.org/sites/default/files/publication/54201/2000265 -Rapid-Re-housing-What-the-Research-Says.pdf. [Accessed June 26, 2017.]

Davis, Mike. "Afterword—a Logic Like Hell's: Being Homeless in Los Angeles." *UCLA Law Review* 39 (Dec. 1991): 325–27.

———. *City of Quartz: Excavating the Future in Los Angeles.* New York: Verso, 1990.

DiMassa, Cara Mia. "Little Tokyo Residents Resent Mental Health Facility." *Los Angeles Times*, Feb. 21, 2008.

Downtown Center Business Improvement District. "Downtown Los Angeles Demographic Study 2013." http://www.downtownla.com /survey/2013/results/DTLA-Demo-Study-2013.pdf. [Accessed March 3, 2016.]

Eng, Lily. "Chief Praised, Rebuked in Crackdown on Homeless." *Los Angeles Times*, Aug. 22, 1990.

Gandy, Oscar H. *The Panoptic Sort: A Political Economy of Personal Information.* Boulder, CO: Westview Press, 1993.

Gerry, Sarah. "*Jones v. City of Los Angeles*: A Moral Response to One City's Attempt to Criminalize, Rather Than Confront, Its Homelessness Crisis." *Harvard Civil Rights-Civil Liberties Law Review* 42 (2007): 239–51.

Green, Richard K., Vincent Reina, and Selma Hepp. "2014 USC Casden Multifamily Forecast." In *USC Lusk Center for Real Estate*, 2014. https:// lusk.usc.edu/sites/default/files/2014-USC-Casden-Multifamily -Forecast.pdf. [Accessed June 26, 2017.]

Gutierrez, The Honorable Philip S. "*Tony Lavan, et al. v. City of Los Angeles, et al.* Order Issuing a Preliminary Injunction." https://cangress.files .wordpress.com/2011/06/lavan-preliminary-injunction-highlights.pdf. [Accessed June 26, 2017.]

Gustafson, Kaaryn S. "The Criminalization of Poverty." *Journal of Criminal Law and Criminology* 99, no. 3 (2009): 643–7160.

Holland, Gale. "Fears Mount over a Homeless Plan That Residents Say Will 'End Venice as We Know It.'" *Los Angeles Times*, Oct. 18, 2016.

———. "L.A. Leaders Are Crafting New Plan to Help Homeless on Skid Row." *Los Angeles Times,* July 15, 2014.

———. "Plan to Turn Cecil Hotel into Homeless Housing Is Withdrawn." *Los Angeles Times*, Apr. 4, 2014.

———. "Treading a Fine Line, L.A. Council Considers Ordinance to Boost Homeless Sweeps." *Los Angeles Times*, Mar. 30, 2016.

———. "Venice Residents Fight over Homeless Housing Project—and Character of the Neighborhood." *Los Angeles Times*, Mar. 11, 2017.

Howard, David B. "Unsheltered: A Report on Homelessness in South Los Angeles." Special Services for Groups, 2008. http://www.ssg.org/wp-content/uploads/Unsheltered_Report.pdf. [Accessed June 26, 2017.]

Huey, Laura. *Negotiating Demands: The Politics of Skid Row Policing in Edinburgh, San Francisco, and Vancouver*. Toronto: University of Toronto Press, 2007.

Irvine, Huston. "Skidrow Serenade." *Los Angeles Times Sunday Magazine*, Mar. 26, 1939: 6, 21.

Littlejohn, Donna. "San Pedro Meeting Erupts over Homeless Storage Center." *Daily Breeze*, Oct. 5, 2016.

Lopez, Steve. "A Corner Where L.A. Hits Rock Bottom." *Los Angeles Times*, Oct. 17, 2005.

Los Angeles Central City Committee. "Centropolis: The Plan for the Central City of Los Angeles." Studies prepared jointly by Los Angeles Central City Committee, Los Angeles City Planning Dept., Traffic Dept., [and others]: 1960.

Los Angeles Department of Mental Health. "Rapid Rehousing: Overview and New Developments." In *9th Annual Housing Institute*, 2016. http://file.lacounty.gov/SDSInter/dmh/246452_RapidRehousing-6-8-16.pdf. [Accessed June 26, 2017.]

Los Angeles Homeless Services Authority. "The Greater Los Angeles Homeless Count." 2017. https://www.lahsa.org/homeless-count/reports. [Accessed June 26, 2017.]

Lyon, David. *Surveillance as Social Sorting: Privacy, Risk, and Digital Discrimination*. New York: Routledge, 2003.

Massey, Douglas S., and Nancy A. Denton. *American Apartheid: Segregation and the Making of the Underclass*. Cambridge, MA: Harvard University Press, 1993.

McDonald, Jeff. "State Ruling May Aid City Crackdown on Homeless: Courts: Decision Will Support Ventura's Plan to Toughen Municipal

Ordinance against Camping in Parks, Officials Say." *Los Angeles Times*, Apr. 25, 1995.

O'Brien, J.C. "Loose Standards, Tight Lips: Why Easy Access to Client Data Can Undermine Homeless Management Information Systems." *Fordham Urban Law Journal* 35 (3), 2008: 673–93.

Office of Los Angeles Mayor Eric Garcetti. "Comprehensive Homelessness Strategy." https://www.lamayor.org/comprehensive-homelessness -strategy. [Accessed Aug. 1, 2017.]

———. "Mayor Eric Garcetti and City Council Approve Emergency Spending on Homeless Housing and Shelter." News Release, Dec. 9, 2015. https://www.lamayor.org/mayor-eric-garcetti-and-city-council -approve-emergency-spending-homeless-housing-and-shelter. [Accessed June 26, 2017.]

OrgCode Consulting Inc. and Community Solutions. VULNERABIL- ITY INDEX SERVICE PRIORITIZATION DECISION ASSIS- TANCE TOOL (VI-SPDAT), American Version 2.0 for Single Adults, 2015.

Parson, Don. "Los Angeles' 'Headline-Happy Public Housing War.'" *Southern California Quarterly* 65 (3), 1983: 265.

Posey, Jacquie. "Penn Researcher Says Ending Homelessness Is Possible." nd. http://www.upenn.edu/spotlights/penn-researcher-says-ending -homelessness-possible. [Accessed June 26, 2017.]

Rosenberg, Jeremy. "Laws That Shaped L.A.: How Bunker Hill Lost Its Victorians." KCET, https://www.kcet.org/departures-columns/laws -that-shaped-la-how-bunker-hill-lost-its-victorians. [Accessed June 26, 2017.]

Sides, Josh. *L.A. City Limits: African American Los Angeles from the Great Depression to the Present.* Oakland, CA: University of California Press, 2003.

Spivack, Donald R. "Community Redevelopment Agency (CRA)." https:// www.scribd.com/document/59101874/History-of-Skid-Row. [Accessed June 26, 2017.]

Stuart, Forrest. *Down, Out, and Under Arrest: Policing and Everyday Life in Skid Row.* Chicago: University of Chicago Press, 2016.

———. "Policing Rock Bottom: Regulation, Rehabilitation, and Resis- tance on Skid Row." Dissertation, Ph.D., Department of Sociology, University of California, Los Angeles, 2012.

Tsemberis, Sam J. *Housing First: The Pathways Model to End Homelessness for People with Mental Illness and Addiction.* Center City, MN: Hazelden, 2010.

US Commission on Civil Rights. "Understanding Fair Housing." Washington, DC: US Govt. Printing Office, 1973.

White, Magner. "L.A. Shows the World How to End Slums." *Los Angeles Examiner (Special Pullout)*, Oct. 12, 1959: 1–6.

Wild, Mark. *Street Meeting: Multiethnic Neighborhoods in Early Twentieth-Century Los Angeles.* Oakland, CA: University of California Press, 2005.

Willse, Craig. *The Value of Homelessness: Managing Surplus Life in the United States.* Minneapolis: University of Minnesota Press, 2015.

Wolch, Jennifer, and Michael J. Dear. *Malign Neglect: Homelessness in an American City.* San Francisco: Jossey-Bass Publishers, 1993.

Documents

My understanding of Los Angeles was enlarged by several fascinating research trips to the Central Branch of the Los Angeles Library and I am grateful for the help of its talented and enthusiastic research librarians. I relied especially on their historical newspaper archives and their government documents collection, which holds copies of the legendary "Centropolis" and Silver Book plans for downtown Los Angeles development. I also enjoyed their collection of historical maps, especially the Sanborn Fire Insurance Maps and Baist's Real Estate Surveys, which helped me re-create the history of Skid Row. Their regular collection also holds a rare copy of a book celebrating the centennial of Rancho Los Amigos, which includes some of the only extant pictures of the Los Angeles County poorhouse.

4. THE ALLEGHENY ALGORITHM

Interviews

Carmen Alexander; Karen Blumen; Fred Brown; Marc Cherna; Kim Berkeley Clark; Erin Dalton; Doreen Glover; Patricia Gordon; May Gray; Patrick Grzyb; Tanya Hankins; Amanda Green Hawkins; Mary Heards; Rochelle Jackson; Janine; Tracey McKants Lewis; Laurie Mulvey; Bruce Noel; Kate Norton; Emily Putnam-Hornstein; Marcia Raines; Judy Hale Reed; Ken Regal; Jessie Schemm; Angel Shep-

herd; Pamela Simmons; Tiffany E. Sizemore-Thompson; Barbara
Stack; Rhonda Strickland; Kenneth R. Strother; Rhema Vaithianathan; Catherine Volponi; and Colleen Young

Published Literature

Ackerman, Jan. "'Why Did You Do That'." *Pittsburgh Post-Gazette*, Mar. 30,
1994: B-1, B-6.

Allegheny County Department of Human Services. "Predictive Risk
Modeling in Child Welfare in Allegheny County: The Allegheny Family
Screening Tool." http://www.alleghenycounty.us/Human-Services
/News-Events/Accomplishments/Allegheny-Family-Screening-Tool
.aspx. [Accessed June 26, 2017.]

Baxter, Joanne. "External Peer Review for *Interim findings on the feasibility of using predictive risk modelling to identify new-born children who
are at high risk of future maltreatment (April 2013)*." Wellington, New
Zealand: Ministry of Social Development, Aug. 2013.

Belser, Ann. "Baby Byron Given Back to His Mom." *North Hills News
Record*, Dec. 28, 1993: A1, A6.

Billingsley, Andrew, and Jeanne M. Giovannoni. *Children of the Storm: Black
Children and American Child Welfare*. New York: Harcourt, Brace, Jo-
vanovich, 1972.

Birckhead, Tamar. "Delinquent by Reason of Poverty." Juvenile Justice
Information Exchange, 2012. http://jjie.org/2012/08/20/delinquent
-by-reason-of-poverty/. [Accessed June 26, 2017.]

Bobkoff, Dan. "From Steel to Tech, Pittsburgh Transforms Itself." In *All
Things Considered*, NPR, Dec. 16, 2010. http://www.npr.org/2010/12
/16/131907405/from-steel-to-tech-pittsburgh-transforms-itself. [Ac-
cessed Aug. 1, 2017.]

Bull, John M.R. "County CYS Director Accepts Florida Post." *Pittsburgh
Post-Gazette*, Jan. 9, 1995: A1, A2.

Cabrera, Marquis. "Florida Leverages Predictive Analytics to Prevent Child
Fatalities—Other States Follow." *HuffPost*, Dec. 21, 2015. http://www
.huffingtonpost.com/marquis-cabrera/florida-leverages-predictive_b
_8586712.html. [Accessed June 26, 2017.]

Center for the Study of Social Policy. "Predictive Analytics in Child Welfare: A Broader View from the Field." https://www.youtube.com/watch?
v=3VaFEWmynYo. [Accessed June 26, 2017.]

Collier, Roger. "New United States Mammogram Guidelines Ignite Debate." *Canadian Medical Association Journal* 182 (2), 2010: E101-E02.

Compac 21 (The Committee to Prepare Allegheny County for the Twenty-first Century). "Preparing Allegheny County for the 21st Century: A Report to the Allegheny County Board of Commissioners." 1996.

Dalton, Erin. "Data Sharing." Actionable Intelligence for Social Policy." http://www.aisp.upenn.edu/wp-content/uploads/2015/11/Dalton -Data-Sharing.pdf. [Accessed June 26, 2017.]

Dare, Tim, and Eileen Gambrill. "Ethical Analysis: Predictive Risk Models at Call Screening for Allegheny County." Centre for Social Data Analytics, University of Auckland, 2016.

Deitrick, Sabina, and Christopher Briem. "Allegheny County Economic Trends 2005." University Center for Social and Urban Research, University of Pittsburgh, 2005. http://ucsur.pitt.edu/wp-content/uploads /2014/11/ACEconomicTrends2005.pdf. [Accessed June 28, 2017.]

Frey, William H., and Ruy Teixeira. "The Political Geography of Pennsylvania: Not Another Rust Belt State." *Brookings Policy Brief*, Brookings Institute, April 15, 2008. https://www.brookings.edu/research/the -political-geography-of-pennsylvania-not-another-rust-belt-state/. [Accessed June 28, 2017.]

Fuoco, Michael A. "Dad Held in Death of Girl, 2." *Pittsburgh Post-Gazette*, Mar. 10, 1994: A1, A13.

Gill, Sam, Indi Dutta-Gupta, and Brendan Roach. "Allegheny County, Pennsylvania: Department of Human Services' Data Warehouse." http://datasmart.ash.harvard.edu/news/article/allegheny-county -pennsylvania-department-of-human-services-data-warehouse-4. [Accessed June 27, 2017.]

Gillingham, Philip. "Predictive Risk Modelling to Prevent Child Maltreatment and Other Adverse Outcomes for Service Users: Inside the 'Black Box' of Machine Learning." *British Journal of Social Work* 46 (6), 2016: 1044–58.

———. "Why the PRM Will Not Work." In *Re-Imagining Social Work in Aotearoa New Zealand*, RSW Collective, Oct. 8, 2015. http://www .reimaginingsocialwork.nz/2015/10/why-the-prm-will-not-work/. [Accessed June 28, 2017.]

Harcourt, Bernard E. *Against Prediction: Profiling, Policing, and Punishing in an Actuarial Age.* Chicago: University of Chicago Press, 2007.

Hawkes, Jeff. "After the Sandusky Case, a New Pennsylvania Law Creates Surge in Child Abuse Reports." *Lancaster Online*, Feb. 20, 2015. http://lancasteronline.com/news/local/after-the-sandusky-case-a-new-pennsylvania-law-creates-surge/article_03541f66-b7a3-11e4-81cd-2f614d04c9af.html. [Accessed June 28, 2017.]

Heimpel, Daniel. "Managing the Flow: Predictive Analytics in Child Welfare." *Chronicle of Social Change*, April 6, 2017. https://chronicleofsocialchange.org/analysis/managing-flow-predictive-analytics-child-welfare. [Accessed Aug. 1, 2017.]

Hickey, Kathleen. "Saving Children, One Algorithm at a Time." In *GCN: Technology, Tools, and Tactics for Public Sector IT*, July 26, 2016. https://gcn.com/articles/2016/07/26/child-welfare-analytics.aspx. [Accessed June 28, 2017.]

The Independent Committee to Review CYS. "Report of the Committee to Review Allegheny County Children and Youth Services" (The Murray Report). Submitted to the Advisory Board of Children and Youth Services of Allegheny County, Feb. 17, 1995.

Kelly, John. "Rapid Safety Feedback's Rapid Ascent." *Chronicle of Social Change*, Feb. 28, 2017. https://chronicleofsocialchange.org/child-welfare-2/rapid-safety-feedbacks-rapid-ascent. [Accessed Aug. 1, 2017.]

Kirk, Stacey. "Paula Bennett Rejects That She Knew about 'Lab Rat' Child Abuse Study." http://www.stuff.co.nz/national/politics/70725871/paula-bennett-rejects-lab-rat-child-abuse-study-greenlit-under-her-watch. [Accessed June 26, 2017.]

Kitzmiller, Erika M. "Allegheny County's Data Warehouse: Leveraging Data to Enhance Human Service Programs and Policies." In *Actionable Intelligence for Social Policy*. Philadelphia: University of Pennsylvania, May 2014. https://www.aisp.upenn.edu/wp-content/uploads/2015/08/AlleghenyCounty-_CaseStudy.pdf. [Accessed Aug. 1, 2017.]

Levenson, Michael. "Can Analytics Help Fix the DCF?" *Boston Globe*, Nov. 7, 2015.

Lindert, Bryan. "Eckerd Rapid Safety Feedback: Summary and Replication Information." nd. http://static.eckerd.org/wp-content/uploads/Eckerd-Rapid-Safety-Feedback-Final.pdf. [Accessed Aug. 1, 2017.]

Ministry of Social Development (New Zealand). "The Feasibility of Using Predictive Risk Modelling to Identify New-Born Children Who Are High Priority for Preventive Services." Feb. 2, 2014. http://www.msd

.govt.nz/documents/about-msd-and-our-work/publications-resources/research/predictive-modelling/00-feasibility-study-report.pdf. [Accessed Aug. 1, 2017.]

———. "The White Paper for Vulnerable Children, Volume II." 2012 https://www.mvcot.govt.nz/assets/Uploads/Documents/whitepaper-volume-ii-web.pdf. [Accessed Aug. 1, 2017.]

Niedecker, Stacy. "Byron's Mother Ready for Family to Be Together." *North Hills News Record*, Dec. 30, 1993: A4.

O'Neil, Cathy. *Weapons of Math Destruction: How Big Data Increases Inequality and Threatens Democracy*. New York: Crown, 2016.

Pelton, Leroy. "The Continuing Role of Material Factors in Child Maltreatment and Placement." *Child Abuse & Neglect* 41 (2015): 30–39.

Piven, Frances Fox, and Richard A. Cloward. *Regulating the Poor: The Functions of Public Welfare*. New York: Pantheon, 1971.

———. *Poor People's Movements: Why They Succeed, How They Fail*. New York: Vintage, 1978.

Pro, Johnna A. "Baby's Death Puts System in Question." *Pittsburgh Post-Gazette*, Mar. 11, 1994: C1, C7.

The Protect Our Children Committee. "Child Protection Report: Digging Deeper to Understand How Pennsylvania Defines Child Abuse." nd. http://www.protectpachildren.org/files/Child-Protection-Report-On-Defining.pdf. [Accessed July 31, 2017.]

Putnam-Hornstein, Emily, and Barbara Needell. "Predictors of Child Protective Service Contact between Birth and Age Five: An Examination of California's 2002 Birth Cohort." *Children and Youth Services Review* 33 (2011): 2400–07.

Rauktis, Mary E., and Julie McCrae. "The Role of Race in Child Welfare System Involvement in Allegheny County," Pittsburgh, PA: Allegheny County Dept. of Human Services, 2010. http://www.alleghenycounty analytics.us/wp-content/uploads/2015/12/The-Role-of-Race-in-Child-Welfare-System-Involvement-in-Allegheny-County.pdf. [Accessed Aug. 1, 2017.]

Reich, Jennifer A. *Fixing Families: Parents, Power, and the Child Welfare System*. New York: Routledge, 2005.

Roberts, Dorothy E. *Shattered Bonds: The Color of Child Welfare*. New York: Basic Books, 2002.

Shroff, Ravi. "Stats and the City: A Data-Driven Approach to Criminal Justice and Child Welfare." In *DataBites*. New York City: Data & Society, June 14, 2017. http://listen.datasociety.net/databites-100-series -stats-city-data-driven-approach-criminal-justice-child-welfare/. [Accessed Aug. 1, 2017.]

Smith, Matthew P. "Authorities Take 'Baby Byron.'" *Pittsburgh Post-Gazette*, Dec. 28, 1993: A1, A2.

Smith, Michael. "Building an Interoperable Human Services System: How Allegheny County Transformed Systems, Services and Outcomes for Vulnerable Children and Families." Smithtown, NY: Stewards of Change, 2008.

Stack, Barbara White. "Criticized CYS Policies to Be Studied." *Pittsburgh Post-Gazette*, Sept. 28, 1994: C1, C4.

———. "CYS Failed to Tell Judge Facts in Case." *Pittsburgh Post-Gazette*, Oct. 1, 1994: A1, A3.

———. "CYS, Father Betrays Girl, 2." *Pittsburgh Post-Gazette*, Sept. 4, 1994: A1, A8.

———. "U.S. Probe of Youth Agency Sought." *Pittsburgh Post-Gazette*, Oct. 4, 1994: B1, B4.

TCC Group. "Peer Review Report 1." Wellington, New Zealand: Ministry of Social Development, 2015. https://www.msd.govt.nz /documents/about-msd-and-our-work/publications-resources /research/predictive-modelling/feasibility-study-schwartz-tcc-interim -review.pdf. [Accessed Aug. 1, 2017.]

US Centers for Disease Control and Prevention. "Adverse Childhood Experiences: Looking at How ACEs Affect our Lives and Society." nd. http://vetoviolence.cdc.gov/apps/phl/resource_center_infographic .html. [Accessed July 31, 2017.]

US Department of Health and Human Services and Children's Bureau. "Child Maltreatment 2015." Jan. 19, 2017. https://www.acf.hhs.gov /cb/resource/child-maltreatment-2015. [Accessed Aug. 1, 2017.]

Vaithianathan, Rhema, Tim Maloney, Nan Jiang, Irene De Haan, Claire Dale, Emily Putnam-Hornstein, and Tim Dare. "Vulnerable Children: Can Administrative Data Be Used to Identify Children at Risk of Adverse Outcomes?" Centre for Applied Research in Economics. Auckland, NZ: University of Auckland Business School, Sept. 2012. http://www.msd.govt.nz/documents/about-msd-and-our-work

/publications-resources/research/vulnerable-children/auckland
-university-can-administrative-data-be-used-to-identify-children-at
-risk-of-adverse-outcome.pdf. [Accessed Aug. 1, 2017.]

Vaithianathan, Rhema, Tim Maloney, Emily Putnam-Hornstein, and Nan
Jiang. "Children in the Public Benefit System at Risk of Maltreatment
Identification Via Predictive Modeling." *American Journal of Preventative Medicine* 45 (3), 2013: 354–59.

Vaithianathan, Rhema, Emily Putnam-Hornstein, Nan Jiang, Parma Nand,
and Tim Maloney. "Developing Predictive Models to Support Child
Maltreatment Hotline Screening Decisions: Allegheny County Methodology and Implementation." Centre for Social Data Analytics, University of Auckland, April 2017. http://www.alleghenycountyanalytics
.us/wp-content/uploads/2017/04/Developing-Predictive-Risk
-Models-package-with-cover-1-to-post-1.pdf. [Accessed Aug. 1, 2017.]

Wilson, Moira L., Sarah Tumen, Rissa Ota, and Anthony G. Simmers.
"Predictive Modeling: Potential Application in Prevention Services."
American Journal of Preventative Medicine 48 (5), 2015: 509–19.

Woods, Darian. "New Zealand's Child Abuse Analytics Study Hits
Political Snag." *Chronicle of Social Change,* Aug. 7, 2015. https://
chronicleofsocialchange.org/featured/new-zealands-child-abuse
-analytics-study-hits-political-snag. [Accessed Aug. 1, 2017.]

Documents

I visited the Pennsylvania State Archives in Harrisburg early in my research
into the Allegheny Family Screening Tool. I found crucial historical
context in the Records of the Department of Public Welfare, especially
Series RG-23: Boxes 8-1618 Carton 26 (Administrative Correspondence), 8–1638 Carton 61 (Interdepartmental Correspondence), 8–1628
Carton 54 (Interdepartmental Correspondence), and 8-1635 Carton
58 (Interdepartmental Correspondence).

5. THE DIGITAL POORHOUSE

Published Literature

*Automating Apartheid: U.S. Computer Exports to South Africa and the
Arms Embargo.* Philadelphia: NARMIC/American Friends Service
Committee, 1984.

Black, Edwin. *IBM and the Holocaust: The Strategic Alliance between Nazi Germany and America's Most Powerful Corporation.* New York: Crown Publishers, 2001.

Brennan, William J. "Reason, Passion, and 'the Progress of the Law.'" *Cardozo Law Review* 3 (1988): 3–23.

Cohen, Adam. *Imbeciles: The Supreme Court, American Eugenics, and the Sterilization of Carrie Buck.* New York: Penguin Press, 2016.

Cohn, Cindy. "Amicus Brief of the Electronic Frontier Foundation (Case 14-4104, Document 57)." 2015. https://www.eff.org/files/2015/02/11 /eff_ibm_apartheid_amicus_brief_final.pdf. [Accessed June 26, 2017.]

Desilver, Drew. "U.S. Income Inequality, on Rise for Decades, Is Now Highest Since 1928." Pew Research Center, 2013. http://www.pewresearch .org/fact-tank/2013/12/05/u-s-income-inequality-on-rise-for-decades -is-now-highest-since-1928/. [Accessed June 26, 2017.]

Ehrenreich, Barbara. *Fear of Falling: The Inner Life of the Middle Class.* New York: Pantheon Books, 1989.

Flaherty, David H. *Protecting Privacy in Surveillance Societies: The Federal Republic of Germany, Sweden, France, Canada, and the United States.* Chapel Hill, NC: University of North Carolina Press, 1989.

Gandy, Oscar H. *Coming to Terms with Chance: Engaging Rational Discrimination and Cumulative Disadvantage.* New York: Routledge, 2009.

Gangadharan, Seeta Peña. "Digital Inclusion and Data Profiling." *First Monday* 17 (5–7), 2012.

Haney López, Ian. *Dog Whistle Politics: How Coded Racial Appeals Have Reinvented Racism and Wrecked the Middle Class.* New York: Oxford University Press, 2014.

Killgrove, Kristina. "How Grave Robbers and Medical Students Helped Dehumanize 19th Century Blacks and the Poor." *Forbes,* July 13, 2015. https://www.forbes.com/sites/kristinakillgrove/2015/07/13/dissected -bodies-and-grave-robbing-evidence-of-unequal-treatment-of-19th -century-blacks-and-poor/#468b84886d12. [Accessed Aug. 1, 2017.]

Massey, Douglas S., and Nancy A. Denton. *American Apartheid: Segregation and the Making of the Underclass.* Cambridge, MA: Harvard University Press, 1993.

Mounk, Yascha. *The Age of Responsibility: Luck, Choice, and the Welfare State.* Cambridge, MA: Harvard University Press, 2017.

O'Neil, Cathy. *Weapons of Math Destruction: How Big Data Increases Inequality and Threatens Democracy*. New York: Crown, 2016.

Rank, Mark R. *One Nation, Underprivileged: Why American Poverty Affects Us All*. New York: Oxford University Press, 2004.

Stone, Deborah A. *Policy Paradox: The Art of Political Decision Making*, 3rd ed. New York: W. W. Norton, 2012.

Taube, Aaron. "How Marketers Use Big Data to Prey on the Poor." *Business Insider*, Dec. 19, 2013. http://www.businessinsider.com/how-marketers-use-big-data-to-prey-on-the-poor-2013-12. [Accessed Aug. 1, 2017.]

Vaithianathan, Rhema. "Big Data Should Shrink Bureaucracy Big Time." *Stuff*, 2016. http://www.stuff.co.nz/national/politics/opinion/85416929/rhema-vaithianathan-big-data-should-shrink-bureaucracy-big-time. [Accessed June 26, 2017.]

Wong, Julie Carrie. "'We're Just Rentals': Uber Drivers Ask Where They Fit in a Self-Driving Future." *Guardian*, Aug. 19, 2016. https://www.theguardian.com/technology/2016/aug/19/uber-self-driving-pittsburgh-what-drivers-think. [Accessed June 28, 2017.]

Conclusion: Dismantling the Digital Poorhouse

Published Literature

Alexander, Karl L., Doris R. Entwisle, and Linda Steffel Olson. *The Long Shadow: Family Background, Disadvantaged Urban Youth, and the Transition to Adulthood*. American Sociological Association, Rose Series in Sociology. New York: Russell Sage Foundation, 2014.

Deloitte Touche. *Public Sector, Disrupted: How Disruptive Innovation Can Help Government Achieve More for Less*. 2012. https://www2.deloitte.com/content/dam/Deloitte/global/Documents/Public-Sector/dttl-ps-publicsectordisrupted-08082013.pdf. [Accessed Aug. 1, 2017.]

Edin, Kathryn J., and H. Luke Shaefer. *$2.00 a Day: Living on Almost Nothing in America*. Boston: Houghton Mifflin Harcourt, 2015.

Garza, Alicia. "A Herstory of the #Blacklivesmatter Movement." http://blacklivesmatter.com/herstory/. [Accessed June 28, 2017.]

Gillespie, Sarah. "Mark Zuckerberg Supports Universal Basic Income. What Is It?" *CNN Money*, May 26, 2017. http://money.cnn.com/2017/05/26/news/economy/mark-zuckerberg-universal-basic-income/index.html. [Accessed June 28, 2017.]

Hiltzik, Michael. "Conservatives, Liberals, Techies, and Social Activists All Love Universal Basic Income: Has Its Time Come?" *Los Angeles Times*, June 22, 2017. http://www.latimes.com/business/hiltzik/la-fi -hiltzik-ubi-20170625-story.html. [Accessed June 28, 2017.]

Holland, Gale. "13,000 Fall into Homelessness Every Month in L.A. County, Report Says." *Los Angeles Times*, Aug. 25, 2015. http://www .latimes.com/local/lanow/la-me-homeless-pathways-20150825-story .html. [Accessed Aug. 1, 2017.]

House of Representatives of the State of Hawaii. *Requesting the Department of Labor and Industrial Relations and the Department of Business, Economic Development, and Tourism to Convene a Basic Economic Security Working Group.* 29th Legislature. http://www .capitol.hawaii.gov/session2017/bills/HCR89_.HTM. [Accessed Aug. 1, 2017.]

Jackson, Thomas F. *From Civil Rights to Human Rights: Martin Luther King, Jr., and the Struggle for Economic Justice.* Philadelphia: University of Pennsylvania Press, 2007.

King, Jr., Dr. Martin Luther. "Remaining Awake through a Great Revolution." Sermon in the National Cathedral. Washington, DC, Mar. 31, 1968 (1968b). http://kingencyclopedia.stanford.edu/encyclopedia /documentsentry/doc_remaining_awake_through_a_great_revolution .1.html. [Accessed Aug. 1, 2017.]

Kotz, Mick, and Mary Lynn Kotz. *A Passion for Equality: George A. Wiley and the Movement.* New York: W. W. Norton & Co., 1977.

McKnight, Gerald. *The Last Crusade: Martin Luther King, Jr., the FBI, and the Poor People's Campaign.* Boulder, CO: Westview Press, 1998.

Movement for Black Lives. "Platform: Reparations." https://policy.m4bl .org/reparations/. [Accessed Aug. 1, 2017.]

Potts, Monica. "The Other Americans." *Democracy: A Journal of Ideas* 32 (2014). http://democracyjournal.org/magazine/32/the-other -americans/. [Accessed Aug. 1, 2017.]

Documents

The online archive of Civil Rights Movement Veterans at http://www .crmvet.org/ is an extraordinary resource. I found many primary materials describing the Poor People's Campaign here, including:

Martin Luther King. *Statement Announcing Poor People's Campaign.* Dec. 4, 1967.

Martin Luther King. *Letter to Supporters Regarding Poor People's Campaign.* Apr. 1968 (1968a).

SCLC ~ Martin Luther King. *Economic Bill of Rights.* 1968.

Unsigned, assumed to be Dr. King and perhaps others associated with SCLC. *Draft: To the President, Congress, and Supreme Court of the United States.* Feb. 6, 1968.

NOTES

1

1. State Board of Charities, 1905.
2. Massachusetts General Court Committee on Paupers Laws and Josiah Quincy 1821: 14.
3. Ibid: 10.
4. Katz, 1996.
5. An 1857 report revealed that 50 of the 177 inmates at the poorhouse in Ulster County, New York, had died in the past year. See also David Wagner, *Ordinary People*: "for nearly thirty years almost every one of the many hundreds of foundlings sent to [Massachusetts state poorhouse] Tewksbury died." (Wagner, 2008: 25).
6. Trattner, 1999: 53–54.
7. *The Washington National Republican*, 1877, quoted in Bellesiles, 2010: 144.
8. Richmond, 1917: 39.
9. Almy, 1910: 31.
10. Priddy from Lombardo, 2008: 128; Buzelle from Trattner, 1999: 100.
11. *274 U.S. 200* (1927), Justia U.S. Supreme Court Center, https://supreme.justia.com /cases/federal/us/274/200/case.html#207. [Accessed July 21, 2017.]
12. Peel, 2007: 133.
13. Nadasen, 2012: 18.
14. Kennedy, 1963.
15. Nadasen, 2012: 12.
16. Ibid: 107.
17. Gilens, 2003: 102.
18. Jackson and Johnson, 1973: 201.
19. Rockefeller, 1959.
20. New York State Department of Social Services, 1975: 1.

2

1. Schneider and Ruthhart, 2009.
2. Sedgwick, 2006.
3. Daniels, 2007.
4. Greenhouse, 1990.
5. Corbin, 2009.
6. Kusmer, 2009.
7. Complaint for Damages and Declaratory Relief, *State of Indiana v. International Business Machines Corporation,* 2006: 22.
8. Finding of Fact, Conclusions of Law, and Judgement for IBM, *State of Indiana v. International Business Machines Corporation,* 2012: 35.
9. Ibid: 4–9.
10. Riecken, 2010: 13A.
11. Higgins, 2009: A1.
12. "'Welfare Queen' Becomes Issue in Reagan Campaign," 1976.
13. Ernst, 2013.
14. Soss, Fording, and Schram, 2011.
15. Leadership Conference on Civil Rights, 2000.

3

1. Boyle, 1947.
2. Lopez, 2005.
3. Irvine, 1939.
4. Posey, nd.
5. Culhane, 2016.
6. OrgCode Consulting Inc. and Community Solutions, 2015: 5–6.
7. Cunningham, 2015: 1.
8. O'Brien, 2008: 693.
9. Ibid.
10. Gustafson, 2009: 669.
11. Blasi, 2008.
12. Lyon, 2003.
13. Gandy, 1993: 1–2.

4

1. U.S. Centers for Disease Control and Prevention, nd.
2. The Independent Committee to Review CYS (The Murray Report), 1995: 5.
3. Putnam-Hornstein and Needell, 2011: 2406.
4. Vaithianathan, 2013: 355.
5. Wilson, 2015: 511.
6. TCC Group, 2015: 5.
7. See, for example, Baxter 2013.
8. Vaithianathan, 2016: 35–41.
9. Ibid: 12.
10. Ibid: 15.
11. Collier, 2010.
12. O'Neil, 2016: 21.
13. Rauktis, 2010.
14. Birckhead, 2012.
15. The remaining half of the variables in the model include the age and number of children in the household, age and number of parents, characteristics of the alleged perpetrator, who reported the alleged maltreatment, mental health status, and drug use.
16. U.S. Dept. of Health and Human Services, 2015.

17. Marc Cherna points out that not all of the predictive variables included in the model are interpreted as negative by the system. So, for example, use of public mental health services *may* be interpreted as a positive, protective factor by the system. It might drive your AFST score down rather than up. Unfortunately, when I asked Vaithianathan and Putnam-Hornstein to release the weights of the variables, which would clarify how important each factor was to the model and if it was negatively or positively correlated with the AFST score, they refused.

5

1. Rank, 2004: 102–3.
2. Killgrove, 2015.
3. Ehrenreich, 1989.
4. Cohen, 2016.
5. Gandy, 2009.
6. Gangadharan, 2012.
7. Wong, 2016.
8. Brennan, 1988: 22.
9. O'Neil, 2016: 38.
10. Vaithianathan, 2016.
11. Cohn, 2015.

Conclusion

1. Kotz, 1977: 249.
2. Potts, 2014.
3. King, 1968a: 1.
4. Edin and Shaefer, 2015: 168.
5. Holland, 2015.
6. King, 1968b.

INDEX